SPIRIT OF THE PHOENIX

Tim Llewellyn was the BBC's Middle East Correspondent for ten years, during which time he covered the Lebanese civil war, the Iranian Revolution, the Iran-Iraq war, the First Gulf War and the Israeli-Palestinian conflict. Since leaving the BBC staff in 1992, he has been a regular broadcast and print commentator on Middle East politics.

'Part travelogue, part political vignettes, part personal reminiscences, Llewellyn captures the essence of this unique and troubled country.'
David Hirst, author of *The Gun and the Olive Branch*

'Tim Llewellyn, a bright and brave BBC correspondent during many of Lebanon's earlier seemingly endless little and big wars, has returned decades later to scrutinize Beirut and its still largely unresolved problems. Read his compelling *Spirit of the Phoenix* and understand how and why that fabled bird of resilient re-birth has survived in Lebanon, but just barely, alas, and missing many of its feathers.'
Jonathan Randal, former Middle East correspondent for the *Washington Post*, and the author of *Osama: The Making of a Terrorist* (I.B.Tauris, 2006)

SPIRIT OF THE PHOENIX
Beirut and the Story of Lebanon

Tim Llewellyn

I.B. TAURIS

LONDON · NEW YORK

Published in 2010 by I.B.Tauris & Co Ltd
6 Salem Road, London W2 4BU
175 Fifth Avenue, New York NY 10010
www.ibtauris.com

Distributed in the United States and Canada Exclusively by Palgrave Macmillan,
175 Fifth Avenue, New York NY 10010

ISBN: 978 1 84511 735 1

A full CIP record for this book is available from the British Library
A full CIP record is available from the Library of Congress

Library of Congress Catalog Card Number: available

Designed and Typeset by 4word Ltd, Bristol, UK
Printed and bound in India by Replika Press Pvt. Ltd.

Contents

Brief Chronology

634–641: Arab Muslim conquest of Syria/Mount Lebanon.

680–681: Maronite Christians split with Byzantium.

969: Byzantines invade Syria. Maronites flee to northern Mount Lebanon.

1110–24: Crusaders invade Syrian coast.

1110–1282: Maronite splits and internal battles over Crusader, regional and spiritual allegiances.

1516: Ottoman Empire takes over Greater Syria.

1523–1697: Ma'an Dynasty (including reign of Fakhr al-Din II) in Mount Lebanon.

1697–1841: Chehab Dynasty.

1831–40: Egyptian ruler Ibrahim Pasha in Syria.

1840: Foreign military intervention in Mount Lebanon ends Egyptian rule.

1842: Ottomans end Emirate of Mount Lebanon.

1841–45: Civil unrest in Mountain.

1860: Civil war in Mount Lebanon. Druze massacre of Christians. Western armies intervene, French in forefront.

1861: Ottomans create mixed governing council (*Mutasarrifiya*) in Mount Lebanon overseen by non-local Christian Ottoman Governor.

1915: Ottomans abolish *Mutasarrifiya*, appoint governor.

1916: Severe famine in Beirut and Mountain.

1918: French armies in Lebanon.

1920: September 1: League of Nations grants France mandate for Syria and Lebanon.

1941: November 26: Lebanon declares independence after British and Free French enter to defeat Vichy French forces.

1943: March: Unwritten National Covenant states Lebanon neutral, independent Arab country with Western ties. Pact sets up confessional arrangement of government favouring Maronite Christians.

1943: September 21: Bishara al-Khuri elected first president of Lebanon. In controversial change of constitution, in 1947, his term of six years is extended by three years – from 1949–1952.

1943: November 11: Free French arrest president and leading members of government.

1943: November 22: Government members released under British pressure. November 22 declared Independence Day.

1943: November/December: France agrees to transfer power to Lebanese Government from January 1, 1944.

1948: May 15: Israeli state established in most of Palestine. Between December 1947 and mid-1949, hundreds of thousands of refugees enter Lebanon.

1949: July 8: Antoun Sa'adeh, leader of National Syrian Social Party, executed by firing squad in Beirut after armed insurrection against Lebanese Government.

1951: July 16: In reprisal for Sa'adeh's execution, Riad el-Solh, Lebanon's first Prime Minister and a founding father of the nation, is assassinated by NSSP agents at Amman airport.

1958: July 14: Iraqi Monarchy and pro-Western Government deposed by force.

1958: July 15: US Marines land in Lebanon after months of armed confrontation between President Camille Chamoun's forces and pro-Nasser and leftist opposition.

1958: July 31: Fuad Chehab elected president. Calm restored.

1967: June 5–10: Israel seizes Sinai from Egypt, Golan Heights from Syria, East Jerusalem, West Bank of Jordan and Gaza from Arab control, in Six-Day War. Lebanon not directly involved.

1968: December 28: Israel destroys 13 civilian airliners at Beirut International Airport in reprisal for Palestinian attack on Israeli airliner in Athens.

1969: November 2: Lebanon and PLO sign Cairo agreements on guerrilla activity inside Lebanon.

1970: September 16: Jordan attacks PLO units in Amman, starting long campaign against guerrillas.

1971: Mid to late July: Jordan defeats and expels PLO and its forces. They reform mainly in Lebanon, in and around refugee camps in Beirut and in the south, near Israeli border. Palestinian operations against Israel from inside Lebanon increase in scope and regularity.

1973: April 10: Israeli commandos kill three Palestinian leaders in West Beirut. Year sees continuing clashes and tension between Palestinian guerrillas and Lebanese army/ security forces, Christian militias.

1975: April 13: Phalangist gunmen ambush bus in Christian East Beirut Ain el-Rumanneh district, killing 27 mainly Palestinian passengers. Phalangists say guerrillas had attacked church. Civil war begins.

1976: June: Syrian troops enter Lebanon to restore peace and control Palestinians.

1977: March 16: Druze chieftain and leftist leader Kamal Junblatt assassinated in home region of Shouf.

1978: March 14: Israel invades south Lebanon after Palestinian attack on bus near Tel Aviv.

1978: March/June: Israel hands territory in south to Christian Lebanese militia leader Sa'ad Haddad; ignores UN Security Council Resolution 425 calling for full Israeli withdrawal.

1982: June 6: After assassination attempt on London Israeli Ambassador Shlomo Argov by fringe extremist Palestinian group, Israel invades Lebanon in 'Operation Peace for Galilee'. By August, Israel occupies Lebanon up to and including East Beirut.

1982: September 14: President-elect Bashir Gemayel assassinated. Israeli forces occupy West Beirut and surround Palestinian refugee camps.

1982: September 16-18: Christian militia massacre many hundreds of Palestinian and Lebanese civilians in Sabra and Chatila refugee camps as Israeli forces hold ring.

1982: September 21: Bashir's elder brother Amin elected president under Israeli aegis.

1982: September 24: US, French, Italian and British peacekeeping force established in and around Beirut.

1983: October 23: 241 US marines and 56 French paratroopers killed in two bomb explosions claimed by two Shia factions.

1985: June: Most Israeli troops gone from central Lebanon but some remain in south to support South Lebanon Army led by renegade Lebanese army Major-General Antoine Lahad. Israelis and SLA establish 'security zone' in area from three to 12 miles (5 to 19kms) deep along Lebanese side of Israeli frontier.

1988: September 22: No candidate elected to succeed President Amin Gemayel. Nation divided among factions, army split. Mainly Muslim government in West Beirut led by Selim al-Hoss; Christian administration in East Beirut headed by Army Commander-in-Chief Michael Aoun.

1989: March 14: General Aoun declares 'war of liberation' against Syria from his outpost in Ba'abda Presidential Palace, East Beirut.

1989: October 22: National Assembly meeting in Ta'ef, Saudi Arabia, endorses charter of national reconciliation reducing presidential authority (Christian) and equalising numbers of Christians and Muslims in Parliament (previously 6-5 in favour of Christians).

1989: November 22: President-elect Rene Mouawwad assassinated. November 24: Elias Hrawi elected. General Emil Lahoud replaces Aoun as C-in-C Lebanese Army.

1989: Aoun fights on.

1990: January–May: Aoun engages rival Christian forces in destructive and debilitating battle for control of Christian region.

1990 October 13: Syrian air force attacks Aoun in Ba'abda Palace. Aoun flees to French Embassy. Civil war officially ends. Aoun later exiled to France.

1991: Militias ordered disarmed, except for Hezbollah. SLA and Israelis remain in control of south near border.

1992: October 31: Rafiq Hariri, wealthy businessman born in Sidon, Saudi nationality, becomes prime minister and begins reconstruction of country's infrastructure.

1996: April 11: 'Operation Grapes of Wrath': Israel bombs south Lebanon, south Beirut and Beka'a Valley to try to subdue Hezbollah. April 18: Israeli attack on UN base at Qana, south Lebanon, kills more than 100 Lebanese seeking refuge there.

1998: November 24: Army commander Emil Lahoud sworn in as president (Hrawi's term had been extended by three years under Syrian pressure).

2000: May 24: Under Hezbollah attack, Israeli forces leave South Lebanon and SLA collapses. Lebanese *de jure* sovereignty restored to Israeli frontier after 22 years; Hezbollah in *de facto* control, alongside Unifil and Lebanese Army units.

2000: October 23: Rafiq Hariri prime minister for second time. Reconstruction well under way but national debt enormous.

2004: September 2: UN Security Council Resolution 1559 framed by France and US demands foreign (i.e. Syrian) troops leave Lebanon. Syria ignores it, and forces reluctant Lebanese Government to extend Lahoud's presidential term by three years. Rafiq Hariri leaves government.

2005: February 14: Hariri killed by truck bomb in Ras Beirut. Syrians or Syrian agents widely blamed. Surge of anti-Syrian rallies and calls for Syrian troops to leave Lebanon.

2005: March 8: Hezbollah organises mass demonstrations in Beirut calling for Syrians to remain in Lebanon.

2005: March 14: Mass rallies ('Cedar Revolution') urge Syrians leave Lebanon. (Foundation of pro-West, anti-Syria, anti-Hezbollah 'March 14' Movement.)

2005: April: Syrian forces have left Lebanon.

2005: June 2: Journalist Samir Qasir, critic of Syrian influence, killed by car bomb. Anti-Syrian alliance led by Hariri's son Sa'ad wins control in parliamentary elections.

2005: September: Four pro-Syrian Lebanese generals charged in connection with Rafiq Hariri assassination.

2005: December 12: Prominent anti-Syrian MP and journalist Gibran Tueni killed by car bomb.

2006: July 13: Israel launches comprehensive assault across Lebanon after Hezbollah captures two Israeli soldiers. Civilian casualties high, destruction widespread, many thousands displaced.

2006: August11: UN Security Council (ceasefire) Resolution 1701. Truce arranged between Hezbollah and Israel. Around 1,000 Lebanese dead, mainly civilians; 159 Israelis killed, mainly soldiers.

2006: November 11: Hezbollah and Amal ministers resign from cabinet over UN plans for Hariri assassination tribunal to try suspects.

2006: November 21: Leading Christian Government Minister Pierre Gemayel (grandson of Phalange Party founder, Pierre, and son of former president, Amin) shot dead.

2006: December 1–10: Thousands of opposition members demand resignation of pro-western government. Opposition sets up tent city near parliament building in central Beirut. In place for 17 months, tying up traffic and virtually paralysing downtown.

2007: January: Street clashes between government (March 14) and opposition (March 8).

2007: May 30: UN Security Council sets up Hariri tribunal.

2007: June 13: Anti-Syrian Walid Eido killed by roadside bomb in Ras Beirut.

2007: September 19: Anti-Syrian MP Antoine Ghanim killed by car bomb.

2007: November 24: President Emil Lahoud steps down after parliament fails to elect successor.

2007: December 12: Possible new Lebanon Army C-in-C General Francois al-Hajj killed by car bomb.

2008: May 8–13 : About 80 killed in clashes between Hezbollah plus pro-Hezbollah factions and pro-government groups. Fears of renewed civil war.

2008: May 25: Parliament elects Army C-in-C Michel Suleiman as president, ending six-month political deadlock. Tent city disappears.

2008: July 11: Agreement on national unity government.

2009: April 29: Four pro-Syrian generals freed after UN court in Hague rules insufficient evidence to convict.

2009: June 7: Pro-Western March 14 coalition of Sa'ad Hariri wins narrow majority in parliamentary elections. Hezbollah accepts outcome.

2009: June 27: Sa'ad Hariri confirmed as prime minister.

Dramatis Personae

Some leading figures in Lebanon's history:

Saint Maroun (circa 350–410AD), Syrian priest and mystic, founder of Maronite Church, later aligned with Rome.

Fakhr al-Din Ma'an (Fakhr al-Din II) (1572–1635), Druze Emir of Mount Lebanon; executed by Ottomans in Istanbul.

Bishara al-Khouri (1890–1964), first president of independent Lebanon (from 1943–1952).

Antoun Sa'adeh (1904–1949), founder in 1930s of Syrian Social National Party, mounted failed coup against Lebanon Government in July, 1949, executed by firing squad in Beirut in same month.

Riad el-Solh (1894–1951), first prime minister of Lebanon and founding father of nation. Assassinated in Jordan by SSNP agent in reprisal for Sa'adeh execution.

Fuad Chehab (1903–1973), Lebanese Army Commander-in-Chief who became president (from 1958–1964) after 1958 civil strife.

Kamal Junblatt (1917–1977), Druze chieftain, leftist leader and influential politician, especially in opposition; assassinated in mountain home district, the Chouf.

Walid Junblatt (1949–), successor to Kamal and a leader of March 14 Movement until August, 2009.

Sa'eb Salam (1905–2000), prominent Sunni politician, many times Prime Minister, and founding father.

Pierre Gemayel (1905–1984), founder and first leader of (mainly Maronite Christian) Phalangist Party.

Amin Gemayel (1942–), eldest son of above and president 1982–1988.

Bashir Gemayel (1947–1982), second son, founder of right-wing Lebanese Forces, assassinated while president-elect.

Pierre Amin Gemayel (1972–2006), son of Amin, assassinated while Minister of Industry.

Camille Chamoun (1900–1987), President 1952–1958, founder and leader of Christian-rightist National Liberal Party and associated Tiger militia (part of Lebanese Forces).

Dany Chamoun (1934–1990), leader of NLP and Tigers in 70s and 80s, murdered at home at close of civil war.

Dory Chamoun (1931–), elder son of Camille and present head of NLP.

Suleiman Franjieh (1910–1992), President 1970–1976, head of Marada Brigades (Christian Maronite) militia, since mid-1970s opposed to Phalangists and Lebanese Forces.

Tony Franjieh (1941–1978), eldest son of Suleiman and political heir, murdered at home by Phalangist militia.

Samir Geagea (1952–), head of Lebanese Forces. Served 11 years jail for alleged war crimes (1994–2005).

Michael Aoun (1935–), head of anti-March 14 Free Patriotic Movement; former Army C-in-C named Prime Minister by outgoing President Gemayel in civil war chaos of 1988; fought Syrians and rival Christians in last years of war; exiled to France 1990–2005.

Imam Musa as-Sadr (1928–1978), revered leader of Lebanese Shi'ites in 1960s and 1970s, founder of 'Movement of the Deprived' and Amal organisations, disappeared in Libya in August, 1978, in mysterious circumstances.

Sheikh Mohammed Hassan Fadlallah (1935–), spiritual leader of Lebanese Shi'ites.

Sheikh Hassan Nasrallah (1960–), leader of Hezbollah.

Sheikh Abbas al-Musawi (1952–1992), founder and second leader of Hezbollah, killed by Israelis in South Lebanon.

Sheikh Subhi al-Tufayli (1948–), first Hezbollah leader.

Rafiq Hariri (1944–2005), Prime Minister during most of 1990s and early 2000s, power-broker behind Ta'ef Agreement, inspiration and organising power of Lebanon's post-war reconstruction, resigned as PM in 2004, assassinated by car bomb on February 14, 2005. 'Cedar Revolution' and departure of Syrian troops soon followed.

Saad Hariri (1970–), second son of Rafiq, head of Future Movement (*al-Mustaqbal*), designated Prime Minister in June, 2009, soon after parliamentary elections won by March 14 Movement.

Rashid Karami (1921–1987), influential Sunni Muslim statesman and political leader, power-base Tripoli; many times Prime Minister in 1950s, 60s, and during and after civil war; while PM in 1987 assassinated by bomb explosion in helicopter.

Rene Muawad (1925–1989), president for 17 days in 1989, assassinated by bomb explosion on November 22.

Elias Hrawi (1925–2006), president from 1989–1998.

Emil Lahoud (1936–), president from 1998–2007.

(Both the last two presidents had their terms extended by three years beyond the constitutional six as a result of Syrian pressure.)

NB: Of the 31 names of Lebanese leaders listed here, 13 died violently, all except one, who was executed, assassinated by political rivals, foreign enemies or their agents.

Acknowledgements

Abigail Fielding Smith, editor of this book, conceived this enterprise and nursed a somewhat erratic writer through the process – I thank her for her diligence, expertise and patience, and also those others at I.B.Tauris who so professionally edited and produced the book. I also wish to thank my close friend Dr. Ghada Karmi, who made vital editorial suggestions but also kept my spirits high and encouraged me when inertia or doubts threatened. In Lebanon, I thank my old friend and colleague Hisham el-Solh, whose contacts throughout the country in whatever area or faction are wide and deep; Sharzad Faramarzi, a long-time colleague (she mostly with the Associated Press) from the days of the Iranian Revolution and various Lebanese excursions; Mona Ziadi and Ed Blanche, also (formerly) of the AP, both replete with knowledge and, almost as importantly, steady friendship and hospitality; Tewfik and Phillipa Mashlawi, at the Middle East Reporter, likewise solid backers and old friends; and David and Amina Hirst, again offering without lien information, experience, hospitality and inspiration. My gratitude also goes to two Beiruti exiles in London, both young women, Hala al-Kara, who worked with me at the BBC and gave me then and so often since personal insights into Lebanon, and Sana Issa, a long-time AP journalist, who is always a source of good advice and sensible Lebanese exchange. I am perhaps most of all in the debt of my old BBC Middle East colleague Jim Muir, who generously and forgivingly lent me his beautiful apartment in Wardiyeh, in West Beirut, when I was visiting Lebanon. Unfortunately he was rarely there himself and unable to protect me from any omissions or errors of fact or interpretation that I may have made. None of the above shares any such responsibilities for this book. Lastly, my thanks to the people of Lebanon, some of whom I have named or indicated in this book, others whom I have spared, who have made such enthusiastic, articulate and informed interlocutors.

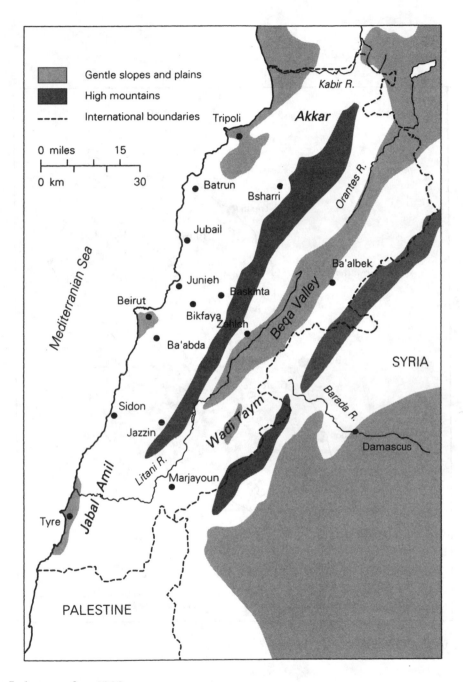

Lebanon after 1920
Topography based on Kamal Salibi, *The Modern History of Lebanon*, 1965

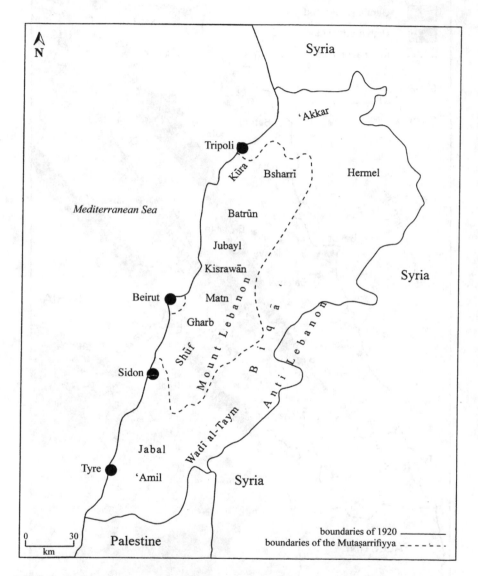

Modern Lebanon

Introduction

For all the beauty of its landscapes and the attractions of its people and culture, Lebanon has coursing through its enfeebled veins all the poisonous currents of international rivalries and regional aggression, and the religious and nationalistic fanaticisms these have engendered that make the Middle East the most dangerous region in the world. There is little sign of this threat diminishing either in Lebanon, a cauldron of all these animosities, or in the wider area. For Lebanon, this state of continuing, terrifying alert has been nearly fatal and could yet prove so.

This book tries to explain how the Lebanese survive the punitive rigours of their geography and history and the never-ending attempts of myriad outsiders to give them every assistance in aggravating their own internal contradictions. It will also show how Lebanon is a template for the Middle East: what shows there is replicated elsewhere; and in reverse, what appears elsewhere is reflected in Lebanon.

As with the Lebanese, it is important not to repine. To begin at the most basic level, there is reassuring news for those who, around three o'clock in the morning, staring wakefully into the dark, imagine hell, the flames, the pain, the eternal despair, whatever it is Hieronymus Bosch sketched out for the errant and sinful. It is this: Hell, or hellish scenes, are usually worse in the imagination or in that substitute for the imagination we call television than when you are there, and Lebanon proves it.

Time and again during the Lebanese Civil War, especially in its earliest stages and again during the later invasions and occupations and assaults that augmented it, we would look aghast at the pictures and hear the reports and rumours coming from that isolated and ravaged country and wonder what could remain of the 'Switzerland of the Middle East',

1

that Mediterranean piece of paradise; the size, it was always said, of Wales or Massachusetts, where one could ski in the morning and swim in the afternoon.

For those on standby to go to Lebanon, journalists, diplomats, Lebanese exiles, the odd salesman of plate glass or generating equipment and their families and friends, such expeditions were viewed with fear and alarm. The advice was ever: 'Is your journey really necessary?' What would the visitor find? Would there be anything or anyone left to find? How would they reach the city from the airport, if there were an airport? When the airport was closed, how would that traveller make the run across the border and the warring mountains to the coastal plain and its cities and capital, Beirut? The answer was: much more easily than they expected.

I once arrived, in early 1976, when the fighting was intense, in the Lebanese resort town of Shtaura, a few miles from the Syrian border, a place where those escaping the dry rigours of Syrian supervision and austerity could stop for a relieved deep breath and a plate of houmous and a *manouche* (a pitta bread and thyme sandwich) before contemplating the journey into the unknown over the mountains and whatever was waiting there. The driver despatched to meet me, one of an extended family of Beiruti Sunnis who ferried around various journalists and cameramen, was quick to reassure me that there was no problem. His scornful attitude towards my worried questions was palpable. His main concern was when I began to buckle my seat belt. 'What kind of driver you think I am?' he said indignantly, releasing the catch, as if to say: nothing to worry about, we rise above all this, no silly precautions necessary – a fatalism jelled with confidence and knowhow that speaks from the Lebanese heart. Ahmed's main concern was not a rocket through the windscreen or an awkward meeting with a ravening band of incensed Christian militiamen, but his own *amour propre* and his determination to rise above everything, even the likelihood of a road accident on one of the minor, mountainside roads the war was forcing us to take.

It illustrated the kind of can-do approach we British associated with Americans during World War II and later, and it is very Lebanese. More often than not, 'can-do' turns into 'have-done', at the practical if not the political daily level.

On arrival in Beirut, the same cheery faces would appear, as if we had come on a Thomas Cook's tour or package holiday, offering food, drink, jokes and reassurance and dismissals of the most recent horrors, despite simultaneous detailed and conflicting descriptions of them. I have often thought that for a Lebanese the worst crime is boredom. Perhaps the reason they hated the post-war years under the Syrians more than the wars themselves was because the restrictive nature of the hegemony forced circumspection. There was a kind of order in those years, but it was boring.

The new arrival would wander out into the streets expecting to see blocks missing and devastation all round, and of course in those areas such as the downtown area, the port, the streets of the suburbs where the rival forces confronted one another, they were and there was, and the signs are there as I write in 2009. But so much more of it seemed to be upright, mended, patched, much as it was before, the shops and some cafes open, most commodities usually available or, if not, very soon to be so. There were moments of dispirited gloom but they were always short-lived. Irrepressibly, back the Lebanese went to work – and to war – after a few days of restocking and recuperation and mutually satisfactory deals, often between enemies. One element never missing for long was *joie de vivre*, the spirit of the nation, the *sine qua non* of Lebanon.

It would be seriously misleading and demeaning, insulting to the many tens of thousands of dead, maimed, dispossessed, exiled, bereaved and ruined over those 15 years, as the war metamorphosed through its different shapes of evil and destruction, to suggest that these horrors had been exaggerated or were not horrors at all. They were horrors the people of Lebanon, and these are not just the Lebanese, still live with and are cursed to live with, unreconciled and without solace for many years to come. War and its consequences almost submerge them. But what kept and keeps striking the visitor about Lebanon and the Lebanese is that insouciant resilience with which they treat adversity and continually rise above it.

This does not trivialise the Lebanese. At its worst, perhaps, it disguises a serious lacuna, something missing or perhaps deliberately for the moment left absent from the Lebanese psyche: pause for self-examination, the asking 'Why?' A psychiatrist might be concerned at the mental health of a people who can so quickly hide their scars, knowing as they do that the hatreds and suspicions and endemic rivalries that sit deep in them are not being reconciled, but lie up there in the long grass.

The intractable problems of the Middle East that so weigh on Lebanon and interfere with its progress mean the Lebanese have had little or no opportunity for reflection or reconciling their differences. They fought a vicious, debilitating and ruinous civil war over 15 years in vain, without change of character or social reform, without any victor and therefore no vanquished, unless all were defeated. The temptation persists among the Lebanese of each persuasion to believe that whoever he or she is or whatever he or she represents, right prevailed, wrong was expunged. It is difficult to work out whether this oblivious attitude to those years of warfare, and their continuance in different forms and at more subdued levels, is a strength or a weakness for the people of this country.

The political structures and make-up of the Lebanese nation have never been revolutionised or even fundamentally reformed; no final line has been drawn under a long period of division. Unlike the Balkans, however riven that area remains, Lebanon has not the stabilising neighbourhoods of the European Union and NATO on one side, Russia on the other, the United Nations (UN) and its many agencies, political agreements and treaties, however controversial, in place. Lebanon dangles by a thread in a region without effective supervision and no foreseeable sign of a just or even effective peace for all. Given this, the Lebanese fall back on what they do best: find refuge in their talents and survivability; their redoubtable skills of trade and creativity; their rich experience of cultural and economic exchange with the worlds to their west and east, unique in the Arab world; their expertise at living hand-to-mouth in style; their ingenuity; their connections; their skill at life itself.

None of this is ephemeral. The Lebanese build, rebuild and work – they put up tower blocks, dig wells, build bridges, fix roads, pipes, telephones and pylons, find generators, open markets and start trade. Nothing is impossible, but everything has its right and closely wrought price. They have also a fascination with the new and the experimental and have the imagination to make proper use of them.

The Lebanese never say die for long. They are happy to challenge the fates. It is this nerve and panache that tends to shock Arab neighbours; with all that internecine killing and chaos, you can hear them ask: How can we take these people seriously? But perhaps it is just because the Lebanese do not take themselves too seriously that they do survive so well, always starting again, and again and again. These dismissive neighbours might ask themselves this: Despite everything, what more pleasant country in the Middle East than Lebanon is there to live in?

Perhaps the Lebanese have little choice in their life-style, but are privileged to have the human resources they have developed over the centuries of open contact with East and West. These are what sustain them in that vacuum where political solution depends so much on powers beyond them: even the most resolute attempt at reconciliation and compromise could so easily be undermined by outsiders. As we shall see as we look at the journey the Lebanese have made down the years, the fractious nature of the country does not lend itself in any way to unity of national purpose. Perhaps the very fact that Lebanon holds together at all in the way it does, keeps popping up and popping back, is a miracle of can-do and make-do.

There are, and always have been, many of all faiths and factions who have wished to stabilise Lebanon and protect it from the reverberations of the Middle East and from itself. The story of how the founding fathers of the nation emerged from under the heels of the Ottomans and Western imperialism and made a country is one the Lebanese can tell with pride. It was an achievement against many odds, odds which have lengthened with the contradictions of the post-imperial age. I sometimes see in my mind's eye a man in a tarbouche gazing wistfully out to sea and thinking: 'For God's sake, bring back the Ottoman Empire.' But he thinks it only for a moment.

The Lebanese are nostalgic but realistic. They demonstrate the spirit of the phoenix; they are a people if not quite a nation yet, constantly reinventing their country, passing repeated tests of their existence while more profound solutions remain for the time being unattainable. During the time I researched and wrote this book, from 2005 to 2009, more conflagrations and more phoenix-like moments have erupted.

Any time might be a good time to write such a book, but now seems a good moment to assess the Lebanon phenomenon, to ask who the Lebanese are, how they arrived where they are today, so full of hope and excitement, always – whatever the crushing blow or visceral disappointment – raising realities from the flames.

❖   ❖   ❖   ❖

The election of a president by the Lebanese parliament on 25 May 2008, after a six-month hiatus over the leadership and at least 18 months of national political paralysis and sporadic but increasingly menacing violence, brought at least temporary relief and even rejoicing to the country. For me, it provided a point, a pause for reflection, from which I could look back and try to assess how Lebanon had reached where it was. But where exactly was it? During the years I had been working on this book there had been no certain point at which to stop and take stock. Lebanon was in limbo. Now, tentatively, with a new and apparently popular leader and with a government of national unity, Lebanon seemed to have provided that punctuation mark.

The idea of this book is to shine light backwards on Lebanon and the Lebanese, to try to illuminate by portraits of people, places, events and situations how Lebanon has fallen into this rhythmic cycle of uncertainty and vulnerability during its 66 years of independence. It might have been easier to make such an assessment perhaps in 2004, before the former Prime Minister, Rafiq Hariri, was assassinated and the Syrians almost immediately withdrew their ruling apparatus from the country. Lebanon, viewed from the standpoint of mid-2004, appeared to have attained some sort of stability, though there were unsettling portents of trouble ahead. But publishing this book in 2004 would have been premature, a permanent risk for anyone writing about the modern Middle East.

After the Syrians departed, a series of assassinations and assassination attempts on leading political and other public critics of Syria ensued. In the summer of 2006 the Israelis invaded Lebanon, in the wake of which differences of view among the Lebanese sharpened with regard to Hezbollah, the Shi'a 'Party of God'. Hezbollah was and is, a resistance, a political force and a uniquely powerful military element inside Lebanon. So, was it a heroic and patriotic movement playing a vital dual role in defending Lebanon against the Zionists and representing the poor and underprivileged, of whom the Shi'ites made up the majority? Or was it an Iranian, a 'Persian' and even a Syrian Trojan Horse, bidding to undermine Lebanon's liberal and multi-sectarian way of life, out of control of the state or anyone else?

These tensions provoked from December 2006 onwards a year and a half of animated political division and of governmental paralysis. The two sides of the argument were defined as pro-Arab, or pro-'Eastern', on the opposition side and pro-Western, pro-American, on the other, government or 'March 14' side (14 March 2005 being the date on which the anti-Syrian Lebanese masses mobilised after the death of Rafiq Hariri, for which many Lebanese held the Syrians to be responsible).

A government challenge to Hezbollah in early May 2008, and Hezbollah's quick and briefly brutal military response, evoking memories of civil war and showing how close to the surface old and new sectarian animosities lurked, with the munitions to back them, frightened the nation and its politicians into compromise. The stasis ended. The violence was damped down as quickly as it had erupted. On 25 May, in Qatar, under general Arab encouragement, the Lebanese leaders agreed on a government of national unity, a political modus vivendi and, not before time, to elect as president the consensus candidate General Michel Suleiman. He should and would have taken his post six months earlier had it not been for a complete failure among leading parties and politicians to agree on how the country should be governed after his taking office. May 2008 broke that stalemate, though the essential differences are by no means resolved.

The new government of national unity and the election of President Suleiman in 2008 were construed as setbacks for American and Western plans for Lebanon, a country which George W. Bush had claimed with nerve but without foundation was an American 'democratic' success story. If Lebanon was a democracy, it had been created so before this George was even born. This book is written before anyone can know who will profit from Michel Suleiman's election; but at least he survived the ceremony and started his term reckoned by even the most sceptical observer to be no one's puppet.

However, it would be reckless even to suggest that Lebanon's internal problems are anywhere near resolution or that internal violence does not present a problem. There are troublesome new elements abroad, as the book will reflect. There is also, possibly more threateningly, the ever-present regional instability, all or any of which can easily blow flames into Lebanon: a US or Israeli assault on Iran and Iranian responses, possibly using Hezbollah; another Israeli invasion of Lebanon; breakdown of peace talks and possible war between Syria and Israel; the dangerous rivalries – exemplified in Iraq, but felt wherever these two branches of Islam co-mingle – of the Shi'a and the Sunni Muslims.

The one positive consistency in Lebanon is the irrepressible, incorrigible nature of the people, hence the book's title, not forgetting that

the Phoenicians, whose ancestry many Lebanese claim (perhaps somewhat spuriously), may have taken their name from that mythical bird.

This book does not attempt to be an academic history, political trea-
tise or even a full explanation; it is a collection of vignettes for the
interested and perhaps partly informed reader, who might, as I do, find
himself or herself submerged from time to time by the complexities of
the Lebanese and their neighbours, characters whose fate and circumstances swim arbitrarily in and out of the Western media, usually ill- or
under-explained, depending on the level of violence and fatalities delivered on a particular day, especially if Israel is involved.

These snapshots are intended to be pinned up and examined with
the aim mainly of showing how the past, especially the recent past,
informs the present, and how Lebanon's eventual stability is as much
with the outside powers that reframed the region after World War I and
who continue to manipulate it as it is with the inhabitants of the region
in general and Lebanon in particular. In the main, in this book, it is the
Lebanese who speak for themselves.

The Making of Presidents

It is Sunday 25 May 2008. Pictures of the new president, who is to be elected this early evening, are being pasted up across Beirut. The Lebanese are good with posters and are deft exponents of graphic design. President-to-be Michel Suleiman is in his blue army commander's uniform, with peaked cap and medals, a handsome, craggy, sincere-looking man in his 50s, gazing meaningfully into an unknown future, to his left, his good side perhaps, rather in the manner of film stars of the 1930s and 1940s. He is more Spencer Tracy than Clark Gable. He is popular – he has kept out of politics – as is his army, the only state institution in the country that the people respect and which has come out well from recent challenges. When Hezbollah and its unruly, some would say thuggish, allies briefly took over Ras Beirut in early May, Hezbollah was quick, having seized control, to hand it back to the army, which had stayed present but neutral, a kind of referee police force. To have become militarily involved might well have fatally divided the force, though how long an army can man the sidelines may well be a tough topic this new leader has to address quite soon.

So, General Michel Suleiman, a Maronite Christian from Amchit, in the coastal area some 20 miles or so north of Beirut, near Byblos, is the beneficiary of his force's popularity and his apparent political neutrality. He is the 12th elected Lebanese president; and while ten of them served their full terms, often in the most bizarre circumstances, there was a year when the country had no president, and two heads of state were assassinated before their feet were properly under the presidential table: one, 21 days after his election; the other, 17 days.

This election has come late and not without its alarms, but the actual process of parliamentary vote and accession itself has been peaceful and has brought the exhausted and frustrated Lebanese a sense of relief. It has not been like other elections I recall.

Bombs, blasts and ballots

The election in 1970 of President Suleiman Franjieh, leader of a Maronite Christian family from the far north-east of Lebanon, the mountain town and district of Zghorta, close to Syria in many senses of the word, a refuge for some, badlands for tribal rivals, was the last in Lebanon for nearly 40 years that was to begin at the right time, be done in the correct way (always allowing for the vagaries of the electoral system), be carried out in the correct place – the National Assembly, in downtown Beirut – and to expire after its due course of six years (albeit in the midst of a civil war).

The next presidential election (due in September 1976) was arranged early, for 8 May, given the chaos in the country and the collapse of any type of mandate for President Franjieh. New, Syrian-inspired and Syrian-drafted legislation was rushed through to enable the early election. The fighting near the port, in and around the old downtown area, which comprised the government buildings, the banking quarter, the National Assembly, Martyrs' Square and much else commercial and cultural, loved and now lost, had rendered the district a desolate, ruined no-go area except for the crazed, the fighters and the snipers. These were often the same people. The traditional Assembly was out of the question as a venue for any parliamentary gathering.

With the Syrians exerting their grip on Lebanon, beginning to try to weaken the leftist-Palestinian forces and restore some balance of power to the Christians (and to impose their own authority), Elias Sarkis, a political apparatchik under the former and perhaps most effective President, Fuad Chehab (1958–64), was the Maronite Christian the Syrians wanted in power. (He had been defeated by Franjieh by one vote in 1970.) Sarkis was not the choice of all the Christians; and by this time the rebellious Left and the Palestinians were at odds with the Syrians. Once they had seen, up to a suspicious point, Syria as Arab ally and mentor, but now they viewed it with hostility as unwelcome interferer and putative controller of Lebanese politics and of Yasser Arafat's Palestine Liberation Organisation (PLO).

The election, on a Saturday morning, took place at a site near the Green Line crossing point, opposite the National Museum, *al-Mathaf*. Here delegates from each side of the hostilities could turn up with reasonable safety and bolt for home as soon as the ceremony was over. We, that is, delegates, soldiers, protective militias and the media scrimmage, gathered outside this new temporary parliament, Villa Mansour, an elegant, tree-shaded residence near the military court buildings and the racecourse, and only a few metres inside the Muslim side of the Rue de Damas, which, more or less, formed central Beirut's frontier between the antagonists.

It was not a comfortable spot to be. As we lurked nervously outside, the delegates were delivered to the villa in armour-plated American limousines and Range Rovers, these vehicles draped with gun-wielding bodyguards, all under the watchful aegis of the Syrian Army and what was left of its Lebanese counterpart. As we counted heads – a quorum was necessary for the election to start – mortars and rockets landed around the villa. It was not a heavy barrage and it was never clear to me, as I crouched there, feeling the occasional breeze of an exploding mortar, whether it was coming from disaffected Christians, resentful Palestinians and their allies (the most probable candidates) or maybe even the Syrians themselves trying to concentrate minds towards a quick result in favour of Elias Sarkis.

We were all scared, but no one died. The Syrians had their way, Sarkis was elected, to take office in the coming September, and with relief we scarpered from this electoral charade at the Villa Mansour, bullets cracking the air above us. When we reached our car, I recall, lent to us by a colleague from Newsweek, Barry Came – it was a maroon BMW, known as the 'Bazzerbout' – my colleague Mike Keats, from the American news agency United Press International(UPI), spotted that one of its rear tyres was flat, possibly punctured by a stray bullet or piece of shrapnel. He pointed at it and said: 'Christ, we can't drive on that. What about Bazzer's rim?'

'To hell with Bazzer's rim,' I said. 'I'm not hanging about for a taxi, let's get out of here.' We bumped to relative safety near the Barbir Hospital and found a cab.

The next presidential election was on August 23 1982, with the invading Israelis taking from the Syrians the part of Masters of Ceremonies. The Syrians were, briefly, out, forced to leave by the Israelis. Israel had control of Lebanon all the way up to and including

Christian east Beirut by this time and their favoured candidate was Bashir Gemayel, a Maronite warlord, leader of the Lebanese Forces (LF; the new, much-widened and much-militarised replacement of the Phalange Party, the creature of his father Pierre), whom they regarded as a (difficult) ally. They reckoned he might be able to fulfil that old Israeli dream of a peace treaty between the two nations.

Again, the downtown area was still rubble, insecure, and the National Assembly at its middle no place for a democratic exercise. On 23 August, with the help of the Israelis, money and menaces, Bashir Gemayel was elected by 62 Lebanese legislators at an army barracks at Fayyadiyeh, where the highway to Damascus curls up the hill, near the Lebanese Ministry of Defence, on the outer reaches of Christian east Beirut. He was never inaugurated. President-elect Bashir was assassinated on 14 September 1982, a story I examine in more detail in Chapter 7. On 21 September, at the same barracks, the Lebanese and Israelis repeated the election process, replacing him with his elder brother Amine Gemayel, another Christian whom the Israelis would try with all their might and wiles to make a partner in peace.

For a while, he was so; but this Gemayel reign, from 1982 to 1988, was notable for perhaps being the most incoherent and damaging period in Lebanon's history. When Amine Gemayel's time was up, no replacement could be agreed and for a time Lebanon had two leaders: one the *soi-disant* prime minister, the Christian army commander of the day, Michel Aoun, who installed himself and his remaining loyal Lebanese troops in Ba'abda Palace, from where he shelled and terrorised his rivals on the Left, in the mountains and in west Beirut, and berated the Syrians. Later on he fell out with the Christian LF, bringing unprecedented mayhem and destruction to the Christian sectors of Beirut.

In the rest of Lebanon, a former prime minister, Selim al-Hoss, remained *en poste,* with some legitimacy but little control of the myriad, incoherent groups that were fighting it out in the mainly Muslim areas. It all made such little sense that the media practically ceased trying to report or explain Lebanon's plight to the outside world.

Order began to be restored, almost, after the Ta'ef agreement on Lebanese political reform (drawn up at the inter-Arab conference in Saudi Arabia in 1989), with President Rene Moawad elected at a Lebanese air force base in Kleiat, in the far north of the country, near the Syrian border, on 5 November 1989. But he failed to meet someone's expectations and was killed on 22 November, Lebanon's

Independence Day and the 26th anniversary of President Kennedy's assassination, when a bomb was detonated alongside his spot in a presidential motor convoy in west Beirut, a not dissimilar attack to the one against Rafiq Hariri some 15 years later.

A candidate more popular with the Syrians, Elias Hrawi, was voted in hastily, just two days later, the chosen location this time being Shtaura, a pleasant little resort in the middle of the Beka'a Valley, close to Syria and easy for the Syrians to protect.

Hrawi ruled not for the statutory six years but for nine, with an extension encouraged if not enforced by the Syrians, who during the 1990s had Lebanon in their grip. This grip was maintained until November 1998, when another Syrian favourite was brought in, a former army Commander-in-Chief, Emile Lahoud. His period in office was also extended for three years, by constitutional amendment and Syrian arm-twisting, in 2004 – but this time Syria's increasingly overbearing and clumsy interference in Lebanon's domestic political affairs brought with it more outright opposition, inside Lebanon and from overseas.

Things had changed, in all sorts of ways, since 1998. Under George W. Bush the world was being encouraged to take a dimmer view of 'radical' Arabs, in other words those to whom could most easily be ascribed the imprimatur 'terrorist' and who did not agree 100 per cent with US foreign policy in the region. The situation in Israel's occupied territories was disintegrating fast and bloodily; the much-vaunted 'two-state' solution for the Palestinians and Israelis was evaporating, except in the minds of Western diplomats and their local stooges; Hamas was gaining strength. Hezbollah, with Iran's help and guidance, had pushed Israel out of Lebanon in 2000. The events of 11 September 2001 had given the Americans and their allies a new and antagonistic view of those Arabs who were not prepared to do what Washington decreed. It was the era of 'with us or against us'. Syria was adjudged 'against'. Most cataclysmic of all, the region, after the American-Britain invasion of Iraq, was, not surprisingly, immured in violence, riven among its main religious and ethnic entities and falling to pieces irredeemably. Iraq's reverberations were felt everywhere. Syria was held to be unhelpful, in the allied view – in Iraq, in Palestine, in Lebanon and in its close affinity with Iran.

It was time for the international community to 'get' Syria and its few friends. By the time President Lahoud had stepped down, in some

13

contumely and without great popular respect, in November 2007, Syria was fighting a rearguard action for influence in Lebanon, and Hezbollah was the new anti-Western bastion, itself losing popularity in Lebanon but not nearly as universally as had the Syrians.

It is hard to believe, on this sunny Sunday morning in May 2008, that this most civilised sector of Ras Beirut, the sharp western edge of the capital, jutting into the Mediterranean, mainly Sunni Muslim but much mixed with Christians, Druze, Shi'a and the bulk of the foreign community who make their homes, places of business and watering places in Lebanon, was just a few days ago in the hands of militiamen. A TV station was burned out, newspaper and political offices were seized, and people were killed and injured in street fighting. Most Beirutis got out of town or stayed home and descended to their cellars, if they had them, or crouched on low floors (the wild men tend to fire high); political leaders' residences and offices were under siege; the killing and savagery was even worse in the city's working-class suburbs, in parts of Mount Lebanon ('the Mountain') and in the north.

Agreement came at the last minute and it is, on the surface, as if it never happened. Last night the restaurants of Ras Beirut were full, all signs of antagonism gone; the downtown area was miraculously cleared overnight of the anti-government protesters in their tent city (see Chapter 13). This glittering arena of high-rises and boulevards, cafes and *haute couture* shops, modern offices and apartment blocks will be filled to capacity over the next few nights with tens of thousands of young Lebanese, just promenading or attending a series of concerts of local Lebanese performers in Martyrs' Square. Their immaculate and polite behaviour will make Leicester Square of a Saturday evening look like a Hogarth print.

Only in a few side streets, as I wander through Ras Beirut, down to the corniche for lunch, do I glimpse the flags and now unarmed men of the National Syrian Social Party (NSSP) and Amal (the Shi'ite political movement), who were used by Hezbollah in recent days to do the shooting and burning for them. Occasionally a group from Amal on motor scooters, waving provocative Amal and Hezbollah banners, drives down Hamra, the main street, irritating everyone;

there are shootings still in rougher areas. But, broadly, the phoenix is up and about.

I first walked these streets, briefly, before the civil war. I became more familiar with them in 1975 and 1976 when the Palestinians and their allies ran them, some of these latter the same groups that are around today. The NSSP, with their symbol of the scarlet Catherine wheel on white on a black background, occupy to this day the petrol station down from the old Mayflower Hotel. Their banners hang over the street near the private Khalidi Hospital. In 1976 the NSSP, or PPS (Parti Populaire Syrien as they were then known), used to have an illegal liquor store on a big stand opposite the garage, smuggled goods, where spirits were available for about US$6 a litre. (The PPS were and are largely Christian, though they mostly fought with the 'Muslim' National Movement and the Palestinians.) The cheap drink helped the foreign press corps take a sympathetic view of the faction.

This area seems to have changed little during the past 40 years: quiet, narrow shaded streets with friendly little stores and kiosks; the flower shops of Jeanne d'Arc; the newsagent opposite the Mayflower; the Mayflower's Duke of Wellington bar unchanged; the Pickwick Tavern up the road (whose irascible publican, the former RAF pilot Jackie Mann, Islamic extremists kidnapped in the mid-1980s); new and intimate restaurants, the Rouge, Kebabji (fast-food kebabs but brilliantly succulent), the Walima – tango night on Thursdays; the Blue Note jazz club in Makhoul Street; the American University's (AUB's) soft red–gold brickwork, bright red roofs and gentle arches glimpsed down at the sea-end of these side roads, lining the northern edge of Bliss Street.

There is a sign advertising the *College Protestant*. We always pronounced it the French way, for some reason, even though it was 'Protestant'. Why did we not then call the AUB *l'universite Americaine de Beyrouth*? It is one of those linguistic imponderables of west Beirut, where everyone slides back and forth from Arabic to French to English, though here English is much more prominent among the under-50s than French. French seems to be a romantic hangover on shop signs and when ordering European food or advertising certain European goods, cosmetics and clothes, cigarettes and perfume. It is still well taught, however, and most Lebanese remain fluent in it, not just the Maronite Christians, who wear French like a badge.

Everyone can feel at home in Ras Beirut. A close Lebanese friend of mine honours his *quartier* in London by calling it 'Ras' Kensington. I know what he means. That is why Hezbollah's intervention here in Ras Beirut a couple of weeks ago is so shocking, even if it were an inevitable outcome of the government's inept ultimatum over the resistance's secret communications and security. People of liberal and not necessarily pro-Western sympathies have been newly set against Hezbollah and the March 8 (opposition) movement (the date that the opposition organised its mass rally in 2005). One of my friends wants a 'March 11' movement – poised neatly between the two sides, where right-thinking and tolerant Ras Beirutis could happily reside.

There has not been trouble like this in Ras Beirut since the mid-1980s, when the country reached its nadir of chaos and internal division and factions fought for control of this desirable slice of the city to no great effect, other than to make it virtually unliveable. These were the years of street battles, of bans on Christmas decorations,[1] of kidnappings of academics, journalists, foreigners and locals, many of them for many years. This was out of character. Ras Beirut is for thinking, reading, eating, strolling, studying, shopping, 'living', jogging on the corniche, even working – nothing vulgar, you understand. This is where the American University of Beirut is located, with its sister institution the American Hospital nearby, the private schools, the embassies and consulates (though the American mission fled to the Christian hills for good in the early 1980s), the smart clothes and book shops and watering holes, the best hotels, as many churches as mosques in this predominantly Muslim sector.

Even when the Palestinian guerrillas manned the street blockades for a while in the 1970s and early 1980s, they were well-behaved, chatty and tolerant most of the time, and smart enough to fade into the background when fighting subsided or moved away from Ras Beirut.

The coming of peace in 1990 restored the calm and the character of Ras Beirut. But all is not quite as it seems. The Hariri complex at Koreitem, just up the street from Hamra, is a fortress now, surrounded by security men, and the streets near it guarded by the Internal Security Force and their armoured vehicles, and the army and their armoured personnel carriers and mini-tanks. This, as the palace and seat of power of the pro-government and March 14 movement of Rafiq Hariri's son and inheritor, Sa'ad Hariri, arch-opponent of Hezbollah, was a target in early May, as was the nearby Hariri Future or *al-Mustaqbal* TV station and the Hariris' newspaper and their movement's offices. Further east, among the classy old oriental villas of the Kantari and Junblatt districts, at the end of the Rue Mexique and opposite the Armenian Protestant church, is the imposing Beirut home of Walid Junblatt, who was then the main progenitor and activator of the Lebanese challenge to Hezbollah. The gangs went there as well, to place him under siege. So Ras Beirut, for all its international esprit de corps, sophistication, maturity, intellectual appendages, cinemas, theatres and general mateyness, became a target. We went back, suddenly, 20 years.

Today, election day (25 May 2008), it is hard to take in the transformation of mood. Even the soldiers sitting or standing in the streets and the tanklets and four-wheel drives seem to be for show rather than for real, on alert. What would they do if the menaces reappeared? No doubt wisely fade away.

There do not seem to be many people about. Have they cautiously taken advantage of a sunny weekend to go to the mountains and beaches? Are people afraid that, as has happened in the past, a presidential election might be accompanied by gunfire and death? Anyway, the ceremony is on TV and is at 5 pm – why waste a sweaty day in town getting crushed in a throng or even blown up?

I eat *mezze* and *sultan brahim* (red mullet) and drink a couple of *Almaza* beers at the Lamb House, on the corniche, then walk back along the coast towards town. The corniche is virtually closed off, though families are sunning themselves and swimming off the rocks along the shore. They are impervious to the black Range Rovers and BMWs tearing up and down, sirens sounding and tyres shrieking on the hot tarmac. There are roadblocks; there are security forces everywhere, especially near the Riviera Hotel. In a residential block next door to the hotel, I am told, are temporarily housed many of the Members of Parliament who will elect Michel Suleiman in a few hours time. We are equidistant from the coastal points at which Rafiq Hariri and Walid Eido, a Sunni government minister, were blown up, outside the St. George Hotel and near the Sporting Club, opposite the Lebanese kebab house where I just had lunch, sipping my beer among the veiled housewives and their children. Is the proximity of this MPs' staging post to the points at which their colleagues had been dispatched into the next world not so long before concentrating minds on this special and long-awaited day?

At home I watch the ceremony on TV, on the BBC. All is smooth and good-humoured, though I am irritated that my friend and colleague Jim Muir, the BBC's long-time, excellent and experienced

Middle East correspondent, is largely shoved aside in favour of some Lebanese commentator in London who obviously has it in for Hezbollah and does not display the knowledge and balance Jim does, when he is given a chance. The new President is ushered peacefully and agreeably, at last, into the Assembly with a healthy majority vote behind him.

First Meeting with the Martyrs 2

One morning in November 1975 I decided to be brave – or curious, or plain stupid – and try to approach the Holiday Inn, in Beirut's hotel district, as fighting had died down, it seemed, and it might be a chance to talk to the Christian Phalangist fighters who were besieged there by the alliance of Palestinian guerrillas and Muslim militias, with whom they were in conflict over this central and international part of the city. Control of this district, near the port, the Central Bank, most of the embassies and the banking and downtown areas, would mean gaining the upper hand – in Beirut itself, anyway – in the civil war, which had then been under way for some seven months.

I walked down through the narrow, protected streets, through Minet el-Hosn and the Junblatti areas, past the beautiful old quasi-oriental houses with their arches and balconies, past the shuttered shops, past where I had seen an old man's body the day before, lying there on his back, shot through the head, his tarbouche rolled a few yards away and his shopping strewn over the road, on towards a corner around which I would have been in full view of the towering Holiday Inn. I took heart, in the middle of what I was already beginning to realise was a futile exercise whose fatal costs might well far outweigh any journalistic gain, from seeing a middle-aged woman walking up the street.

She had just rounded a corner from an open area where she would have been easily targeted by snipers in the hotel, had they been minded. But then I recalled a colleague of mine telling me a few days before that he had been inside the Holiday Inn, during a truce, and had met a vivacious young female with a long-barrelled rifle and a telescopic sight.

'I recognise you,' she told my friend, a BBC correspondent.

'How?' he said. 'I don't think we've met.'

'Oh yes, I've seen you many times,' she said, 'through this.' She pointed to her gun and its attachment. 'I've had you in the cross-hairs.'

Was I still going to do this?

The woman and I crossed and she said nothing. No one else, unsurprisingly, was about. I crept nervously onwards. As I was just about to round the corner from which the woman had appeared unscathed, there was a single shot. I do not know why or at whom or if it was just target practice, possibly some unlucky cat the victim. I jumped a foot in the air. Then I turned and went back to the hotel. Many weeks later, when the Christians had finally been flushed from the hotel, a party of us walked slowly up to the rear of the Holiday Inn from the coast side, to find the charred, monolithic ruin empty.

Thirty-two years later, the façade of that Holiday Inn is exactly as it was in late 1975, except that now grass grows where the limousines once parked, the wrecked buildings around have been replaced by glittering new ones, but the Inn is beyond redemption, standing as a ravaged monument to the civil war; a warning, however, that is so familiar it may no longer be heeded. It is a 24-storey shell, too big to knock down and too expensive to reclaim, the scorch marks and shell holes there as they were registered towards the end of 1975.

The Christians lost the battle of the hotels, at the centre of which was the Holiday Inn, to the Palestinians and the National Movement – each side in Lebanon had their own clear idea of what 'The Nation' was and meant – and the fighting surged eastwards to the downtown area and along the Green Line that more or less followed the Road to Damascus through the city and up into the hills to the east.

To try to make a late entrance to that history, it is good to take the shortish walk from the Holiday Inn towards the coast, turning west; a beginner's tour of Beirut's upheavals, where the civil strife focused in 1975 and afterwards, and where the ranks of the martyrs and their mentors remain on walls, as statues, in posters and in memory.

My tour is on a sunny day in June 2007. The city is in a state of nervous breakdown, as not only is the political situation fraught and divisive, but just a few days earlier a senior government Member of Parliament (MP) had been assassinated by a car bomb. This too will be part of the walk. As I stroll down the hill, past the creamy Phoenicia Hotel, Beirut's finest now, but also in its day burned and battered by the rival militias, nervous flunkeys order me not to walk in their grounds but out in the street. They have Very Important Guests to worry about. The hotel is a favourite with businessmen and princes from the Gulf. The streets here abound with men in plain clothes and walkie-talkies, mobile phones, soldiers, security, paramilitaries, mini-tanks and armoured personnel carriers. When people say 'Beirut is back to normal,' I think, 'Perhaps this is what they mean. Armed men everywhere and the machinery of war clogging the streets.'

Around the side of the Phoenicia and its crenellated balconies and limousines, to the west, is the St. George Hotel, in the Bay, a building that was once the home of the *glitterati*, the drinking place of diplomats and spies, journalists and hangers-on, and the favoured resting place of the rich and privileged. It is a square-rigged, elegant, four-floor block that could have been lifted in from the Riviera. It was from here that The Word on the Middle East emanated in the 1950s, 1960s and early 1970s; where news and rumours of coups and troubles in the Arab world beyond peaceful Lebanon were circulated and where expats and agents and newsmen brewed the mixture of facts and speculation that made Beirut, and this hotel, the press centre of the Middle East. The brew was so heady that even the taxi drivers deft enough to claim a pitch outside were an integral part of it, and many of them went on, long after the St. George had been burned out, to be fixers, TV producers and journalists as the 15 years of civil war played out.

The hotel battles of October to December 1975 ended the St. George's grand old life. Christian forces occupied it; the Palestinians and their allies finally took it. It was wrecked and burned but stayed intact as a shell, another monument. The hotel expired but the next-door marina and pool kept going. Today, as I pass, two young beauties in bikinis covered by towelled bathrobes step out of a Mercedes outside the Palm Beach Hotel opposite and scurry across the road to the St. George and its chaises longues and cold cocktails and beers. This may be technically 'mainly' Muslim west Beirut, but you would not know it at the St. George pool.

The pool remains as it was before the war and after it subsided in that area in 1976 – the lissom, brown-bodied girls, the self-regarding studs in gold chains, the Lebanese *jeunesse doree* whose Arabic chatter switched to French as soon as a foreigner neared.

As I watch the girls cross the road in front of the St. George, clutching their little bags and their lotions and MP3s, I suppose they know that they are on the tarmac where, in February 2005, the St. George was the site of another turning point in Lebanon's tormented course.

On Valentine's Day that year, just before 1 pm, Rafiq Hariri, the flamboyant Lebanese former prime minister who had masterminded and raised the finances for Lebanon's reconstruction after 1990, was driving in his motorcade from parliament towards his home, via the coastal route that cuts through the hotel district towards the east–west corniche. This took him past the front of the St. George Hotel. (The hotel was to be refurbished after so many years and plans were afoot to bring it back to its former glory, as had been the case with most of the other hotels in the area, with the exception of the gaunt and scarred mass of the Holiday Inn.)

As his motorcade drew level with the old hotel, there was an enormous explosion under or near his car – it is still not absolutely clear – killing him instantly, fatally wounding his close friend and associate Bassel Fuleihan and killing 14 other people. The blast shifted the St. George on its foundations and ended any plans for its future. Much more than that, it blew recovering Lebanon off course. Hariri's assassination spelled an end to Lebanon's steady, 15-year recuperation and renaissance. The Syrians, who immediately came under suspicion as authors of the bombing – it was in the familiar style of Syria and its agents – were instantly pressed under the weight of great internal Lebanese outcry and international pressure to leave Lebanon. They did so within a few weeks, in some humiliation. They had had a near 30-year presence and what could only be described as, since 1990, 15 years of hegemony, much of it with the co-operation of large numbers of Lebanese. It was the end of the new beginning.

Two-and-a-half years later, as I walk past the St. George, the bomb site now cleared, the road repaved, the St. George still squatting there sullen and abandoned, perhaps for ever, there is no physical sign of the detonation and its dreadful results.

The political consequences remain. Lebanon reverberates from the death and destruction of that day. Nothing has been the same since. The enthusiasm and euphoria that were almost universal among Lebanese as the Syrian soldiers and their machinery of secret services and political agencies departed (ostensibly) soon dissipated. Hope was sidelined by political machination of the old and familiar style.

For the moment though, on this walk, it is the historic and iconic sources of this modern discontent and disequilibrium that are evident: this along the corniche being only one of such sorties through Beirut or other towns and villages of Lebanon that could tell the story in the faces of martyrs or the wrecks of buildings.

A couple of hundred yards or so west of the St. George, as the bay comes more clearly and widely into view and the corniche rolls out ahead, is the little enclave of Ain Mreisse, where a tall, long triangular plinth bears the striding imprint of the late, great (or infamous, depending again on which side of the street you walk) Egyptian President, Gamal Abdel Nasser; and across the street from him is the tiny Nasser Mosque, of a pale, pinkish-grey brick and weak-custard-coloured arched windows, not unlike those in a Welsh Nonconformist chapel.

In fact, from the outside, apart from the imposing minaret, the mosque could well be a Welsh Nonconformist chapel. Small it may be, but Nasser and his supporters, who this mosque commemorates, now a memory rather than an influence, was a powerful element in Lebanon's upheavals, in the near-civil war of 1958 and again in the 1970s. Even now, in Lebanon, Sunni Muslims of the middle and working class remember him as a representative of Arab Nationalist and Sunni authority, a defiant leader of power and presence, who defied Israel and the West, who saw off the British and French in 1956, who challenged pro-Western Christian Lebanese leaders in 1958, and who came to terrible grief in 1967 when Israel conquered the Arabs so definitively. But still, long after his death, some of them kept his spirit alive – or at least tried to – when in small Nasserite militia groups they fought alongside the Palestinians and Druze against their Phalangist-Christian opponents for a larger Muslim say in Lebanon's affairs and a more equitable distribution of the political pickings.

Nasserism is a memory now. For many Arabs, even Sunnis, despite the depredations they have lived since his death in 1970, it is not always a good memory. He spoke more than he delivered, he was more an idea than a result, except perhaps for those inside Egypt who suffered under his socialistic experiments, lost their livelihoods and were often forced to leave their mother-country. He lives on, though, as an Arab leader of courage and inspiration in an age of puppets and potentates. One looks at his confident image, stepping out across Ain Mreisse, with regret and nostalgia.

There is a lot of nostalgia about in Ain Mreisse. Just behind the Nasser regalia, staring down on his great Sunni contemporary, is the legendary Imam Musa Sadr, the Shi'ite cleric of similarly convincing powers of persuasion and mass appeal who began the whole motivation and mobilisation of working class and peasant Lebanon, especially the Shi'ites, in the early 1970s. It was he who created Amal, or Hope, which became a powerful militia in the middle of the civil war, but which also and coterminously, after his mysterious disappearance in 1978, became corrupted and shorn of its idealism and appeal. It was – by the end of the 1980s – replaced by Hezbollah, as the Shi'ites' representative, army and political embodiment.

Amal flags still hang in Ain Mreisse, a reminder that the party still exists and has strength and representation in parliament and government, and is tolerated and used by Hezbollah in the game of power-seeking. By the portrait of Imam Musa Sadr is a poster of the present Speaker of the Lebanese parliament and a leading player in the political confrontation between government and opposition, the Amal leader, Nabih Berri.

During the later years of the civil war, especially after the Israeli invasion of 1982, Ain Mreisse became a focus of Shi'ite refugees from the south and the southern suburbs, the 'Dahiyeh', running from the indiscriminate bombs and shells and the fighting between their Palestinian neighbours and the Israelis, Amal at that stage being their political arm. Amal and the Syrians ran the neighbourhood, which became a slum for ten years, families stacked into the blocks that had once housed the smartest restaurants, the night clubs, the hotels. Ain Mreisse since 1990 or so has been recapturing some of its old charm, but now the threat is the swinging ball of the demolition team and the towering crane piling up yet another empty high-rise as an investment opportunity against the day – which surely must come? – when Lebanon once again prospers without adversity.

Now maybe four of those elegant four-storey Mediterranean houses, with their arched windows and red-tiled roofs, remain, squashed on all sides by tower-blocks, like diminutive old ladies with uncalled-for escorts. Most of these memorable Beiruti coastal dwellings, with their echoes of the Ottomans or French-colonial gentility are falling into disrepair.

At the end of this strip is the site of the old American Embassy, a not very attractive block, but one of human scale in its day, when – as older Lebanese remember it – American diplomats were friendly and approachable and could be seen at parties, functions, on the AUB campus and in the street, not, as they are now, bunkered away in a fortress compound in Awkar, in the Christian hills of the Metn, some way north of Beirut, venturing out only in armour-plated limousines with armed guards, their ambassador a consul to whom Lebanese government leaders go for their instructions rather than a discreet diplomat. The Americans today are trying to be to the Lebanese what the French were 100 years ago, though they are not as skilful, resourceful or any longer all-powerful as the French were then.

There is a reason for this change of American pose and attitude, and it could all be said to have started here, where a high-rise apartment block has risen on the site of the former mission. A new generation of Lebanese probably have no idea of what was once here or what happened. It was the first major attack by Islamists on a US diplomatic mission. It happened in April 1983, after the USA had sent a Marine force in to help supervise the end of the Israeli invasion of Lebanon and because, under President Ronald Reagan, the mission had altered. The US Administration had decided to start using its military weight against the Muslim – mostly Shi'ite, Druze, Palestinian and leftist – militias it decided Lebanon would be better off without.

It was not a wise tactic. Israel's army of occupation held much of the southern half of the country and remained in the mountains to the east of Beirut. The USA was known to be an uncritical supporter, financier and armourer of Israel. The machinery which dealt such death and destruction to Lebanon's population had very largely come from or been paid for by the USA.

On 18 April 1983, a suicide bomber driving a van with about 2000 lb of explosives managed to inveigle his way into the Embassy compound and blow up himself and his deadly delivery in the entranceway. The whole of the front of the mission collapsed, killing 63 people, 17 of them Americans and eight of them agents and employees of the CIA, including the CIA director for the whole of the Near East. It was later judicially determined in the USA that a new organisation, almost unknown in 1983 outside Iran, Hezbollah, had been responsible. This may well be a little retrospective points-scoring as Hezbollah was inchoate in 1983, but the general principle of total Islamic guerrilla war against the USA and its allies was presaged in this western corner of Ain Mreisse. Worse was to come.

The walk becomes a promenade past here, the broad pavement of the corniche usually a swarm of strollers, joggers, traders on bikes with breads and ice-creams, chiclets and sweets, picnickers and families on the rocks down below the railings by the sea, the men and boys in trunks, the women in robes and *hijab* – the familiar headscarves and modest dress of this part of the Muslim Arab world – sweating it out in the sun while the men relax, swim and fish. This is where Beirut's working class Muslims normally come to relax at the weekend. Today, however, the corniche is virtually deserted, though it is a warm June day (16 June 2007), a Saturday, when normally it would be jammed.

All I can see is a legless beggar wheeling himself along on a kind of tray with wheels. I buy chiclets from him and notice a familiar-looking figure standing by a lamp standard. He looks like a taxi driver I once knew, but he turns out to be someone else, one of a type, a Sunni with a face that is familiar in style and texture from Alexandria through Haifa, Sidon and Beirut to Tripoli and Tartous: bronzed, lined, cheery, wide and framed by frizzy white hair. He hails me like a long-lost friend and we talk about the old days and drivers we knew, and although he tells me, on discovering I am British, that he was at El Alamein, subsequent clues in the conversation indicate that he would have been about 12 years old at the time. I ask about the empty corniche. His taxi is on the eastbound side and we could safely crawl across to it on our hands and knees the traffic is so light. 'It's the situation,' he says.

In Beirut, it is so often the situation. Three days earlier, a few hundred yards further along this same seaside road, a Lebanese MP, a Sunni Muslim named Walid Eido, was killed by a car bomb, as were his son and driver, who were in his car with him, two security guards and four passers-by, including two young players in one of Beirut's two top football teams. They had been at the Sporting Club, a popular seaside club with pool, restaurants and other sporting facilities, in the shadow of the great Ferris wheel that is as much a landmark of Beirut's as its cousin was of Harry Lime's Vienna. The landmark shares the lethal and sinister nature of its situation with post-war Austria, too. Mystery will ever surround the nature of Mr Eido's assassins; but, whoever they were, they were as professional and dedicated to eliminating their target and anyone else who got in the way as those who blew up Rafiq Hariri – whose death site we passed a mile or so back – two years and four months earlier. Perhaps they were the same people, or from the same band of killers or hired by the same patrons.

I leave the driver, Ali, and walk on to the site of Eido's demise, or as near to it as I can reach, past the broken windows of nearby hotels and the desultory Lebanese soldiers and security men hanging round the tape that closes off the shattered alleyway, still piled with the wreckage of the blast and the burned-out cars. There is nothing to see now. There is just that fear in the air that there is so often in Beirut, in Lebanon, for the people who live there, who thought until 14 February 2005 that perhaps that fear had lifted and that better and safer times lay ahead. If they had thought that they should have every sympathy; but they forgot that they live in a bad neighbourhood, where war has by no means finished, where international forces of West and East are at each other's throats with renewed vigour – an intensity that has grown since that Embassy attack in 1983 – and that their own leaders play perilous games with these powers, these enemies. The story of Lebanon does not change, despite the incorrigible spirit of its people, or maybe even because of it.

The fault lines of the civil war, for most of its varied life, certainly the first ten years, were very much along the Christian–Muslim divides: in the downtown area by the port and in the districts of east and west Beirut that impinged upon it; and along the Damascus Road that cuts south and south-east through the city and the poorer suburbs, then winds up through the hills, where those traditional rivals the Druze and the Maronites formed the hard basis of the battle. These Lebanese fought each other with particular ferocity after the Israelis relinquished their occupation of the hills above Beirut, the Shouf, which had lasted from mid-1982 to late 1983. Two Israeli invasions, in 1978 and 1982, only served to aggravate the tensions in Lebanon, as well as deliver tens of thousands more casualties and displace hundreds of thousands more people, including the removal from Israel's northern doorstep of the military and political infrastructure of the PLO.

One focus of these fault lines, especially in the first years, was the area we have just explored, in the hotel district and its surrounds. But as the 1980s drew on, the fighters turned in on themselves, Druze and Shi'ite fighting for control of west Beirut, Shi'ite militia and Syrians besieging and bombarding the Palestinian camps of south Beirut in a final effort to subdue the PLO, or what was left of it after the Israeli invasion and the expulsion of the bulk of the Palestinian guerrillas in 1982 and 1983.

27

There seemed to be little sense to it and the world withdrew what little care and attention it had ever focused on the country, except, that is, to interfere for advantage. There seemed, in 1984, to be little advantage to be found in the ruins of Lebanon. The Christians also turned on each other, with particular venom and destructiveness, the right-wing militias finally facing the rump of the Lebanese Army and its friends in two years of battles that, finally, brought an end to the war. The war was over in 1990, but there was no reconciliation, no recompense and no real solution; merely a slightly new set of constitutional rules that moved towards correcting the balance of power between Sunni Muslims and Christians; and, to enable it, a Syrian hegemony that was to last for 15 years. And when it ended, the situation for the Lebanese was little, if at all, better than the status quo ante of 1974.

Up Among the Christians

In a spacious 'La Coupole'-style eatery in Gemmayzeh, a district to the east of the port that has become a thriving source of bars and cafes and a haunt of the Beirut pleasure-seekers since the early 1990s – old buildings remain in the shadow of the new downtown Hariri glitz, a hint of the Old Beirut – I hear a young Lebanese woman at the next table say: 'One good thing about confessionalism is that we can never have a dictator. No one would permit it.' I admire her sentiments and agree with her, silently, though I wonder whether a dictator, a benign one perhaps, is not exactly what Lebanon needs as it veers without national leadership through the storms of the Middle East and the vagaries of its own politicians' venality. (The nearest Lebanon had to a dictatorship was under the rule of President Fuad Chehab, who kept order in Lebanon through what many would argue were its finest and most prosperous and peaceful years, from 1958, when he was elected, to be followed by Charles Helou in 1964, both of whom ruled in the same spirit and with the same methods, largely through the disciplinary and intrusive force of military intelligence and the beneficent effects of the flow of oil money through the country's banking system, businesses and traders. For reasons we shall explore later, the end of Helou's administration in 1970 more or less coincided with the beginning of Lebanon's gradual disintegration.)

A Lebanese political columnist has put the case to me succinctly, cynically but with some pertinence: 'In the Arab Middle East you can have a nation state or you can have democracy. You can't have them both.' I ponder this. Jordan is about the only Arab country I can think of where the two concepts co-exist, uneasily, but even there the democracy is well restricted and the nation state is an uneasy amalgam of East Bankers and Palestinians which survives with Western aid and Israeli permission, just.

Here in Gemmayzeh, because of where we are, I assume the young woman I am eavesdropping is Christian. If so, she and her friends, talking in English to a foreign couple, are 'progressive', not always a characteristic connected with Lebanon's Christians but perhaps more so these days, as the young tire of the mouthings of their leaders and the lack of progress in their humanly resourceful and talented country.

They are talking of the idiocy of the charges that in the 2006 July Israeli invasion Hezbollah used civilian, human defensive shields to try to hold off the air and artillery bombardments. 'Of course civilians were killed,' says another woman. 'Israel was attacking villages and suburbs. Where else would Hezbollah put their guns? And how can you defend against such attacks with women and children?'

It is true on both or all sides of the lines in Lebanon that many educated young people like this talk freely and often against the grain of the political perceptions they have grown up with, the Christians preternaturally suspicious of Muslims and especially the propensity of Hezbollah to draw Lebanon into conflict with Israel. Sunni Muslims share this fear.

One cannot help feeling, however, that such cross-cultural sentiments and beliefs – as paraded in the days of peaceful revolution after the assassination of Rafiq Hariri and the departure of the Syrians – are soon mangled by reality. Women marry and have children, usually inside their confessional boundaries, and their husbands need jobs and advancement. In Lebanon that comes through a system of patronage based on tribalism, family and influence. The system has always absorbed those who would buck it. Many have tried over the decades and failed.

Politicians who advocated systems of politics based on the popular vote soon found that the extended family and therefore religion was the mainstay of trust in Lebanon: even if the electoral system were changed to one of pure universal suffrage of the European style, the eventual distribution of offices, jobs and patronage would devolve along confessional lines.

The origins of the Maronites

The origins of the Maronite presence in Lebanon are arguable, but, broadly, it seems the Church was founded in the sixth or seventh century by followers of Saint Maroun, a fifth-century religious man who would have lived in the Orontes river (now the Asi) area of northern Syria. (The Asi rises near Hama and flows to the Mediterranean on what is now the south-eastern coast of Turkey, near Antakya, or Antioch.) It is supposed that the Church's founders were Monothelites, believers in the Two Natures, divine and human, but one will of Christ, a belief that put them at odds with Rome in those early years.

The Maronite people were most probably members of tribes who had moved north and west, with many others, from South Arabia and Yemen to Syria, although some Maronites like to think they were descended from the Mardaites, people from Anatolia, what is now central and eastern Turkey, a conceit which allowed them to emphasise what many of them regarded, still regard, as essential – to depict themselves as special and separate, even to posing as non-Arabs, as ethnically different from their fellow countrymen in Lebanon and Syria (just as they are so accepted in Cyprus). This is almost certainly not the case, but it was often stressed to me during the civil war by Maronites that they were not Arabs, even that they spoke 'Lebanese' rather than Arabic.

One leader from the Bsherri area concocted a lexicon of 'Lebanese', which was Arabic transliterated into Latin script, incorporating local expressions, words and phrases. It did not catch on. The Maronites were always Arabic speakers, except in their liturgy – and not only speakers but often masters and teachers of Arabic.

The Maronites settled in Mount Lebanon mainly during the tenth century, on the run from attacks in Syria by Byzantine, Eastern Christians, who saw the Maronites, with their tentative links to Rome at that time, as aliens and rivals. Whatever their beliefs, doctrines and forms of prayer, a mixture of Eastern and Western rite, the Maronites traditionally behaved as a tribe as well as a sect, a defensive political entity in the region where, in the tenth century and beyond, they were squeezed between the expanding Muslim empires and dynasties and the followers of the orthodoxy of Constantinople. The high fastnesses of Mount Lebanon were the ideal refuge: they could come out and go down at will; it was much harder for outsiders to penetrate upwards.

31

Bsherri and the Holy Valley of Kadisha, an almost impenetrable gulch at the foot of the highest peaks, were to become for some 900 years the refuge of the Maronite patriarchs. (*Kadisha* means 'holy' in Syriac, the language the Maronites still use in their liturgy, the literary form of Aramaic, the Semitic language that Christ spoke.) They had been on the run from various persecutors for almost a thousand years, Byzantine Christian and Muslim among them.

The sanctuary was largely successful; the Byzantine Christians never cracked it. Not until the Ottomans seized power over the area in the fifteenth century were Bsherri and its district penetrated; even then the Maronites managed to preserve their de facto autonomy.

At first, however, as the tenth century turned into the eleventh, the Maronites had to deal with the Mamluks, the warlike, Muslim Turkic tendency that ruled Egypt and Syria from Cairo, with whom they forged reasonably harmonious relations, and, later, the Crusaders, who found in these Christians a much sought-after welcome as they made their first foray towards Jerusalem from Antioch, through extremely hostile territory, in the late eleventh century. The Maronites did co-operate with the Crusaders, who took for themselves an imposing and long-lasting possession of Tripoli; and this apparent piece of treachery has often been held up by the Maronites' opponents as proof of their duplicity and lack of loyalty to the Arab East they inhabit. Much of this is unfair, however. Many sects, including the Sunni Muslims, helped out the Crusaders when it suited them, when the invaders' support might have been useful in local disputes, and the Maronites themselves periodically raided the Crusaders in search of loot or their own advantage in some now apparently counter-intuitive alliances. In those days the region was a mixture not just of Maronites and Sunnis, themselves often in different groups and gangs, but of Shi'ites, Kurds and Orthodox Christians.

Not all Maronites were happy about the first formal union between the Maronite Church and Rome, which took place in the late twelfth century, while the Crusaders were still present in Syria and in Jerusalem. It was only with Mamluk help that the Church managed to suppress anti-Rome Maronite rebellions and civil strife – the Mamluks themselves having excellent commercial relations with the powerful Republic of Venice: Catholic, militaristic, seaborne and rich.

Rome, however, remained uneasy about the Maronites. They were thought to be too 'Eastern' in outlook and rite. Further, they had defied the Pope by electing their own patriarchs to the See of Antioch, which covered what is now northern Lebanon as far south as Tripoli (Rome recognised the patriarchy of the Melkites, who we now know as Greek Catholics, also Eastern-rite Christians who recognised Rome). However, troubles within the Church, the divisions between rival popes and then the long-drawn-out and failed efforts to unite the Western and Eastern Churches, Rome and Constantinople, in the fifteenth century and the subsequent triumph of the Ottomans, who captured Constantinople in 1453, saw the Pope reaching out to those in the Levant whom he knew he could, to some extent, trust: the Maronites, who for their part were keen to acquire Western protection in the uncertain Muslim world in which they survived.

Three years after the fall of Constantinople, the Pope recognised the Maronite patriarch of Antioch, and in 1510 Pope Leo X recognised the Maronites as a special historical Church of the Eastern rite, a 'rose among thorns', as he put it, though it is not clear who exactly the thorns were – other Christians or the majority of Muslims who surrounded them and by now ruled over them. In this hostile environment, but inside their own well-protected areas, the Maronites had developed a system of rule that was as secular and tribal as it was spiritual.

Certainly, the religious class were at the head of the community; but they were served and protected by a strong class of centurions, militaristic leaders known as *muqaddamim*, muqaddams, part-religious and responsible to the religious leadership, but with an element of the official gang-leader about them, a strand of leadership not reflected in quite the same way in other communities. It gave the Maronites the image and the reality of toughness and survivability, and made them attractive and reliable allies to the different Western traders and priests who did their business in the Levant.

The Church of Rome was also beginning to acquire other anxieties that made a trusted Eastern ally the more necessary. The Reformation, by the end of the sixteenth century, was knocking hard at Rome's doors. After the Synod of Qannubin, at the remote monastery in the Bsherri district, in 1608, the first Maronite patriarch of Mount Lebanon was one John Makhluf, which meant that the Holy Mother Church had given its official blessing and recognition to the Maronite tendency and confirmed its true and essential links with Rome.

However, as the Ottomans increased their hold on and penetration of the Syrian hinterland and Mount Lebanon itself, bringing with it powers of taxation over all non-Muslims, the prosperity of the area began to decrease and life became more difficult for the Christian inhabitants. There were also intrusions by local Shi'ites and others. Maronites began to emigrate southwards, to the Druze area of the Shouf, in the hills east of Beirut and points south above the coast, towards Sidon and, later on, to Kisrawan, north of Beirut and also nearer the coast.

Until the early nineteenth century the Maronites did well in these new areas, without trouble from the natives, whom they joined and often overtook. In the Druze areas they worked in and gradually dominated the expanding silk trade, growing silk and exporting it (see Chapter 8). In Kisrawan they moved up the social scale, gradually establishing themselves as a feudal, land-owning class of entrepreneurs, dominating much of the trade with the West.

It would not always be thus, however. The Ottomans, in strength, had been content to allow these developments among their subjects. After all, the Sublime Porte took its cut of whatever Christian prosperity emerged and burgeoned. But the Ottoman Empire was beginning to creak by the end of the eighteenth century and into the nineteenth. It began to shrink and sunder. As the European powers became more influential, first protecting the Ottoman entity, later picking it apart, so did the constituents of the Levant turn on each other and seek advantage where they could, alongside new and powerful collaborators.

This day, the Saturday of the holy weekend, 2007, I drive up to the heart of Maronite country to see where, it might be said, the idea of Lebanon began. This is in Bsherri, nearly 7000 feet up in the mountains of the north-east. The coastal highway north from Beirut towards Tripoli is soon running under the span of the mountains, a towering statue of Christ overseeing the tawdry view below, of high-rises and garish billboards advertising bikinis and jeans on lissom, pouting girls, in an array of come-hither poses. Muslim areas of Beirut are not without their Western displays of half-naked girls and dark-eyed temptresses, depending on exactly which part of Muslim Lebanon; but somehow here, on the Christian side, it becomes a display of strength of nerve, of defiance almost. 'We are modern,' the highway billboards seem to say. 'We are as the West. Know it.' The latest advertisement, all over Lebanon, is of a blue-eyed blonde encouraging her sisters to take out loans for face-lifts from an American bank.

North of Jounieh, the flourishing port city about ten miles north east of Beirut, the Christians' main harbour during the civil war, there is still a diversion round one of the bridges that takes the main Tripoli highway across a ravine.

Why the Israelis chose to knock this one out a year earlier, during their massive assault on Lebanon, is something only they can know: one imagines that their aim was to put their potential friends among the Christians against Hezbollah.

It has not worked. First, the Christians are not really any longer such potentially close friends of the Israelis. If they blamed anyone for their bridges being destroyed in 2006 it was the people who bombed them, though it has to be said that now, a year after the invasion, that patience with the Shi'ite resistance is beginning to expire and not just among Christians. My driver, Sa'id, a large, beaming, bronzed man with a generous set of very white teeth, who could not be anything other than a Sunni, in a very Sunni American eight-cylinder saloon of early 1980s vintage, reflects this impatience. He has no good word to say of the Shi'ites, a disturbing reflection of how the fault lines in Lebanon are changing. In fact, he is positively insulting about them.

I am, however, more worried about where I am taking Sa'id, up into these glorious hills at the end of the highway snaking up from near the second city of Lebanon, Tripoli, an overwhelmingly Sunni Muslim port where Sa'id would fit in far better than in the Christian fastness of Bsherri. This is the route to the original site of the Cedars of Lebanon, the Christians' and the nation's everlasting, biblical symbol. The cedar is the centrepiece of the national flag and has been co-opted by many groups and militias. There are not many cedar trees left up here now, most of them having been cut down by greedy entrepreneurs over the past decades. There are more further south in the Druze-controlled forests of the Shouf; but this is where one might say the Christian Maronite frame was hewn, out of these remote canyons and mountains, where the hands of their many enemies would find it hard to reach.

It is a panoramic vision as we climb from the coast, through small villages and past pines and firs, the air thinning and – this is early spring

– the cloud cover lowering and bringing with it a fine rain. As we near Bsherri, there are posters carrying the attractive image of Sadrika, the wife of Samir Geagea, the head of the Lebanese Forces party (LF) and chieftain of this area, and a leading protagonist and fighter in Lebanon's wars, past and present. Bsherri is a town of red-roofed houses that hangs off the cliff-edges in a bowl of mountains. The livelihood here is apples and grapes and, when they come, tourists, but probably the most important source of income is remittances from abroad, from the Gulf, from South America, from Australia, from Europe.

The Maronites have always emigrated in large numbers, in good and bad times. There are more of them abroad than there are in Lebanon (probably about a million resident at any one time in the country), a tendency which is eloquently spelled out as Sa'id and I drive across the Bsherri limits: a massive blue hoarding offers in white lettering, in English, French and Arabic, the availability in a town office of expert advice from a local lawyer on how to go about acquiring an Australian visa.

The young people who greet us, supporters and relatives of Samir Geagea, are typical of the almost blindly dedicated political workers who serve different masters on the Christian side. There is a whiff of hero-worship here that, it seems to me, contrasts with the more pragmatic solidarity of the Shi'ites, with their bosses and commanders. I get the feeling that to these young Christian Maronites a man like Samir Geagea – to any outsider a ruthless warlord – is other-worldly, almost saintly in his world beyond doubt or failure. They carry a banner. There is something evangelical and mystical here. It is in the air. We ask Sa'id, the only Muslim for miles around, whether he would like to come with us on our tour around Bsherri District, but he is happy to stay with his car, in the town. I later find that he has attracted much attention from the locals but has not been troubled. I reflect that 25 years earlier, had I for some reason been mad enough to bring him here, I would not have left him alone; had I done so he would probably have had his throat cut.

It is up here, in April, with the wind-charged rain beating at us, driving fiercely down the canyon from the snow-capped mountains towering over us, that I sense the harsh origins of the Maronite separateness. These were people forged in adversity, living in the desolate winters, snowbound and isolated, emerging cautiously to trade with coastal and desert neighbours and scurrying back to their caves and frugal settlements. In winter these villages are regularly cut from the outside world. In summer they are cool outposts only half an hour's drive from the damp, hot blanket of the Mediterranean coast. What a lonesome and often paranoid view these Christians must have had of the immediate outside world and how inevitable it was, as we shall see, that they would find their reassuring but dangerous alliances so much further afield, in the alien West.

They did become an integral part of, perhaps the reason for, the special nation that was to emerge, as a refuge of often-quarrelsome sects and minorities. But even though the Maronites over the centuries became a central and even dominant part of Levantine, Lebanese life and politics, trading with, living with, even marrying into other groups, and emigrating and travelling like their different neighbours, they retained and even now retain that separateness, that quickness to return mentally if not physically to their Mountain, a mountain in the mind as well as in its remoteness and well-defended perimeters.

The making of the Maronites

A long string of Maronite martyrs was already extant when the Maronite patriarch established himself in the Monastery of Qannubin, which is cut precariously into the rocky edges of the canyon of Kadisha. The link between the fifth and twentieth centuries is easily made by one of the Maronites showing us around the monastery. 'To understand Lebanon,' says John Geagea, a 30-something host, a businessman, 'you must go everywhere, visit every faction. But if you do not come here and see this you do not understand how Lebanon began or what it has become.' Pointing to a tiny cell, maybe 15 feet by 5 feet, with a view down the Kadisha pass, an eyrie from which approaching enemies could have been spotted, John says: 'It was in a room just this size that they kept Samir Geagea for 11 years.' He is referring to the incarceration of the Christian LF leader, effectively by Syrian command four years after the end of the civil war in 1990, much of it in solitary confinement. Samir Geagea was the only militia leader to face a sort of justice in the years that followed the end of the fighting; but to his followers it was no justice at all, merely a Syrian-inspired revenge against a man who refused to toe the line, to bow his head to Lebanon's new masters.

To his followers, such as John and Samir Geagea's sister-in-law, Denise, another guide today, these years of imprisonment, during which only his immediate family and his lawyer were allowed to see him, have bestowed on Geagea an almost unearthly aura, enhancing a familial and tribal loyalty that goes back to his days in the mid-1970s as a young Phalangist fighter and emerging leader under that other iconic Christian figure Bashir Gemayel.

Unlike Bashir, Samir Geagea is the 'martyr' who has survived, who, first, should have died at his many enemies' hands and, had the Syrians stayed in Lebanon, as well they might have, could have ended his useful days in prison.

As it is, Samir Geagea is a typical product of Maronite myth and legend, history and actuality. He is a tyrant and bogeyman to his enemies, some of the most entrenched of whom are his Maronite Christian neighbours just a few miles away in the territories loyal to the Franjieh family, in Zghorta. Equally, Geagea is a hero and warrior-commander to his supporters. He exemplifies the Maronite story: like him, the Maronites have been unpopular in the Arab world, mainly because of their ethnic cleansing of Muslims and Palestinians from their areas during the civil war years of 1975–90, and because so many of them behaved as out-and-out Western-focused Christians in an area of Muslims and more Eastern-thinking Christians. They have, it is true, been ruthless, with others and with themselves, when they felt their survival was at stake, a feeling they carry constantly. In the mid-1970s and early 1980s this feeling was severely inflamed, with reason.

It is not surprising that on this harsh, beautiful mountain the inhabitants carry on feuds that go back centuries. For all the religious and social similarities the Maronite Christians share, they can fight and slaughter one another with as much fervour and ferocity as they might ever apply to those of different sects or nationalities; even their churches have not always been sanctuary from carnage.

Slaughter inside the sect: Feuds, bosses, men of honour

In this north-east corner of the *Jebl Lubnan* literally, (Mount of Lebanon) we are in the heart of Lebanese Christendom: Tripoli down on the coast to the west, looking out across the Mediterranean; Syria over the giant rise to the east; with both of which places the local inhabitants have had strong historic links. The Arabs of Syria ruled here in the seventh and eighth centuries, this sector of the Mountain coming under the District of Homs, now in modern Syria; the Crusaders, the Mamluks and the Ottomans trying to bring the region under their (limited) control from Tripoli for more than 800 years. In modern times, the mountain above Tripoli is still the redoubt of the Christians. Whoever is nominally in charge, these are notoriously canny and resilient hill people who are resistant to excessive intrusion by outsiders, as is witnessed in one of the main divisions inside the Christian community.

Feuds the length of Mount Lebanon, inside clans and sects as well as between them, have that remorseless and, to the outsider, inexplicable durability that marks the vendettas of Corsica, Sardinia, Sicily and the mountainous reaches of Italy. At their heart are not merely rivalries over land, power and votes, but the vibrant concepts of honour and respect, not just of the family or village but of the district and its *za'im*. *Za'im* is simply the Arabic word for 'boss'. In Lebanon, however, it has a more resonant cachet – it means the 'big boss', the 'strong man', perhaps even 'the enforcer', and he has always been at the centre of Lebanese tribal politics and the loyalties and disciplinary systems that go with it.

The *za'im* is essentially the local chieftain, who commands or at least expects the obedience and service and often the money from those he protects and serves in his district. He will expect tribute near election days, and his men will in return offer protection when needed against rival factions, and advice and help in local disputes. The battles this system has provoked are as savage, if not as broad in scale, as those between the Confessions or major parties, within a community, Christian or Druze for example, as between these two sects.

Bsherri District has had a long rivalry with Zghorta, the seat of power of the influential Maronite Franjieh family, about 12 miles to the northwest of Bsherri town. Ehden, another Franjieh stronghold, is only five miles away. These are very local quarrels and no less vicious for that. The relationship between the Franjiehs and their political and local rivals, respectively the Gemayels and the Geageas, combines a toxic mix of local militias, neighbourly loathing and national power-seeking.

The Franjiehs' most famous recent son was Suleiman, a family enforcer and *za'im* who held the presidency of the Republic from 1970 to 1976, a spell which saw the start of the civil war and the first entry of Syrian troops into the country in an effort to stop the fighting and mediate, in a pretty forceful way, between the contestants. Suleiman Franjieh held on – just – throughout all this, managing to remain close to the Syrian power-brokers, whom many if not most of his co-religionists mistrusted and hated. If this President was more brawn than brain, it would be nonetheless unfair to lay all the blame for these destructive years at his door.

Suleiman's family had been traders who became wealthy during the early nineteenth century, then began to assert themselves politically. His grandfather began the family's rise to prominence with a position in the *Mutassarifate,* the governorate of the whole Lebanese Mountain that the Ottomans established in 1861 after the mutual massacres by the Druze and Christians in the 1850s. These wars had been the point at which the Western powers, particularly the French, but also the British, the Austro-Hungarians and the Italians, had started to press their acquisitive ambitions in Greater Syria. The Ottomans thought to regain order by establishing a governorate of councillors from a careful balance of the sects under the aegis of a Christian, but not Lebanese, governor.

Suleiman's father Kabalam was the first real politician of the family. He was elected to the Lebanese legislature formed under the French, after World War I; and his eldest son, Hamid, took on his father's role as a legislator both under the Mandate and after Independence. He was apparently a much-respected man who might even have been considered eventually for the presidency – but he was the victim of a stroke in the mid-1950s and the family's political succession fell to the next-in-line, Suleiman, a very different style of political activist.

Suleiman Franjieh was a real *za'im*, a *za'im* with form. In the early 1950s he and his cohorts had shot it out with a rival Christian family during Mass in a village church, a gunfight in which about 25 people were killed. For a year and a half Suleiman took refuge in Syria, with whose future leaders, including the Assad family, he became well acquainted. When he became President of Lebanon in 1970, it was the same year that Hafez al-Assad, Commander of the Syrian Air Force, took power in Syria.

As the 1970s progressed, Suleiman Franjieh found himself, as President and as a Maronite, embodying the authority of the state in its increasing problems with the emergent Palestinian movement. As sporadic clashes between the armed forces and the Palestinian guerrillas turned into open warfare, the strife evolved – the army disintegrated, broadly along confessional lines, and disaffected Lebanese from an array of political and tribal sources joined the Palestinians in their insurgency against the tattered Lebanese state and the Christian militias. Out of this chaos, the Christian Phalangist party emerged as *primus inter pares* among the defenders of Christian Lebanon and what it saw as the core of state authority.

The Phalange was a modern political structure, less feudal in nature than most of the other Lebanese parties, of whatever leaning, but very much at that stage under the sway of its founder, Sheikh Pierre Gemayel. His younger son Bashir, a dynamic *za'im* in his own right, led the party's military wing, the LF.

This made an uneasy formula in any quest for Christian Maronite solidarity. The Franjiehs, with their Syrian connections and sympathies, objected strongly to the Phalangists' flirtation with Israel, which was arming and training Christian fighters in their struggle against the common enemy, the Palestinians; they saw the relationship as a treacherous alliance which would prejudice Lebanon's Arab status and relations to the East and eventually blow up in the Phalangists' faces, which it later did. It went further than this. The Franjiehs objected to the grip Phalangists had on many residents, in their own Zghorta area, the arm of this powerful party stretching from its own home territory of Bekfaya, nearly 30 miles south-west of Zghorta, only 12 miles from Beirut. In other words, the Franjiehs, to say the least, were not getting total 'respect' in their backyard. Beyond this, the Franjiehs were having explosive clashes over various business and financial interests with pro-Phalangists in the Tripoli area, again very much the Franjiehs' area of influence.

The enmity was compounded in March 1978 when the Israelis invaded Lebanon and seized a swathe of its southern border region, putting a former Lebanese Major, Sa'ad Haddad, a Greek Catholic, in charge of it under Israeli supervision and with Phalangist compliance.

In June 1978, Bashir Gemayel sent a group of Phalangist fighters under the command of one Samir Geagea to attack the villa belonging to Suleiman's son and heir, Tony. In the assault, Tony, his wife and their baby daughter were killed, and the vendetta was intensified. It cannot be a coincidence that Bashir Gemayel chose a man from a Bsherri family to carry out this contract, and as the Gemayels faded from power during the 1980s it was Samir Geagea who seized control of the LF and the main political cadres of the Maronite Christians, though by the end of the 1980s the latter were not long from collectively losing much of their political power.

The stories of these feuds illustrate some of the realities of Lebanon, even with the Christians by no means as strong as they once were. First, these people can be extremely ferocious in defence of their land and rights, and religion. Any idea that they could easily or even possibly be subsumed under some Islamic Republican rule, whether Sunni or Shi'ite, is so far-fetched as to be unthinkable. Their internal divisions also make them unreliable allies, as the Crusaders, the Ottomans and the Israelis were to find out, in their different ways. They are, in the end, troublesome hill people when necessity drives, emerging to play their part in the wide world when it suits them, but finding strength and repose in their mountain refuge when enemies real or imagined threaten.

The Maronites are resourceful and tough. Without them Lebanon would have been, and is, unimaginable: they are the unique element. History was kinder to them in the first few hundred years or so of their sojourn in Mount Lebanon than it has been in the past 150 years.

Lunch with Priest and Parishioner

4

If I feel detached from the relative reality of Beirut and the coast up here, it is not surprising – detachment from the realities of their enemies was the reason the Maronites gathered up here in Bsherri and elsewhere in the mountains in the first place. At lunch, in the home of the chairman of the district council, are George Geagea and his wife, his cousins John and a young TV journalist Diamante, Antoine, the custodian of the museum of Khalil Gibran (this most famous artist son of Lebanon was born in Bsherri) and the local priest, Father Charbel. The whisky, wine and beer are on a silver tray and the usual melange of Lebanese *mezze* is before us (though no meat today as it is Easter weekend).

I stay off the liquor as getting to grips with local history needs clear thinking. Father Charbel's Maronite story differs from the received wisdom of most historians I have read, ascribing their empowerment in the Mountain to the early preachings and conversions of the followers of Saint Maroun, not the more familiar story of forced immigration from northern Syria.

He is an intense, dark-haired young man with a look more of the Caucasus, or Balkans even, about him. He does not take a drink. I notice that most of the guests in this massive living room gazing down the valley are fair and blue- or green-eyed. But this is not rare in Lebanon or anywhere else in what was Greater Syria, and maybe my observations are more attuned because I am deep among the Christians and looking too hard for those often spurious ethnic differences that many of them like to stress.

Most of his story, however, fits with that of the more orthodox histories, especially his emphasis on the ever-strengthening links with

43

Rome and the survival of the Maronites through various persecutions. He also stresses the fact that it was under the Muslims of the Ottoman Empire that the Maronites solidified the special status of Mount Lebanon and thus the foundation of what eventually became the state of Lebanon.

Persecution is an important badge of identity and *raison d'etre* in this region. 'We are a social and political system,' says Antoine, looking reasoned and academic in his cardigan, sipping a weak whisky. 'There are more factors cementing us than religion. What has bound us together are centuries of persecution. This has given us strength. And our links with the West have made us the ideal middle men between East and West. Do not forget that the Emir Fakhrieddin [the powerful and rebellious Druze leader of Mount Lebanon in the late sixteenth and early seventeenth century] allied with us to secure Western support against the Ottomans.'

I do not point out that the Emir, though a great and successful leader, ended his life decapitated in Istanbul by an Ottoman headsman. Life so often is cut short for eminent and revolutionary Lebanese leaders. Those who show their heads too clearly are likely to lose them: 'Mount Lebanon was always a shelter for everyone in the region, not just Maronites – a refuge, a place to hide, where people can worship how they like or live how they want to live, without interference.' As long, I reflect, as they are no threat to the Maronites, thinking again of the defensive and often murderous singularity of the Maronites during the civil war.

'We are the guarantors of Lebanon's independence,' says George. 'The Syrians have systematically tried to knock down all our main leaders and build up marginal people.' Antoine sees an Israeli dimension in Syrian hegemony over Lebanon, now, in 2007, ended (for the time being): 'Israel enjoys this ... it is in Israel's interests to have despotic regimes next door. It does not want democracy here. It needs enemies, not friends.' Sentiments one might have expected more from the other side of Lebanon's ideological divide. Nothing is ever straightforward here; the conflicting conspiracy theories would baffle a Borgia.

These (but by no means all) Maronites are pleased with their new post-2005 alliance with their old enemies the Druze and many of the Sunni Muslims. 'What is crucial now,' says John Geagea, the Bsherri council chief, 'is that for the first time the Sunnis are saying I am Lebanese first and Muslim second. They did not do this before.' They often did, in fact, but this is a statement, a slogan almost, I am to hear over and over again from non-Sunni supporters of the pro-government March 14 movement.

Many Sunnis fought and lost their lives fighting for Lebanese independence, against the French and even against those who saw Arab nationalism and (or?) subservience to Syria as logical ways forward for the emergent Lebanese. But it is indicative in the present, post-civil war context. I can never quite decide whether Lebanese memories are too long or too short; the answer is, almost certainly, selectively either.

Samir Geagea is the most eminent, or perhaps notorious, modern-day son of Bsherri. Among my guides and friends in Bsherri, such fierce and passionate devotion is expressed towards him that they seem to have been in The Presence. I am to find him impressive and scary. Samir Geagea daunts one for a number of reasons – he was an enthusiastic and brutal fighter for the Maronite cause, brave and bloody and extreme, a protégé originally of the equally militant and single-minded Bashir Gemayel.

Bashir's death (see Chapter 1) ended his long and not always successful flirtation with the Israelis during their invasion of Lebanon in 1982. Following these traumatic events and in the upheavals that followed, by 1986 the 34-year-old Samir Geagea had effected a kind of reverse takeover of the Nationalist and Maronite movement, bringing Bashir's Phalangist military wing, the LF, under his wing. The LF remained the most powerful Maronite body, under his command, until the civil war ended in 1990.

The other reason Samir Geagea demands respect is that between 1994 and mid-2005 he survived 11 years of virtual solitary confinement in a small cell, buried below the Lebanese Ministry of Defence. Ironically, his great Christian opponent, then and now, General Michel Aoun, also fell foul of the Syrians in the final years of the civil war. He also lived to appear again as a contender in the Lebanese political arena, in his case surviving 14 years of exile in France.

He and Samir Geagea were both reincarnated after the Syrians' physical if not political departure in March 2005, following the assassination of Rafiq Hariri – Geagea released from custody, Aoun returning from exile.

Samir Geagea had fought hard against the Syrians, as indeed he had fought earlier against the Palestinians, Druze and Muslims, but he had ended by fighting General Aoun in the intra-Christian savagery that finally ended the war and the fortitude of the Lebanese to withstand it after nearly a generation. This vicious Christian internecine warfare lost Geagea many supporters among the Christians. He lacked public support when the peace turned against him.

Where other warlords slotted back into the toing and froing of Lebanese political chicanery, co-operating with the Syrians, Samir Geagea went his own way, his head well above that dangerous parapet. Unlike his more pragmatic (and more typically Lebanese) fellow polit-ical personalities of all sects and strains, Geagea spent the first years of Syrian overlordship, 1990–4, making it clear he was vehemently opposed to Syria's interference in Lebanon and nailing his eternal Maronite-Independent-Lebanese colours to the mast. Whatever one makes of Samir Geagea, he is consistent in this.

This was too much for the Syrian/Lebanese authorities, who, his supporters believe, with some justice, tried to frame him for the bomb-ing of a church in the village of Zouk Mikael, on the coast near the port of Jounieh, deep in Christian territory just a few miles north of Beirut. Nine people were killed.

After a long and to say the least deeply suspect 'judicial' process, under close Syrian oversight and amid repeated allegations of deten-tion and torture and one Geagea colleague suddenly dying in custody, Samir Geagea was cleared of the church bombing, but convicted of responsibility for three assassinations of Lebanese leaders and the attempted killing of a fourth. Here it is often argued by his many oppo-nents, by no means all of them Syrian stooges, that the blood on Geagea's hands – often shed at the expense of fellow Christians, such as the Bsherri'ites' rival Franjieh clan, just over the hills from Bsherri and the cedars, and the supporters in the late 1980s of General Michel Aoun, not to mention thousands of innocent citizens of all sects – means that his imprisonment was deserved.

It might equally be argued that if Samir Geagea was to be jailed for the mayhem in which he participated between 1975 and 1990, then there were many equally deserving of punishment who live on in wealth and power.

In July 2005 he was finally released into the (almost) Syrian-free community. When I visited him, after my day in Bsherri, it was in yet another bunker – this time one of his own making and choice in a hotel in a village called Bzouma, above Jounieh in Kisrawan, not far from Harissa, where the giant statue of Jesus Christ lifts its prayerful arms from the hills overseeing the ocean below.[1]

To reach Samir Geagea – or the 'Hakim' as he is familiarly known, a term of respect that roughly translates as 'Doctor-Commander', or 'Wise-One' – means penetrating with much prior advice an outer guard of Lebanese state Internal Security armed guards, who place a mirror under your car to see if you are trying to bring in a bomb, and then an inner guard of the Hakim's own men, who take no chances, driving guests in an armoured four-wheel drive SUV the few-score yards across the hotel courtyard to the building's entrance. In the lobby, all mobile phones are removed and cameras and recorders are closely examined, held at the door, rather in the manner of cowboys' six-shooters at a Dodge City dance hall.

I am greeted in this splendid, closely guarded hostelry by one of the Hakim's long-time fans and aides, Denise Fayad, who is 30ish and as beautiful as her elder sister, Samir Geagea's wife Sadrika. Denise and Sadrika were among the few regular visitors of the Hakim in his long military confinement. Both are devoted servants of the Geagea cause. Sadrika became his representative on Earth while he was in jail, much to the resentment of others in the LF. Her position by his side remains undiminished. As usual in Lebanon, politics is at core a family business.

I am given coffee and cake while we await the summons of the leader downstairs. I asked for an hour of his time but am granted an hour and a half. Samir Geagea is a gaunt, balding man with a thin black moustache and the look of a bird of prey, though considering his 11 years in the severity and isolation of a military jail he has not aged as much as I would have expected in the 13 or so years since I last saw him. This was just after the troubles ended. He and his LF were struggling to survive (they were severely reduced after his incarceration and have never recaptured their old stature).

Samir Geagea, whatever his record in the mutual slaughter that has characterised Lebanon, is not a man who has massed great personal wealth and there are no telling stories circulated of personal corruption, though the authoritarian and arbitrary ways of his LF in the years of their power made them unpopular among many they were supposed to represent.

He comes across as direct, honest and not without humour. Unlike many politicians he seems interested in his guest and the world about him. He is not entirely wrapt in egomaniacal self-absorption, or at least gives the polite and effective appearance of not being so. In a recent series of articles published by a leading Lebanese newspaper to commemorate the 32nd anniversary of the beginning of the civil war, a number of factional and national leaders were asked if they thought they should apologise for the dreadful bloodshed and quarter-of-a-million-strong death toll that that war produced. All of them except Samir Geagea hedged and compromised. Geagea said, 'I publicly and honestly apologise.'

'Bsherri made me what I am,' he says. 'I am influenced by its geography, its climate, its history and by the philosophical mysticism within its society ... placed as it is between the Valley of the Saints, the Valley of Kadisha and the birthplace of Khalil Gibran. When I was a child I was imbued with this atmosphere. When the people of Bsherri talk they talk of heroes and history, they don't talk about the price of things, economics and everyday matters.'

'Each region of the Mountain has its mystique. Jebl Amal [the Shi'ite area of the Mountain, in the south] was for the downtrodden. Bsherri,' he laughs, 'was where you went not to be downtrodden.'

The characteristics of the people there, he says, are tenacity, independence: 'We are unbending, unflinching. The people of the Mountain are tough, the people of the shores are intellectual. The revolutionaries came out of the Mountain. We were always a place of refuge and independence, whereas the people of the coast were, for example, exemplary citizens of the Ottoman Empire. If you ask me how we make one country out of this I say you need a little bit of everything to make a world.'

He tried to combine studying medicine at the AUB with becoming involved in politics. Politics meant history to him and he wanted to change history; he wanted to help people through medicine and through politics. But in 1975 the civil war came. He found himself literally in the front line as his house in the Christian suburb of Ain el-Rummaneh, in south-east Beirut, was directly across the main road that divided the Christians from the mainly Shi'ite Muslims of Chiah: 'We expected them across the divide every day.'

What was the threat in the war? Islamic, Arab, Palestinian, leftist?

'I saw it as a direct military threat from the Palestinian guerrillas.

They were trying to take control of Lebanon. I thought that then and I still believe it now. If they had managed to control Lebanon they would have had a strong card in their hands, and this is what brought Syria in. Not to save us Christians but to keep the Palestinians in their place. Even then, I intuitively thought that Syria was a greater threat to us even than the Palestinians. It was a sheer question of the size of the country. The Syrians convinced many Christians that they were coming to our rescue but it was not the case. They wanted control of Lebanon.'

Here he speaks for most Christians and many other Lebanese. Is he not forgetting though that Lebanon was a part of Syria: distinctive and different, maybe, but still much a part, and never surely beyond its influence or presence, whether benign or otherwise?

'The Syria–Lebanon relationship you can compare with Iraq and Saudi Arabia or France and Belgium.' (If only it were so. Much of what Samir Geagea says contains real sense, but these analogies, in my view, are not sustainable.) 'There was,' he goes on, 'always a kind of state here in Lebanon; before the Ottoman Empire and after the Ottomans. Now the people of the coast like never before are making it clear through the March 14 movement that they want one state including the Mountain and the coast. It's crystal clear that's what most of the Lebanese want and Syria can claim what it likes.'

He says that when he emerged from prison he witnessed an enormous metamorphosis in Lebanon and among the Lebanese: 'The Sunnis are now sharing with us our slogans from the beginning of the civil war, 30 years ago: "Lebanon First". [Fuad] Siniora [the Lebanese prime minister in April 2007] has said that the Syrians should understand that there is an independent entity at their border.'

This process of change among the Sunnis happened gradually as a result of the experience of Syrian occupation, but the catalyst was the assassination of Rafiq Hariri: 'Now the Sunnis are asking the Palestinians to give up their arms, for the delineation of frontiers with Syria, for an embassy exchange, for Hezbollah to surrender their arms. There is no more talk of Arab nationalism, only of Arab friendship. The Sunnis like us are looking as much to the West for engagement as to the Arabs.'

Samir Geagea regards the present stand-off between the coalition of (some of) the Christians, and most of the Druze and Sunnis on one side and (most of) the Shi'ites on the other as unfortunate. He wants, he says, to find a way of reaching the Shi'ites, to bring them into the coalition, but it is obvious this cannot and will not happen before there is, as he puts it, regime change in Syria and/or Iran. At the time he speaks this does not look imminent, despite the best efforts of the US government that is supporting Geagea and his allies. (The USA did not do much to help him in the early 1990s, when they were keen to retain Syria's support in the coalition against Iraq. Funny how things change – that was also the time when the USA and Britain switched the focus from Syria, Iran and a fringe Palestinian group based in Syria, the Popular Front for the Liberation of Palestine – General Command whom they had fingered as suspects in the Lockerbie airliner bombing of 1988, to Libya.)

Are the Shi'ites Lebanese?

'They are by approbation and citizenship but not by affiliation, not when they put the Islamic *umma* before the nation.' (Not all of them do, even in official Hezbollah-speak, though it depends to whom one listens and when and where they speak.)

Samir Geagea admits that Hezbollah were more effective than the state of Lebanon could ever have been in getting the Israelis out in 2000 after 22 years of occupation of the south; he points out that his militia were more effective against the Syrians than the state was or could have been. But 'you cannot have a state without inconveniences. We cannot live without a state. If we had Lebanese soldiers along the Israeli border they would not have invaded ... after all they did not bother us between 1949 and 1969 [when the Palestinian guerrillas first started operating from Lebanon]. If Israel attacked our state we would all be the resistance.'

It is interesting how these Christian arguments alter, depending on circumstances. The Maronites created a state within a state between 1975 and 1990, not that dissimilar from that the Shi'ites later created in the 1990s and 2000s, when the Christians thought the Lebanese nation weak, corrupted and misled, a feeling echoed in 2007 by the Shi'ites and their allies.

The Hakim says that Lebanon is made up of different entities who have evolved at different stages: the mountain people became autonomous, the Sunnis made excellent citizens of the Ottoman Empire, the Shi'ites were forgotten. (This is broadly true, though the Ottomans did recognise the particular character and limited autonomy of the Mountain and its inhabitants.) 'Lebanon is now at the same stage as Switzerland was in the Middle Ages. But now we have at least apparently reached equilibrium with the Sunnis. For how long, I do not know. If another Nasser came along?'

He does not think Lebanon will break up, but it is difficult to say. It all depends on the durability of this new equilibrium and on the steadfastness of the Sunnis. But I think it might depend on a lot more than that. Lebanon's internal affairs have never been wholly or even mostly internal.

One problem for the Christians who support Samir Geagea and the Phalangist party of Amine Gemayel is that many working-class and lower middle-class Christians back former General Aoun, who is in an electoral and possibly even class-based alliance with Hezbollah, who also depend on the backing of the street. The old guard, who carved up Lebanon's territory and wealth as it suited them, and who ran the country largely for their own satisfaction, that of the rich and the entrepreneurial, and who made and broke alliances with fellow Lebanese and foreigners as they saw it financially and politically fit, are finding a unity of the oppressed of all sects forming against them.

In some cases it has religious overtones, as with hostilities developing between Shi'ites and Sunnis. There is in Lebanon the over-arching struggle between Iran and Syria, on one side, and the West on the other, which has become more definitive in the years of George W. Bush and the 'war against terrorism'. Samir Geagea himself is of humble origins and not a player in the pass-the-parcel of Lebanese wealth and influence; yet for all his resilience and the almost fanatical obeisance of those close to him, it may be that he has lost touch with political realities in his years of isolation.

The Bus to Civil War

5

The Maronite community, so crucial a part of the identity of Lebanon, did not come well out of the civil war. It did not fare well in terms of its reputation during those 15 years. This was unfair. The foreign and local press, so much a part of the battle zones that opposed the Christian Nationalist forces, were much to blame. The main Lebanese newspapers were in west Beirut, which was largely sympathetic to and very much under the aegis of the Palestinians and their Muslim Lebanese colleagues and co-fighters in the National Movement, led by the Druze chieftain and sometime cabinet minister Kamal Junblatt, a striking, esoteric, mystic, enigmatic and incredibly strong-willed leader: their editorial lines, in varying degrees, tended to see the Christian Forces as 'over there' and 'isolationist'.

The foreign media also tended to identify with the Palestinians, in a tense, love-hate relationship. This often depended on the Palestinian group involved and the editorial tendencies as Palestinians saw them at any particular time of a particular Western TV or radio channel or newspaper, particularly the Americans and British. (In those far-off days there was still a perceptible difference between American and British official attitudes to the Israeli–Palestinian question. The British were more *historically* suspect, with some good reason. But the British government at that time had a more balanced view of the Middle East, particularly the Israel–Palestine problem, one it maintained until towards the mid-1990s and the advent of Tony Blair.) The Palestinians were by no means adept at public and press relations, and suspicious of the media, especially the Americans and British. But they were there and available, up to a point, and had friends and supporters in the coffee shops, bars and hotels and on the AUB campus and in the west

Beirut drawing rooms, who were able to explain the Lebanese and Middle East complexities with a Palestinian and/or Arab Nationalist twist.

Journalists and diplomats in that part of town, west Beirut, where all of them lived and worked, which had, by the quirk of confessional line-drawing, become behind Muslim-Palestinian lines, but remained a very mixed Christian and Muslim quarter, were more than ready to identify with the Muslims and Palestinians. They (we) saw them as underdogs and outsiders battered and reduced during recent Middle East history, much of it unfairly encouraged and delivered by the all-powerful nations from which these (we) very journalists and diplomats came.

I remember animated tutorials in various pubs as a young Christian lieutenant in Fateh and other Palestinian friends tried to explain to me the tormented history of the region, especially the Palestinian question, a dreadful episode in Britain's colonial story.

For many of us, before, during and after the civil war, much of the coverage of the region had been of the misfortunes and mistakes of the Palestinians and the Israelis, with 'our' side reporting from the Arab perspective, while our colleagues did the same from 'their' side in Jerusalem or Tel Aviv. There had been little fair analysis. Background went begging. It is much the same in the popular TV and other news media today.

Until 1975, Lebanon had been more or less incidental in Middle East reporting, much ignored and even more misunderstood. The country was reckoned by those on the editorial desks of London and New York, if not so much Paris, to be marginal and complicated, which was, in a way, true. Journalists based in Beirut who had tried to alert their desks to the looming troubles in Lebanon, in 1972, 1973 and 1974, had mostly found their copy spiked. How could paradise be in danger?

Even now, ignorance about Lebanon is rife, even among other Arabs. People say to me, 'Isn't it a shame what happened to Lebanon? I remember it in the sixties,' as if the 'events' of 1975–90 (and beyond) were some natural disaster, like an unforeseen hurricane, rather than ones made by corrupt politicians and thoughtless, self-interested statesmen, inside and outside the region. As if Lebanon were not a post-colonial disaster guaranteed to happen. As if Lebanon were positioned, say, between Sardinia and Corsica rather than sand-wiched between two of the Middle East's most enduring and bitter antagonists, Israel and Syria. As if Lebanon were not playing reluctant host to an army of dispossessed, well-armed and well-financed guerrillas with the sympathies of much of the world and all the Arabs behind them?

Despite public identification with Israel and their governments' broad policies in the Middle East, which favoured Israel, Western diplomats stationed in Beirut tended privately to empathise with the Palestinians and their allies. Many of these envoys were Arabists and, in the case of the British, many of them had enjoyed the privileges and expertise of tuition in Arabic at the Middle East Centre for Arabic Studies, in Shemlan, in the foothills of the Shouf. These emissaries found themselves giving instant courses in regional politics, history and behaviour to the young men and women of the Western media, many of whom, as the crisis deepened, had arrived from Europe, the USA, Canada and Australia and crisis spots much further east. They were not familiar with the Arab world.

The spin was pro-Arab and often anti-Israeli, and while Israel's actions before and during this period had indeed done nothing but aggravate what internal tensions existed in Lebanon, and that spin was therefore probably largely justified, as the war continued and the Maronites' association of convenience with the Israelis emerged into public knowledge, it was not surprising that the Christian cause suffered even more in the overseas public's perception.

Neither were the Christians their own best friends. They were the ones who were 'isolated', physically and politically. For many of these 15 years, a journey from one side or the other ranged from impossible to darned uncomfortable, there being a Green Line whose few crossing-points were either closed by snipers or artillery or about to be made unnegotiable by such.

Thus, at many crucial stages of the war, especially in the first years in the mid-1970s, the Maronite leaders, such as Pierre and Bashir Gemayel, Camille Chamoun and his sons Dany and Dory, and other luminaries such as Abu Arz (Father of the Cedars), and many other interlocutors further down the chain of command, not to mention the authorities of the Maronite Church itself and the beleaguered Presidents, Suleiman Franjieh and later Elias Sarkis, were unable to unburden themselves personally to leading foreign diplomats and journalists, as well as being cut off from more than half the Lebanese population.

Worse, there was little opportunity for any of the diplomatic corps or media to indulge in that background chit-chat and socialising that lends weight and sympathy to the case being put. The Christians felt, and were, misunderstood. In the west of the city, we foreigners and our friends saw them, in their turn, as the enemy, the firers rather than the dodgers of shells and rockets. There is inevitably a tendency, however firmly resisted, to see the point of view of the man or woman in the ditch next to you, rather than that of the person who has consigned you to that ditch.

April 13: The massacre on the bus

The whole campaign started badly for the Christians. I am reminded of all this starkly on Friday 13 April 2007. It is the 32nd anniversary of what is officially now recognised as the start of the war, and this year is the first time it is being commemorated in a quasi-official way, the Lebanese having tried during the past 17 years or so to brush aside the events of 1975–90, rather than come to terms with them. This year, ironically, two years and two months after the shock of the Hariri assassination, the icons of the civil war are being exhibited as talk of a new conflagration begins to impinge on the lips and ears of a newly nervous Lebanese populace.

One of my least favourite places during the years of battle was the Museum, *al-Mathaf*, at the main crossing point between the two sides. In the wide-open rotunda that faced the Museum, with its Roman columns and majestic frontage, was the space across which travellers from east to west or vice versa had to drive as fast as possible to avoid snipers or explosives. It was a mouth-drying, sphincter-tightening, tyre-squealing surge across 50 yards or so of no-man's land, to the cover of the walls and buildings opposite.

Today, I am visiting the Hippodrome, or racecourse. In happier days it was one of those collection points where love of and investment in the horses brought all sects together in common cause and peaceful celebration. In the mid-1970s, however, I and many others had come to regard this area with trepidation. A journey to the racecourse during the Troubles meant almost certainly that one was in for a trip to the 'other side'. Even after a successful crossing a Western journalist could expect a frosty reception from those Christians, and there were many of them, who felt they were misunderstood, getting a bad press. The fact was, they were. (After all that, one had to return, the gauntlet-run prospect hanging in the back of one's mind throughout the visit.)

More than 30 years later, the racecourse has been turned into a memorial for the event that is judged to have started the war. At its centre is the burnt-out wreck of a bus, still recognisably such. It is a charred and battered 1950s Desoto with a vermilion bonnet and pale blue front bumper, these now the only distinguishably coloured bits of the rusted remains. Perhaps its rightful place would be in the nearby Museum, with the other artefacts of Lebanon's tortured history. The bus's owner, who lives in the south, refuses to sell his relic, but is pleased to show it to the public on this occasion.

It has been an unlucky bus. After the massacre of 13 April 1975, when 27 of its passengers were gunned down and killed, generally accepted as the spark that ignited the civil war, it was briefly re-commandeered as public transport in the early 1980s, but it was put out of action in a crash. Later, while parked uselessly in the Mousseitbeh area of west Beirut, a mixed working- and middle-class Muslim sector, not that far from the old Green Line and scene of some of the battles for position between the different groups during the miserable mid-1980s, it was hit by a missile. Yet still it survives, a neat metallic reminder of Lebanon's survival skills.

Since then the bus's role has been purely representational. Today it stands, roped off, in a solitary, grim position, in the lee of a row of Roman columns, not far from the rear of the Museum and its priceless, classical artefacts. Nearby are placards showing pictures of the original scenes of 13 April, the bodies of the victims, the blown-up front-page headlines and photographs of the Beirut morning papers of 14 April, and under canvas awnings various politicians and journalists old enough to remember those ugly days are giving interviews to other journalists and politicians.

One organiser of this event I speak to is the daughter of a recently assassinated Christian politician who was an outspoken opponent of the Syrians. I am overcome with British restraint and say nothing, but realise later that in Lebanon, as in Ireland, to speak of death, however close or intimate, is not considered obtrusive. Like most of the others at this sad little scene she is sheltering under a large umbrella. It is a bleak, damp day with April showers gusting across the wide-open racecourse. The weather, and perhaps that characteristic reluctance of the

Lebanese to face these grim aspects of their past, have made the memorial something of a flop.

The few people here seem to represent no particular faction, though a few politicians have shown up to say their bland pieces. (I manage to find one important man, a high-up in the Phalange Party who knows more than most people do about the intricacies of the civil war. He promises to see me in his office; he later cancels. Many of the more cautious political figures are lying low in these unhappy days, and even the incautious ones are speaking from well-protected safety.) Badges, umbrellas and tee-shirts with 'I Love Lebanon' slogans are neutral, and apart from these few, dedicated rememberers, there is only a posse of Lebanese soldiers and four-wheel-drive security vehicles guarding the scene. I reflect that it is likely, in Lebanon's present state of nervousness, that few but the chattering classes are in any mood to be reminded of 13 April 1975, and the mayhem that followed, bringing the nation to its knees and under outside control.

Sunday the 13th: The start of it all

Ain Rummaneh was not a good start for the Christians. What happened that day was seen by many as purely and simply a massacre perpetrated by them against innocent civilians. It was that, but it was not the whole story. Well before 1975, Lebanon was undergoing seismic internal ructions, many, if not most of them, the result of tensions between the state and the Palestinian guerrillas of the PLO and other groups. These were regularly turning into armed clashes. (The underlying reasons for this I discuss in Chapter 7.

On Sunday 13 April, the imposing figure of Pierre Gemayel, founder in 1936 and long-time leader of the right-wing Nationalist Phalange Party, the Voice of the Maronites, was attending the opening of a new church in a location very near what was soon to become a focal part of the confrontation lines between Christians and Palestinians and Muslims, in the working-class Christian suburb of Ain Rummaneh. This is just across a main road from the poorish and mainly Shi'ite Muslim district of Chiah. The road was soon to be a closed route across which the two communities fired an incessant barrage of machine-gun fire, mortars and rockets to no great effect other than enormous property damage and human casualties. Nobody ever took anyone else's ground, a fairly familiar story throughout the civil war as it affected Beirut and its neighbourhoods.

As the opening celebrations began, Phalangist guards stopped a car with obscured number plates, which they took to be containing Palestinian guerrillas. The chances were they were right. Shots were exchanged and one of the men in the car was wounded. A little later another, similarly disguised, car tried to crash a Phalangist guards' barrier near the new church, and the car's occupants this time opened fire on the Christian militiamen, killing one of Pierre Gemayel's personal bodyguards and three other men.

It has since been reported, but never confirmed, that both these incidents involved members of what was known as the Rejection Front of the Palestinian movement – that is to say radical elements at the fringes of or even outside the mainstream PLO and possibly beyond Yasser Arafat's reach.

In the wake of these shootings a bus full of Palestinians and their wives and children was making its way east across the city from the Corniche Mazraa area, a long boulevard that cuts from the Beirut coast inland and eastward towards the Museum. Near the corniche's eastern end in those days were stationed and living many of the Palestinian guerrillas, with their families and their entourages, who had arrived in Lebanon in their sad and bloody exodus from Palestine by way of Jordan and Syria. Many of their offices, barracks and meeting places were here, not far from the Fakaneh area, where the PLO had its headquarters.

These Palestinians, many from the Iraqi-backed Arab Liberation Front, one of the noisome groups that often made trouble for Arafat, among many others, had been part of their own very different celebration – the first anniversary of a Palestinian guerrilla attack on the northern Israeli village of Kyriat Shmoneh – and were on their way home to the refugee camp of Tel al-Za'atar, in the Christian district of Dekwaneh, in the eastern part of the city.

Either because he was lost or because he decided to take an ill-advised short-cut, the driver took the bus through the part of Ain Rummaneh where the Phalangists were in a rage after the attacks on them earlier that day. As soon as they sighted the vehicle and its Palestinian passengers, the Phalangist militia men opened fire, and kept firing. The passengers were trapped, the bus stranded amid the Christian attackers in the narrow street that runs past the church. By the time the security forces arrived and stopped the shooting, 27 people had been killed, among them women and children.

As news spread of the incident, road blocks and barrages went up along what were soon to become the familiar 'fronts' between Christian and Muslim areas, and the process of city-wide ethnic cleansing was launched. After a day of fighting, Pierre Gemayel aligned himself and his forces with those of the Lebanese Nation and Army (which had been having its own troubles with the Palestinians and dissident Muslim Lebanese groups in recent years), stating that no groups should have authority beyond that of the state.

This was a clear reference to the PLO and all who supported it. A ceasefire was imposed and eventually the Phalangist leader did hand over two of those responsible for firing on the bus. But the pin was out of the grenade. The lines were formed and ready. From this day on Lebanon was in its steady decline – years of internal strife that took many forms. Perhaps even more and lastingly damaging and deleterious to its and the region's fortunes, Lebanon's torment attracted the attention of the Israelis, who were, during those years of civil strife, to mount two invasions, one of them awesome in effect, and launch a 22-year occupation of large swathes of the country, aggravating and enhancing what were already serious internal problems.

The Syrians also became involved, if indeed they had not been involved from the very beginning, the most attentive but not the only interested Arab party in Lebanon's makeup and security. But it was the Syrians who exercised decisive power. Thirty-two years later, as I look at the wreckage of that bus, it is hard to say which of these parties prevailed, if any. But most certainly, the end of the civil war spelled not only an end to Christian superiority in Lebanon, but within the Christian hierarchy it ended the leadership status of the Phalangist Party, who until the 1980s had represented the fiercest and most determined face of Maronite defiance and exclusivity.

Phalangists, and more Martyrs

When Sheikh Pierre Gemayel founded the Phalangist Party, he was inspired by Generalissimo Franco's fascists and the disciplines he observed at the Berlin Olympics of Adolf Hitler and his blackshirts. Sheikh Pierre was a tall man with a head like a proud eagle; he was a prime mover in Lebanon's fight for freedom. His forebears had been forced into exile towards the final days of the Ottoman Empire because of their involvement in the struggle against the rule of Istanbul, and Pierre himself, with his *Kataeb*, or Phalanx, carried on the struggle against the French, whose mandatory rule followed on the collapse of the Ottomans in World War I. The Gemayels come from the town of Bikfaya, a few miles up into the hills east of Beirut, where the clan has been prominent since the sixteenth century.

Two of Pierre Gemayel's sons became president of the nation: one, Bashir, for three weeks, a bomb ending his life even before he could be inaugurated; and his elder brother, Amine, his successor, who held gingerly and unsuccessfully on to power through the middle of the 1980s, a rein over some of the most profound chaos in Lebanon's modern history. This climactic turbulence continued after his term expired in 1988 and was only ended after wasting battles among the Christians themselves and Syrian intervention, which had been approved in Washington and by the Israelis. Political reform, of a limited sort, and Syrian hegemony followed, and thus finis was written to Christian overlordship in Lebanon.

The motif of martyrdom remains strong for the Gemayels. I set off for their Phalangist HQ from that great monolith, the tombstone of the Holiday Inn, and head towards the port. To get to the khaki-coloured blockhouse that is the Phalangist HQ, I have to skirt the downtown enclaves, Rafiq Hariri's memorial, the apartment buildings and hotels, boulevards awash in designer labels and the fancy embellishments of the world of Gucci and Farhi and Dolce and Gabbana. Hariri's Solidere Company made this phoenix rise from the cinders of war, to the horror of many, who would have thought fitting some more useful and to-scale rebuilding of the shattered city centre, and who judged his development of the area to be made possible only by enforced seizure of the ruins and the land; and to the joy of many others, probably the majority, who saw in this new and futuristic representation of Gotham a statement about Lebanon's notional bright new future.

I have to skirt it now, however, as Beirut is experiencing with exasperation in government quarters the fourth month of the tented camp occupation by opposition protesters of a half-mile-square zone near the parliament building. The occupiers are mainly Shi'ites from the Hezbollah movement and Christian backers of General Michel Aoun, who is, at this time, in alliance with Hezbollah. For those who always found Hariri's concrete dream-come-true an irrelevance, the occupation is no more than an irritant, a sideshow. But for supporters of the Hariri clan, the government and the March 14 movement that lives on his memory and forms the backbone of the existing government – which is in a war of words and ideology and maybe more with Syria, a powerful opposition and the sitting president, Emile Lahoud – this manifestation, this prolonged sit-in is a calculated insult and a signal of malicious intent from the East, Syria and Iran and the perceived Forces of Darkness.

There is hardly anyone in the tented camp, but it is a physical fact. It is made even more real by concentric circles of razor wire and fencing, guard posts, armoured vehicles and rank upon rank of security and armed forces and various brands of policeman. It is possible to negotiate all this and reach a boulevard cafe for a cappuccino or sandwich and beer in the sun or one of the offices that relocated in this dreamland, but many not bound to be there just cannot be bothered. Business is bad. From the port, looking south and back towards the area, I can see the stark, metal outlines of the four martyrs, back in exactly the same spot – the old Martyrs' Square – as they had been from the 1920s to the early 2000s, but during the 1970s riddled with shot and shell as they stood alone in the middle of the fighting that swept back and forth across the downtown district.

Now, restored, the four figures stand against the skyline: a woman carrying a torch representing freedom and a young man the future, and two men recumbent, representing the 33 martyrs, six of them Lebanese, who were hanged on the orders of the Ottoman envoy Jamal Pasha in 1916 for communicating with the Empire's Western enemies and for trying to defy the Sultan's rule. It was a harsh period for the insurgent Lebanese. The Young Turks, militant leaders who had taken over in Istanbul in 1908 and were ruthlessly and nationalistically Turkish rather than all-embracingly Ottoman, held power under Enver Pasha. These men were reasserting themselves forcibly throughout their Arab possessions, as the vultures of the West, particularly the French and the British, circled over the carrion of the disintegrating empire. The Lebanese rebels could not be forgiven or spared, either for their uprisings or their clandestine contacts with the West, who they thought might help them. (Although it was to prove, not surprisingly, that as the Ottoman Empire fell, independence for its subjects was far from Western minds. Lebanon, like Palestine, Syria and Iraq, was part of the spoils of the Great War, not a prize for freedom-lovers and self-determinists.)

Next to the martyrs of 1916 is the Hariri Mosque, burial place of Lebanon's most famous modern martyr, with its four minarets (in somewhat leaden imitation of the Sinan Mosques above Istanbul's Golden Horn) and its garish turquoise dome. This has been the site, since Rafiq Hariri's assassination in 2005, of so many political mani-festations, both for and against him, for here also are the parliament, the main offices of the banks and the Grand Serail, the seat of Lebanon's government, itself originally built by the Ottomans and refurbished after the war by Hariri's hand and capital.

One is never done with martyrs here. As I walk towards the Phalangist building, I see its western wall covered with the portrait of a good-looking young man. He was just one in a series of assassinations that began with the death of Hariri. He was the grandson of Sheikh Pierre (who died peacefully in 1984 aged 78, despite many attempts to kill him over the 50 years or so of his political life and leadership), and the son of former president Amine (who is at time of writing still alive). He was Pierre Amine Gemayel, and was 34 years old and Industry Minister when he was shot dead, in November 2006, by unknown gun-men. He is one in a long line of murdered Lebanese politicians and other public personalities who have one characteristic in common: they had been strongly and publicly opposed to the Syrian presence in and influence over Lebanon, and supporters of the essentially pro-Western government that has ruled since the elections of spring 2005. Many Lebanese put two and two together, remember their history, and assume these killings to be part of a Syrian plan to bring Lebanon back into the Damascus fold, an assumption strengthened by UN investiga-tions into Hariri's and his sympathisers' subsequent deaths. Under UN authority, the Lebanese detained four pro-Syrian Lebanese generals who faced trial by the UN Special Tribunal in the Netherlands.[1]

Any attempts to investigate Lebanon's past – and my visit today to the Phalangists will be no different – are coloured by these events. They have put politicians, commentators, academics and other citizens alike into a slough of uncertainty. The creeping cull in parliamentary ranks of government members and supporters means that the Syrian-favoured opposition, of Hezbollah and General Aoun's Free Patriotic Movement, is gaining ground constitutionally. This is paralysing the pro-Western government. Five months after President Emile Lahoud's term officially

ended, it is making impossible the parliamentary election of his successor – who has to be a Maronite Christian. A candidate, a former army
commander, has been agreed on, but not the makeup and modus
operandi of the government that should serve under him.

Syrian, Hezbollah and other Lebanese opposition to the Tribunal
and the stalemate in national leadership and governance are at the
heart of the modern Lebanese crisis and easily demonstrate the state's
split personality, one which the West and the East are fighting to unite
to their own liking and advantage.

More clear now perhaps, this struggle between East and West for
dominance in Lebanon has always been basic to its troubles. In the
1970s, though, the Phalangists did not have the unqualified Western
support that today's Lebanon government enjoys, or survives. As I
approach their HQ building, the clear view of it brings back vivid and
disturbing memories. I remember it as an outpost that was the last
Christian redoubt at the edge of no-man's land.

Between the *Kataeb* House and the Palestinians and their allied fighters there was less than half a mile or so of rubble and often unrecovered
bodies, a free-fire zone for the mortars, rocket-propelled grenades and
heavy machine-guns of the different sides, neither force in the end making any significant headway but battering into ruinous submission the
Ottoman and French colonial buildings. The battles early on destroyed
and forced into history the vibrant, mixed communities that had met,
done business, ate, drunk and even romanced under their arches, behind
their walls and among their columns, strolling in the souks, sipping coffee in the shade of the arches, queuing for the latest James Bond or
Egyptian tear-jerker at the cinemas, bar-hopping and visiting night-
clubs. All this was blown up, for ever, and the sterile, fake-European
walkways and skyscrapers of the new downtown are not bringing it back.

A few-score yards from these offices great mounds of earth protected the Phalangists' villa from their enemies across the divide. We
could peep through spy-holes and look across the wasteland to where
the 'other side' peered back, looking for some remote target, some fool-
ish young man darting between positions, perhaps, someone trying to
retrieve a corpse or badly wounded colleague, someone just being careless, or even, for target practice, a wandering cat or stray dog.

Then we would make the hair-raising trip back to that 'other side', at
which point the protective wall outside the *Kataeb* House would in its
turn become again 'the other side', and we could look back at it from

behind the barricades in the ruins of Rue Allenby and Avenue Weygand and the Bank of Syria, alongside the Palestinian and Muslim snipers. All this is a bad memory now, in the 2000s, and would be unimaginable for any Lebanese under the age of 30 – except that the nation has almost ever since suffered new and different indignities, violent and political, internally and externally delivered and motivated.

The Phalange HQ is no longer a place of menace or siege mentality. No young fighters swagger outside the doors with Virgin Marys painted on the stocks of their automatic rifles; there are no militia-girls with crude wooden crosses dangling on their full, olive-skin décolletage.[2]

No. Now the few and unarmed guards at the door are friendly and relaxed and invite me to sit and have coffee and read a Phalangist news sheet while I wait for Yusuf Abu Khalil, the Number Two in the *Kataeb*, a long-time political leader of the movement and former editor of the Phalange newspaper, *al-Amal*, which I am clutching as I am ushered up to see him. It is important to understand the Phalange, depleted though they may be as new forces have emerged inside Christian ranks and new powers have been brought to bear. The Phalange supported Syrian intervention in Lebanon in mid-1976, when it looked as if the Muslim–Druze–Palestinian alliance might prevail, pulling Lebanon irrevocably into an Arab-Muslim Middle East, or making it into another, at least temporary Palestine. At that time the Syrians were entering the country in force to make sure the PLO and its allies did not upset Lebanon's balance, did not make the PLO a force too great in the Levant. In those days, the Syrian regime of President Hafez al-Assad regarded the Palestinian struggle against Israel very much Damascus business. The Americans and Israelis both encouraged the Syrian intervention as long as it aimed to suppress Palestinian power and did not approach Israel's notional area of concern in the south.

The Phalange soon realised that the Syrian presence challenged the Maronites' unique power in Lebanon's political trade-offs and confessional system. The party then made a serious strategic error, in 1977, thinking that since Syria had saved the Christian Maronites from at worst defeat at the hands of the Palestinians and Muslims and at best fundamental reforms of the Christian-weighted political system, the Syrians could, should and would now go home and leave Lebanon more or less as before. They soon reverted to their old policies of resistance against Damascus and flirtation with the Israelis. Fighting between Syrians and Phalangists broke out as soon as 1978. In the end,

65

the Phalangists failed, were replaced, reduced, but even their Christian replacements ultimately disintegrated. Syria's opponents are now a very different, rainbow alliance.

The Phalangists were always at the heart of independent Lebanon and prominent among those who created this nation that is so different from its neighbours and yet so irrevocably conjoined with them. Yusuf Abu Khalil is one of their typical old guard, a neat, elderly man in a dark suit and discreet tie with white swept-back hair. He is short and slim, with all the menace of a family lawyer. He could be behind the desk of a solicitors' firm in Surbiton, except that these days he would not be allowed to chain smoke. He tells me that the *Kataeb* was the first political party to be set up in Lebanon, and, in this region of icons and patriarchs, inevitably, behind him on the wall, is a large portrait of his mentor, Pierre Gemayel.

The *Kataeb*, he says, were created in 1936, eight years before Independence, to solidify the idea of Lebanon as the only secular and civil society-based nation in the region. The party was small and divided at first, but its members resolved their differences when Pierre Gemayel became leader in 1937. The party is 99 per cent Christian, and he is quick to make this point in a roundabout way when he says that while the *Kataeb* wanted to reinforce the idea of Lebanon as secular, the Moslems wanted it to be part of Syria. This is not totally accurate, as many Druze, Sunni and Shi'a fought for independence, and supported then and now a Lebanon separate from Syria; but there is an element of truth in it as, to varying degrees, the Muslims, and even some Christians, have emphasised Lebanon's place in the wider Arab world and its dependence for survival on the support of and sometimes orders from the stronger Arab neighbours, most obviously Syria.

Yusuf says the French wanted to delay independence, and retain a military presence in Lebanon – true of France before World War II, Vichy France and the France of de Gaulle, to whom the Allies had restored France and its colonial and mandatory possessions. There were demonstrations and clashes with French security. In 1943, he says, the Muslims agreed that if the French left they would recognise Lebanon as independent of Syria, and under the combined pressure of the Lebanese of all faiths and France's Allies (all this was happening before and during France's own Liberation), independence was granted in 1943.

Until the late 1970s, says Yusuf, on about his eighth cigarette since I met him half an hour ago, the Phalangists were the political heart and strength of the Lebanese Christian Maronites and other like-minded Christians. They violently opposed the PLO's armed presence in Lebanon, which became a disruptive factor for the delicate Lebanese polity in the late 1960s and early 1970s. In the mid-1970s, they created the LF, under the leadership of Gemayel's younger son, Bashir, as their armed wing. (He had risen to the top of the Phalangist security system in his early 20s, partly as the result of yet another act of martyrdom, that of William Hawi, head of the party's military security council, who was shot dead by a Palestinian sniper at Tel al-Za'atar camp in the eastern suburbs of Beirut in 1976.) Yusuf says the LF were brought up 'in the mentality of war'. Bashir's second-in-command was Samir Geagea. After Bashir's assassination in 1982 the LF developed a mind and strength of its own as a political as well as military entity. It broke away from the Phalange to replace it, eventually, and for the next ten years or so, as the strongest party in the Christian regions.

Yusuf says: 'They fought against the Muslims in the civil war, and so they kept those feelings in place,' implying that the *Kataeb* is now, as we speak, in the mid-2000s more rational and tolerant. This may be so, but there is a certain amount of *force majeure* in play here, as the party is certainly much less influential than it was in the 1950s, 1960s and 1970s. Its leader and former President, Amine Gemayel, elder brother of the assassinated Bashir, is a much less flamboyant and charismatic character and, in the eyes of most Lebanese, a feeble substitute for his younger brother – whose picture is still displayed in many Christian districts.

Amine Gemayel ruled or rather tried to rule Lebanon at a time when even the bits that had fallen apart were falling apart: after the horrendous 1982 invasion by Israel, with whom he tried to effect an ill-fated peace treaty, and up to the climactic blood-letting of the war years when his presidency ended, no successor could be found. His appointee as military ruler-cum-prime minister, Michel Aoun, took on both the rival Christian militias of the LF and, fatally, the Syrian Army. Amine Gemayel's period in office and its aftermath was perhaps the most disastrous stretch of Lebanon's civil war, though it did in its consequence exhaust the combatants, bring a local and an Arab but mainly a Syrian solution, of sorts, and with it 15 years of relative peace if not total sanity (never forgetting the continuing Israeli occupation of the south of Lebanon, which was to last ten more years). But there was no real reconciliation or any recognition of what had gone wrong and how it might all be put right.

Yusuf Abu Khalil admits that there is Christian fanaticism and a deep fear of Hezbollah (not confined to Christians, by any means, and, it has to be said, not shared by all Christians either). The LF are, he says, therefore in favour of cantonisation, though they do not announce this publicly (cantonisation happened de facto between 1975 and 1990, with especial efficiency and rigour in the Christian sector, but was physically if not mentally dismantled after the civil war ended). Yusuf says a federal Lebanon would not work, which is one area where the Phalangists disagree with the LF; he is probably right.

A free and equally accessible Beirut is the very hub of Lebanon (it is to Lebanon as Jerusalem is to the Palestinians, and the enforced Israeli separation of Jerusalem from its hinterland has shown what a nonsense the absence of a natural commercial and political capital makes of an entity).

Even if the city were divided and linked to different and somehow autonomous cantons, it would only entrench the enervating and violent divisions of the civil war: Lebanon's heart would have been eviscerated.

Yusuf says the *Kataeb*'s aim is to remove Lebanon from the international arena of conflict: 'For 30 years now the Arabs and Iran have been using Lebanon to fight Israel.' This is true, but the Lebanese have never been strong or coherent enough to resist outside interference and blandishments, and their geographical position and their endemic reliance on outside sponsorship, East or West, makes it unlikely they can, even if some Tito- or Mandela-like figure is in the wings, of which there is no sign. If Yusuf is right about the *Kataeb*'s aim, it is a dream.

With Israel at its southern border, Lebanon's role as another Arab obstacle to Israel's progress and peace of mind, however that might ever be attained or delivered, means that it is a front-line state, whether the Christians or anyone else wish it that way or not.

Yusuf is honest about Israel. In the mid-1970s he was one of the Christian leaders who actually sailed down to Israel, coming ashore at Haifa to meet senior Israeli generals, intelligence people and politicians.[3] 'It is not our fault,' he says, 'if our interests coincide with those of Israel. During World War II the Western powers co-operated with the Soviet Union. My enemy's enemy is my friend.' He is angry that, as he sees it, the fight with Israel is carried out on Syria's behalf from Lebanese soil when no bullet has been fired for 34 years or more across the Golan

Heights. He says that UN Security Council Resolution 1701 is about breaking all those links between Lebanon and outside forces.

Resolution 1701, after much delay by the Americans and their British sidekicks, who hoped Israel would flatten Hezbollah, but were disappointed, ended Israel's devastating but ill-fated invasion of Lebanon in the summer of 2006. The resolution called, *inter alia*, for 'the disarmament of all armed groups in Lebanon, so that ... there will be no weapons or authority in Lebanon other than that of the Lebanese state', and in the hands of UN forces where specified. Yusuf and the Phalangists and the government of the day are in favour of this, which is very much in the spirit of the Ta'ef Accords of 1989, which brought a peaceful end to the civil war and new constitutional arrangements. These aimed to give the state back its authority, and more political power to the (Sunni) Muslims at the expense of the Christians. The Shi'ite Muslims did not prosper through Ta'ef or the war itself, but eventually through fighting and ultimately removing the Israeli forces from south Lebanon, and their own powers of self-discipline and organisation.

Under Syria's aegis, Hezbollah retained their arms as a legitimate resistance. They intend to keep them. Unlike Yusuf and his political allies, the Shi'ite and Christian (Aounist) opposition see the USA as the brains behind and main author of 1701, the enemy of the Arabs and friend of Israel's, and therefore a significant outside force itself.

When Yusuf says Iranian influence has reached the border with Israel through Hezbollah he is correct. However, it is a fact that can hardly be removed by force, unless Israel defeats Hezbollah and renders it harmless. Then Lebanon would be back to the mid-1980s, divided into a Syrian-controlled if chaotic and quarrelsome northern sector, and an Israeli-dominated south, with the whole process of internal resistance and possibly real civil war beginning again. The Shi'ites and Palestinians and like-minded anti-Israeli, anti-Western Arabs of Lebanon and their neighbours in Syria, let us say more than 2 million people in Lebanon and 19 million in Syria, are not going to disappear or become inured to Israel and the USA with a third of Lebanon under foreign occupation.

Yusuf does not seem able to view this question of 'influence' from another angle: that American, Western, Israeli influences are to many Lebanese equally threatening and to be deplored. But then, as an old-fashioned and unreconstructed Maronite political adviser and writer, he would see those influences as positive, some or all of them to be used to protect his community, and Lebanon's identity, from the threatening clouds of Islam and Arabism, in their rawest forms, to the East. This is at the core of the argument about Lebanese identity, each side at its most extreme edges blind to the other's concept of what Lebanon should be. Yusuf's vision does not allow him to consider that during the past two centuries the Western Powers in their various forms and their different stages have divided the Arabs, for their own profit, often at the point of a gun, and in the case of the creation of Israel planted an alien and aggressive state in their midst.

Yusuf would not and does not point out that while he, his colleagues and the West wring their hands over arms shipments across the Lebanese border and coast from Syria and Iran, they are quite happy about the billions upon billions of dollars worth of arms delivered to Israel, much of it a gift from the USA, and the burgeoning and sophisticated indigenous Israeli arms industry, itself engendered and supported by the USA. Yusuf does not mention that it was these armaments that were used so many times to bombard his own land.

As to Hezbollah and its weapons and Resolution 1701's full implementation, Yusuf is a bit of a dreamer. There has always been a dream element in Christian politics, along the lines of 'Why don't all those Muslims just go away and leave us alone?' He is not, however, dreaming when it comes to knowing that the West is capricious, suiting itself rather than its supposedly Christian clients. 'We cannot rely 100 per cent on the US,' he says, a lesson that many have learned over the decades.

'After all, the US put Syria here in the first place.' (The Americans gave Syria permission to assert itself in Lebanon militarily in 1976 and 1990. On each occasion the Syrians saved the Christians, the first time from the Palestinians, the second time from themselves.)

However, he adds, 'The US want to weaken Syria and Iran because of Israel, and that coincides with our interest.' Yusuf thinks that if Iranian and Syrian influence was reduced, the Shi'ites would turn back to Lebanon and hand their authority back to the state (but why would they, given their experiences of the past 50 or more years?). 'There would be the Lebanese Army to defend them,' he says. Against Israel? Against anyone?

He does make sense though when he says that 'Hezbollah can never liberate Israel but it will never let it rest in peace.' The reverse is equally true, but on past experience it will not stop Israel trying. Hezbollah and Iran both know that the Lebanese resistance to Israel and the support for the resistance inside Palestine have been an inspiration to the Arab world. They give notice to Israel and the USA that they cannot forever have everything their way in the Middle East, without cost or come-back. Lebanon's trouble, as ever, is that it is the main arena for this contest, outside Palestine itself. Everyone makes his point in Lebanon.

Yusuf epitomises much old-fashioned Maronite thinking. The Maronite Christians are in a very real sense the people, the entity with-out which the Mountain and thus Lebanon itself could never have existed. In that sense they are essential to Lebanon's '*Lubnaniyat*', or Lebaneseness, and survival as such, if not now as powerful a unit as they once were in state affairs and often beyond those. They are a key part of Lebanon's separateness, its identity and its very construction. But for a period they suffered from hubris and saw themselves *as* the state. When that state was severely challenged from the late 1960s onwards, by Palestinian power combined with reformist and disgrun-tled Lebanese factions, they withdrew into a paranoid shell. All others, Muslim, Druze, even other Christians, were dangerous outsiders and potential if not actual enemies.

This paranoia was exacerbated by the Maronites' perception of the region they inhabited, whether exemplified by intensifyingly political Islam, by Arab nationalism, by Palestinian intrusion, arrogance and irredentism, or by Syrian interference and bullying; and by diminishing sympathy for their political and military isolationism in the West, even among the French. The end of the civil war saw the Maronites' power much reduced. They remain, however, in different groupings and alliances vitally important to Lebanon's unique character and struc-ture. Young, educated but poor, working-class Christians who cannot find jobs yet, and who cannot afford to emigrate like their wealthier cousins, are a groundswell of resentment and political dissent, as have been the more publicised and high-profile poor among the Shi'ites; they are finding common ground in wanting the Lebanese system of *laissez-faire* economics and clan-based patronage reformed.

The better-off Maronites are becoming better informed and more confident, especially since the departure of the Syrians, and more open to outside contacts and influences. No one party or leader any longer has complete power over the majority of them, as the Phalangists and LF had for so long, until it all blew apart in 1989.

However, in critical times one cannot be absolutely certain that –
were the threat or imagined threat so great – a psychological retreat to
the circled wagons in the Mountain might not happen in panic or
extremis.

Another Kind
of Christian

6

On the eve of the 2007 bus memorial at the racecourse, I went to the Saroulla cinema/theatre complex in Hamra, the centre of west Beirut, to meet an enterprising young woman called Hania Mroué, one of a new generation of Lebanese trying to make her country aware of its past and to drag it into some more rational and co-operative ideal of nationhood. This week she has organised a film festival with the theme 'Journalists on the Edge'. That night we watch the sinister and rather lugubrious German film 'Circle of Deceit', directed by the new-wave director Volker Schlondorff in 1981. The film is bizarre. The central character, a visiting German journalist, is more complicated and fool-hardy than most of the correspondents I worked with over 20 or so years – though perhaps not than the photographers, a breed made near-suicidal by professional necessity. (The 'hero' has a mad photog-rapher on assignment with him.) 'Circle', made right after the period whose events it tries to depict, does communicate the mindless horror of the mid-1970s. It brings back with a rush the chaos and killing, the darkness of spirit and vengeful murderousness on all sides.

The young audience, like Hania herself, were most of them unborn, babies or infants, some growing up abroad with their exiled parents, when the civil war started. It is an apt curtain-raiser for the memorial events of 13 April. My thoughts are back in those evil times most of these educated youngsters milling about in the Saroulla complex can-not have known. But they are concerned. In that uniform of jeans and navel-exposing tops and tee-shirts they are distinguishable from their British contemporaries only in that they are smarter, better behaved and better turned out: they may be the iPod generation, plugged in to blogs and downloads, but these Lebanese youth are interested in, if puzzled by, a past it is not impossible they may be doomed to repeat, albeit in a different form. They are a contrast to the young English I know who are uninterested in anything that happened much before the year they entered school. They are young, but old enough to have absorbed by osmosis, from their parents, even from vague memory, a feeling of curiosity about their country's violent heritage.

Some friends of mine from those days have bit parts in 'Circle of Deceit'. They have enough experience of the war years to appear authentic, especially Jack Dagilaitis, an American academic and civil rights enthusiast who arrived in the 1960s, braved the war and the Syrian era in Beirut and stayed on, like many other hard-core, foreign lovers of Beirut and its spirit of survival. He would live nowhere else, he tells me.

One of the stars of the film is Fouad Naim. He is well known on stage and screen in the Middle East, a Christian who reminds me of Omar Sharif, with his dramatic, dashing good looks. But this Christian Lebanese has no time for sects and confessionalism. In the film, however, he plays a mountain chieftain – presumably based on a Dany Chamoun- or Bashir Gemayel- or Tony Franjieh-style figure – who lives in splendour in a fortress-like villa, holds court by a pool decorated by slinky Western and local women, but also runs a militia and kills people, which is, after all, what you do with a militia. It is a good piece of non-type casting by Volker Schlondorff, as is Jack's portrayal of an American spook.

Earlier in the day, sipping coffee in the cinema lounge among chain-smoking students and talking to Hania Mroué, I was introduced to Fouad Naim's wife, who owns the building and is the inspiriting figure and financier of the theatre and gallery it contains. It is a serendipitous meeting, one of those intimate revelations of Ras Beirut, where everyone knows everyone and everything is connected. Fouad's wife is the celebrated actress and character Nidal Achkar, a legendary beauty, dressed in black today as she is in mourning for her mother Raoufa. She is therefore mostly at her house in the mountains at this time, receiving condolences from hordes of friends, admirers and relatives. I am lucky to have bumped into her.

The meeting is also fortuitous because, thinking about those days of the mid-1970s, as I now do, I recall a strange bunch of fighters from the PPS, now known as the NSSP.

They intrigued me partly because their philosophy was unique, their history violent and significant, despite their minority status, and they were, mostly, Christians of the Greek Orthodox faith who fought on the side of the Palestinians, Muslims and Druze.

Nidal is a devoted daughter and supporter of the NSSP. She invites me to her home in the mountains to tell me why. It is a typical Lebanese story, of intransigent and idealistic mountain Christians, of their spread down into the city, of their involvement in the turbulent story of Lebanon's independence and its tribulations since.

Nidal's home is in Dik el Mahde, in the Metn district, in the hills north-east of Beirut, a 45-minute drive from her theatre in Hamra. It is a very different world, with a haunting glimpse of the Mediterranean through her garden of pines and cactus. Her villa sits in the cool shade of the trees, full of memories, of a childhood of poets, artists and civilised chatter, but also of sieges, ruins and flight. The gateway is, like so many others in modern, nervous Lebanon, barred and guarded. Nidal is stately, as an actress should be – I can see her a few years on from now as a splendid Lady Bracknell; she is still a little too young, and would be perfect as one of Tennessee Williams' matriarchs – but warm and effusive. As she sweeps about her exquisite, airy home, ordering coffee and sweets and ushering me into her presence, her political enthusiasms and beliefs pour forth.

It is difficult to associate this upper middle-class family with a party with such a violent background and such a controversial reputation. Yet why? One thinks of Diana Mosley and the blackshirts, or Vanessa Redgrave and the Workers' Revolutionary Party. Nidal is more politically centred than either of those two ladies, her attachment to the NSSP familial and ideological; perhaps she shuts out its militant side, or maybe believes that that dark side is a necessary part of Lebanese politics and survival.

The NSSP is a paradigm of the Lebanese experience, a story in itself of the almost impossible intricacies of Lebanon's system and its wider regional involvements: mountain-based and mainly Christian, yet essentially secular, non-tribal (only the Lebanese Communists and Ba'athists also claim to be so); Lebanese, yet in favour of a Greater Syria; founded and run by visionaries and thinkers; yet accused of plotting mayhem and suspected of involvement in murder.

It is a long haul of the imagination from the splendour of Nidal's 1000-square-metre drawing room, with its modernist paintings, family portraits, inlaid Damascene sideboards and cabinets, elegant sculptures, Chinese porcelain and Persian rugs on marble flooring, to the young men with the distinctive crimson flash on their arms, who sailed through the Beirut streets with their machine-guns and cannon-toting pick-up trucks, off to battle at the front or in the hills. All that seems in the past now, yet the NSSP somehow retains its reputation for rough and murderous tactics. The 'Syrian' in its title does not help it in Lebanon these days.

Even 'Syrian' is a bit of a misnomer. It is only recently that the Syrians, against whom the NSSP fought in the war, have allowed the party an official place in their tightly ordered political system. It was banned there between 1955 and 1970 because of its alleged involvement in the murder of a Syrian general. 'There's always a plot against us,' says Nidal, somehow oblivious to the charge that it is her NSSP that is so often at the centre of fatal conspiracies.

The party was founded by an enlightened and fervent young idealist called Antoun Sa'adeh in 1932. He believed in the four 'Arab unities': Egypt and the Sudan; the Maghreb (the north African Arab countries west of Libya); the Khalij, the Arabian Gulf; and the 'Fertile Crescent' that is to say, Greater Syria and Iraq, Syria including Palestine, Jordan and Lebanon. Oddly, the Fertile Crescent was to be embellished and completed by its notional star, Cyprus. Although the PPS proclaims its secular nature, one cannot help noticing the Greek Orthodox influence. Sa'adeh was Greek Orthodox. The Orthodox, the inheritors of Byzantium, are the biggest Christian sect in the whole region (as delineated in the Fertile Crescent). This helps explain the addition of Cyprus. Regional unity on PPS lines would have given the Levant's majority Christian sect a cohesive power among all the other Christian confessions.

For all its reputation for thuggery when needed (the NSSP is not alone among Lebanese political parties in this), this party has a profound intellectual and philosophical base grounded in its brilliant young founder. For all his education and eloquence, however, Antoun was to end his life, still only in his early 40s, in front of a Lebanese military firing squad. He was a heroic martyr to supporters and worshippers such as Nidal; he was a traitor to many others. Antoun Sa'adeh was the essential product of the rebellious Lebanese Mountain, yet preached all his life the oneness of Syria.

He was born in 1904 in the mountain village of Shweir, nearly 20 miles northeast of Beirut, a district with a history of opposing outside authority that goes back to the first Islamic dynasties of the Omayyads and Abbasids, in the seventh and eighth centuries. His father, Khalil, was a brilliant physician, an intellectual who agitated against outside authority in any guise and wrote many works, including novels. One was 'Caesar and Cleopatra', in English. He studied the Russian Revolution and wrote a book about it, and published an Arabic–English lexicon. Dr Khalil also started Lebanon's first tuberculosis clinic, in the early years of the twentieth century. He was Renaissance Man. However, he fell foul of the French in 1909, correctly but ill-advisedly openly accusing the French Consul in Beirut of trying to avoid paying for theatre tickets Khalil had organised for Consulate staff. The Ottoman authorities (still ruling Greater Syria at the time) told Dr Sa'adeh he would be wise to leave the country.

The incident is an illustration of how powerful and how domineering the French already were a good 13 years before they were awarded Mandatory Rule over Syria and Lebanon by the League of Nations, in 1922.

It was while the older Sa'adeh was in Egypt that Antoun experienced what were perhaps his formative years – those of World War I. For the Lebanese, these years were agonising. The war played its part, but there were two other, equally tormenting factors: the brutal rule of the Ottoman ruler of the area, Jamal Pasha, who saw as one of his main tasks the repression of Syrian–Lebanese nationalist aspirations, using the gun and the gallows unsparingly; and a famine, between 1916 and 1918, that reduced the population of Mount Lebanon by a third. This famine was partly caused by a plague of locusts over the whole of Greater Syria, devouring crops and leaving the land bare, a crop-destroying heat-wave on the Syrian plains in 1916 and the depredations of the Turks as they commandeered agricultural livestock and beasts of burden for the army they were throwing in desperate battle against the invading British. The Turks compounded Lebanon's misery by laying seige to the main port, Beirut, and for a long while preventing sorely needed imports of grain and other supplies.

By the middle of the war, aged only 12, Antoun was in *loco parentis* for his two younger brothers, Edward and Salim, and his younger sister, Grace (their mother, Nayfeh, had died in Egypt in 1913, giving birth to Grace; his father had soon afterwards left Egypt for Argentina). They managed to survive in an orphanage school in the Christian town of Brumanna. This was run by an English dentist and his fellow physicians from the Syrian Protestant College in Beirut (later the AUB). The Turkish leaders had allowed these exiles from a belligerent state to remain in Lebanon for two reasons: their ministrations were welcomed by the rulers, and they continued to train young Arab doctors for conscription into the medical corps of the Ottoman army.

It was during this basic process of forging a personality and the courage to survive and take responsibility that the young Antoun learned to resent outside authority, even at the age of 15 objecting to the authoritarian attitudes of the French as much as to the brutalities of the Ottomans, who were trying in vain to cling to their Arab lands and subjects.

Meanwhile, Antoun's father had launched Arabic-language newspapers first in Argentina then in Sao Paulo, in Brazil. In 1920, Antoun joined him there after trekking across the USA to stay with relatives in the outer reaches of New Mexico. Here the young man had found life boring and constricting and he soon moved on to Sao Paulo. Here he was set on the course of political engagement and activism that was to inform his short life.

Like his father, and very much under his aegis, Antoun believed in and preached modernism, secularism and 'Syrianism', refusing to adopt the defeatism and deracination of so many Syrian–Lebanese immigrants in the Americas. He opposed the acceptance of European rule-by-mandate in Greater Syria after World War I. By Syrianism, he meant the geographical unity of Greater Syria, which included modern Syria, Lebanon, Palestine and what was to become Jordan. This one state, both father and son believed, stood a better chance of maintaining the area and its people safe, strong and integrated than if it were carved into segments ready for delivery to the British, the French and the Zionists. Both men developed a deep horror of the religious fragmentation that broke out again in Lebanon after the Great War ended and the unity of the fight for national independence ebbed away as the West took control. Each Sa'adeh, father and son, insisted that without betraying their Arabism, the peoples of the Levant had to modernise, to shake off old and regressive thinking and tribalism.

It was no doubt easier for the young Antoun to sustain his opposition to French rule, and the separate Lebanon that came with it, in the far reaches of South America than it was for his compatriots back home, under that very rule and learning to survive and manipulate it. He returned to Lebanon in 1930, a good-looking, well-tailored, athletically proportioned young man, aged 26, with the best intentions of radical reform within him. He began to assemble a political party, the PPS, that he intended would make his ideals into a reality in his native land.

Nidal's father, Assad, a Maronite, whose wife, Raoufa, was Greek Orthodox, was a devoted follower of Antoun Sa'adeh. Assad even followed him to Brazil during the years of World War II, when events forced him to flee Lebanon: he was not popular with the French, fighting as he was for independence. His Holy Grail of the unity of Greater Syria (the Fertile Crescent) made him equally unpopular with Arab Nationalist Muslims and Lebanese Nationalists.

The fight for independence is often more complicated by what those struggling for it see as the way ahead once they have acquired it than it is by the rule of the colonialist. This was so in Cyprus, Kenya, India and indeed Palestine. Internal differences among freedom-fighters vitiated their campaigns as much as did the worn-out British rulers. The same was true of France and Lebanon before and during World War II. Conflicting ideas about what Lebanon should be remain at the core of its fragility. The NSSP is just one minor but representative element in the mix.

Between 1962 and 1968 (when the 'Chehabist' era came to an end), Assad Achkar spent much time in jail as a result of the party's rebellious activities and their family home was attacked by Phalangists in 1961. The family element, as ever, is strong, Nidal unwaveringly retaining the political beliefs of her father.

Despite her party's insistence on secularity, the confessional element played a strong and negative part in her party's misfortunes. The family's Phalangist neighbours in the Metn could not accept that her father, a Maronite, was a loyal activist in a party that contained Muslims. 'They thought he was a heathen, against Christ, not to be in the *Kataeb* (the Phalange),' she says, seated in one of her plush, slate-green and maroon divans, sipping Turkish coffee. Now in her 60s, she is still a beauty, wearing gracefully a black linen *abaya* with edgings of delicate arabesques. 'We were always a party of believers,' Nidal says, wistfully. 'This house was always full of them, writers, poets, painters, politicians – I grew up listening to them.' It is not exactly the same house. Angry Phalangists attacked again and burned it to the ground in 1976, evicting the mother and her children, who fled to Jordan and beyond until the violence abated. The house we are in was rebuilt, with the stones of the old, a little down the hill from the site of the original home. It has been rebuilt in resplendent Mediterranean–Oriental style, arched windows and doorways, high ceilings, quiet and shade, echoes and murmurs. Who could countenance murder here?

Nidal's brother, Ghassan, does not doubt that many could and would. And they did. Ghassan was until the last election a deputy for the NSSP in the Lebanese Assembly. He joins us, a laconic man who slumps on another sofa and is amusingly dismissive of a political system he says cheated him out of his seat in 2005. He says a rump of fair-weather Armenian and Maronite supporters switched their vote on him at the last minute. No doubt money played its part. No doubt there are other versions. Anyway, today Ghassan is gardening and thinking. 'We do not agree with Syria on many things,' he says. 'But we have sided with them because they are the last Arab country standing against Israel.' Perhaps he is being a little unfair to Lebanon, which officially remains at war with Israel. It certainly has no peace treaty with Israel, and will never have one until or unless Syria signs one. Lebanon also houses Israel's most forceful physical opponent, Hezbollah: 'This Syrian regime is not the one we wanted, but in this crumbling Arab world it is the only choice.'

Ghassan thinks Syria bit off more than it could digest when it moved in on Lebanon. 'It did not have a sufficient number of astute and dedicated people to take over our country and run it,' he says. He is remarkably honest for a man who represents a party said by its opponents to be in Syria's pocket and alleged to carry out its commands. 'The top echelon is fine,' he says, 'but go down the scale a little...' and he names some eminent Syrian handlers of the Lebanese 'file' who were happy to work with certain Lebanese collaborators in looting the country and presenting to their seniors in Damascus the picture of Lebanon's condition and affairs they wanted them to see: 'They could have come to Lebanon and woven social ties and economic ties and built on the connections that exist here between the families, but they didn't have the vision.' He says the PPS/NSSP were always against the idea of Syria trying to take Lebanon by force – the relationship and the marriage had to grow from mutual experience and benefit.

The tragedy of the Christians, continues Ghassan, is that they thought Lebanon could exist independently of its surroundings. His sister and I laugh out loud when he adds, with the acerbity of a Raymond Chandler: 'The Christian Lebanese were like people who thought they could sell chiclets in a room full of people with machine-guns.' I recall the street vendors rolling their trolleys of cigarettes or

bread up the middle of the road, bellowing 'Marlboro', with the reverberations of the last sniper round still in their ears. The metaphorical
meaning of his quip is exemplified by the current stand-offs and verbal
exchanges between political leaders, who seem to have learned nothing
from years of strife. They play with the fires of regional and international menace. Perhaps it would have been better for the Syrians to
have stayed; but as Ghassan has pointed out, they turned out to be
obtrusive and greedy, alienating the Lebanese on all sides and – it
seems well possible – turning to their old violent interventions when
their fortunes diminished and they lost their grip.

Equally, as Ghassan and Nidal know, Lebanon can never be rid of a
close Syrian connection, whether the Lebanese like it or not. It is in the
blood, the family ties that have stretched across what is now the border
for many hundreds of years before there were any borders; it is in the
shared history, language, culture, music, traditions, food and religions.
The West introduced frontiers and customs posts, passports and immigration, and tried to solidify inside European-model nation states the
fluidity of the Arab world.

But this is the modern world. These tribes have accepted their new,
enclosed identities. The question for Syria and Lebanon is whether
their connection can be more benign than malign. Syria has hankerings
after reuniting the whole family. The NSSP and Nidal's family are
sympathetic to that idea, though not perhaps in the fashion in which
Syria has tried to exert itself as over-all controller.

Syria stopped the state fracturing completely, in 1976 and again in
1990, and brought stability to Lebanon. But its rule became heavy-
handed in the late 1990s and positively intrusive after the old President
Assad died in 2000. His far-sighted overview of the region died with
him and could not immediately be revived by his young son, Bashar,
who succeeded him. The old guard at the top in Syria, with their nervous and authoritarian view of the systems and inhabitants of both
countries, prevailed, even though Bashar at first tried to use his late
father's name and authority to carry out political and economic
reforms in Syria. A freer Syria might have meant a lighter touch in
Lebanon. It was not to be. Meanwhile, the Syrian *mukhabarrat*
(Intelligence) and the pro-consuls at their posts over the hills in
Lebanon proved to be beyond his grasp.

Syria lost its grip in Beirut finally in 2005 and has not regained it.
Lebanon left to its devices has shown renewed signs of dividing and

fracturing. A divided and fractured Lebanon is very much part of Israel's plan, says Ghassan. It is a widely held view among all factions: he mentions the break-up of Iraq, the 'Bantustan' programme in Palestine, the dangers even in Syria itself, where a minority of Alawites rule over a Sunni Muslim majority and strong Christian and Druze minorities in an authoritarian, Ba'athist state whose sudden demise could, as in Iraq, bring implosion and disintegration. 'For Israel,' says Ghassan, 'the only way to be safe is to be the strongest state in the midst of fragmentation.' If he is right, the tendencies in 2007, as we sit and contemplate Lebanon's misery amid the draperies of this gracious palace, are much in Israel's favour. The uncertainty and division remind me of a hymn: 'Change and decay/In all around I see'.

From the NSSP point of view, the strength of the Arabs is in the region, in the people, in their patience: 'We have had the Seleucids, the Mamluks, the Ottomans, the French and the British. They have all come and gone but have not broken the weave of the area.' But in his certainties and his hopes Ghassan is choosing to ignore Palestine, whose weave was unravelled – shredded – in 1948 by the creation of Israel, a phenomenon that could not have been made possible but for British intervention and connivance. Lebanon and Syria would not be antagonists had it not been for the French decision to mould a small and Christian-dominated nation from the fabric of Syria.

As for Hezbollah, a relatively recent phenomenon, Israel created it by militarily occupying southern Lebanon for so long; Israel made it the power it is today. Some Lebanese would argue conspiratorially that this was deliberate. Conspiracy theories are easy to dismiss when you are not the ones conspired against, and this is a region where Sykes–Picot,[1] for example, is as fresh in the mind of a Lebanese or Palestinian today, 90 or so years on, as, say, 9/11 is in the minds of a Briton or American, less than six years on. Deliberate or not, perhaps, as with Hamas in Palestine, Israel's scheme to create dissension among its neighbours by encouraging Islamists against nationalists has not turned out quite as it hoped. If Hezbollah is a threat to anyone it is possibly more of a threat to Israel than it is to Lebanon if the Lebanese can keep their heads, as obviously Ghassan intends to.

'We can work with fundamentalist groups as long as they fulfil two criteria: they are against Israel and for the unity of Lebanon. And I believe that Hezbollah is Lebanese to the bone – Iran cannot tell them what to do and nor can Syria if it is not in Lebanon's interests. They were much more fanatical five or six years ago. No one can make an Islamic state in Lebanon. It would be permanent war. They have seen the war between religious sects that has happened in Iraq and it has taught them a terrible lesson.'

There is logic in this ex-politician's remarks and evidence that he is correct. The trouble is that in Lebanon, where each faction, tribe, party, warlord and leader watches the other with fear at worst and suspicion at best of any advantage in the other's camp, where any gain is perceived as gain at one's own expense, any alliance viewed with the utmost gravity, logic does not operate much of the time.

To counterbalance a sense of disadvantage, Group X will seek a new alliance, perhaps with an outside force, a meeting in Damascus, a visit to a Palestinian camp, a coffee in the southern suburbs, an afternoon at the American Embassy, an all-expenses-paid weekend in Paris, courtesy of the Quai d'Orsay or the presidential Palace – in other words, some outside alliance, foreign or regional that the relevant party or grouping will feel gives it the edge over its rivals. In turn, the group itself risks becoming the tool of its new mentor. Few Lebanese factions, if any, have the strength, discipline and hard-wired ideological commitment of Hezbollah.

What a miasma of paranoia this lovely place is. It is up here in these tree-lined mountains and tumbling villages, hawk-eyed over the ocean, that I feel it most; here is the backbone of Lebanon, the retreats of the dissidents, freedom-lovers, fugitives, refugees, separatists and bigots, with their lines down to and outlets in Beirut, the one city which reflects them, personifies them and carries their confusions to the nation.

A short, troubled history

I had been reminded of Antoun Sa'adeh before I bumped into Nidal Achkar. Walking up from the row of hotels and restaurants that cluster along the coastal west Beirut enclave of Raouche, on the corniche, near the landmark Pigeon Rock, towards Hariri's Future TV station, I noticed a bust planted outside a modest office block at the top of the hill that leads up from the Sea Rock Hotel. Young men lurked in the lobby, eyeing me.

The bust was of the late Mr Sa'adeh. Not long ago the PPS flag would have been flying outside and the lobby contingent would have been carrying Kalashnikovs. In fact, not long after I noted the office and decided to look into the party's history, in the spring of 2007, it was attacked, the party believed by some rivals to be involved somehow or even directly in the spate of killings of leading, pro-March 14 (government) politicians and supporters.

In the mid-to-late 2000s, the fraught relationship between the Lebanese government and its supporters and the regime in Damascus meant many if not most Lebanese were convinced that any notable member of society who died suddenly and violently had been despatched by Syria or its agents, a conviction not entirely unjustified given much past circumstantial evidence: during the many years I lived in or was connected with Lebanon, Damascus made certain that no one individual in Lebanon rose too far to threaten the precarious confessional balance of power or political order: Kamal Junblatt's assassination in March 1977 and Bashir Gemayel's in September 1982 were two cases in point.

The NSSP comes under suspicion now as a Syrian agency, but it has had a troubled history with almost everyone during its 75 years. I describe it not so much because of the importance of the party itself, which is limited in terms of domestic Lebanese power-sharing, but because of what it illustrates about the close connections between Lebanon and its neighbours, and the ephemeral nature of the borders that intersect the Levant. The party is not as *outré* as it sometimes might seem when it rejects these artificial lines between Syria, Lebanon, Jordan and Palestine.

The creation of Israel in 1948 and the consequent catastrophe for the indigenous Palestinian Arabs reverberated throughout the region, not only in the shape of hundreds of thousands of refugees swarming in terror and in despair across neighbouring Arab borders (I shall look at the direct impact on Lebanon in Chapter 7), but in a massive undermining of Arab confidence and pride.

A new set of triumphalist colonialist-settlers, well armed and well financed, Western-backed interlopers, largely of European origins, had arrived in the region to continue and build on the divisive and acquisitive intrusions of the old Europeans, most particularly the French and the British.

In Syria, in 1949, the Syrian Commander-in-Chief, Husni al Za'im, saw the defeat of the Syrian forces in the disastrous campaign in Palestine as the direct responsibility of the civilian government in

Damascus. He threw that body out in a military coup. Za'im was a great believer, at that stage, in the PPS's philosophy of the unity of Greater Syria. His Damascus coup re-inspired Antoun Sa'adeh to take up the struggle for it against the leadership in Lebanon (he had been relatively quiescent after Lebanon gained independence from the French in 1943). He did not, essentially, believe in the concept or viability of the Lebanese State.

The Palestinian debacle, Sa'adeh thought, as did Za'im, was proof of his own country's leadership's ineptitude and weakness, and of the flawed nature of Arab nationalism, which, unlike his tighter idea of Greater Syria and like-minded peoples, tried to bring the variegated tribes of the Maghreb and the Gulf and Egypt–Sudan under one wing. He knew this was unwieldy and unworkable and he has so far been proved correct; but his next moves were to go fatally awry.

Not for the first time, Lebanon's constituent parts were torn between the magnets of Arab unity, Greater Syria and Lebanese Nationalism, whose most extreme exponents in the Christian camp were doubtful even about Lebanon's 'Arab identity'. The latter were suspicious of any close connections with the wider Arab and mostly Islamic world. Antoun Sa'adeh saw his chance of exploiting these uncertainties and stormed into their centre with more outspoken ideological enthusiasm than careful circumspection and assessment. The Lebanese authorities, backed by the increasingly powerful Phalangist Party, itself only a few years younger than the NSSP, saw Sa'adeh as disturbingly close to General Za'im's Syrians, and acted to suppress him.

In June of 1949 there was a battle between Phalangist militia members and NSSP fighters in the Beirut district of Gemmayzeh, then a poor area near the port, at the western edge of Christian east Beirut, where the party published its newspaper. This building was burned down. Lebanese police subsequently arrested party members and accusations were voiced that Sa'adeh and his men were plotting to overthrow the government and merge the country with Syria.

Sa'adeh fled to Syria to join Za'im and was granted asylum. Here he tried to change great words and fine thoughts into deeds of arms. From Syria he announced an armed uprising against government posts in the Beka'a Valley, the long, wide fertile stretch of territory that separates the mountains of Lebanon from the Anti-Lebanon range, which more or less forms the eastern border between the two countries. The idea was that NSSP armed units would push up into the Mountain and on into

Beirut. They were stopped almost as soon as they started. The Lebanese Army crushed them before they could get up out of the Beka'a (it is interesting to note here that this is a good example of how the Lebanese Army's purpose – and few successful military endeavours – has always been internal security rather than facing down any external foe).

Sa'adeh, if not his party, was suddenly history. His fair-weather friend Za'im did a *volte face* and made up with the government in Beirut, with a little interventional diplomatic help from Saudi Arabia and Egypt, the 'Arab' factor here coming into play. The last thing either Saudi Arabia or Egypt wanted was a powerful Syro-Lebanese bloc to their north. Syria and Lebanon decided to smooth over various differences that had emerged in the few years since their independence, and the Greater Syria idea took its place in the dream factory.

Its continued presence there has been confirmed over the years by the steady disintegration of Iraq, the bad-blood separation of Lebanon and Syria in 2005, the instability in Lebanon, the evisceration of Palestine, the domination of Israel and Jordan's peace treaty with the Jewish State.

The people of the region have much to regret. The resources and human talents of the Near East, pooled, would be an Arab powerhouse in the region, a good enough reason, one supposes, for many interests to guarantee that it does not happen. For example, up against a united economic and perhaps military entity on its northern and eastern borders, Israel would not have found it so easy to dominate the Middle East. Perhaps Israel might not have existed at all, certainly not in its present, superlatively and uniquely over-riding form. On the other hand, it is impossible to know how the different Arab components of Greater Syria might ultimately have fitted together in such a grand attempt at modern nation-building over the years after the Great War and given the fissiparous Arab tendencies that had been magnified and exploited by the Western powers.

As for Sa'adeh, his erstwhile ally General Za'im had him handed over to the Lebanese in Damascus, and he was taken to a military court in Beirut. There he was charged with conspiring to overthrow the Lebanon government and – that old favourite – 'collaboration with Israel', a deeply hurtful and unjust charge against a man who had always vehemently opposed Zionism and its works. He was shot by a firing squad on 8 July 1949, joining the long and open-ended roster of notable Lebanese martyrs.

His legacy is important, however, and his party and its ideas remained a symbolic and even sometimes central part of the Lebanese matrix. It emphasised for many Lebanese the special nature of the Near East and its separateness from the wider stretches of Arabia, the harsher interpretations of Islam, its outlook to the West as well as the East. Sa'adeh's followers kept the light burning at no small cost to themselves, trapped as they were between conflicting forces and sectarian tribalism: Christian exclusiveness, Islamic fervour, Arab nationalism, Egyptian–Syrian unity, Western meddling and manipulation, Zionist chicanery and intervention, Palestinian nationalism and revolution, Marxism and socialism, Nasserism.

The NSSP tried again to assert itself at the New Year's Eve turn of 1961 into 1962. This time they took on perhaps the most powerful and effective system that ever ruled free Lebanon, the government of President Fuad Chehab, a former commander of the army who had performed expertly in the brief Muslim uprising against his predecessor, Camille Chamoun, in 1958. Chehab understood the Lebanese people, and the army. He used firm but relatively benign military discipline and his good relations with the Arab states, including Gamal Abdel Nasser, the Egyptian president, to powerful internal effect. He stood aloof from the parties, kept the army intact as an arm of the state, and imposed internal order in a disinterested form that appealed to Lebanese of all inclinations. President Chehab appeared to have that rare commodity in Lebanese leadership circles, a social conscience.

The NSSP's attempted New Year's coup was another suicidal enterprise. The rebels appear to have been disgruntled by the defeat of Chamoun's anti-Nasserite forces. Army units, led by officers who were members of the NSSP, and supported by militia fighters, occupied officers' quarters at the Ministry of Defence at Yarzeh, just up the hill from the presidential palace, and took a number of senior officers captive.

They were routed by soldiers loyal to General Chehab. The failed putsch did nothing but rally the public, especially the Christians, around the government. Mass arrests followed.

What the coup attempt did was to entrench military intelligence at the centre of government for the next eight years or so. It was one way of bringing order and it worked. It was as near as possible a benign military-style dictatorship of officers and technocrats that the NSSP had by its violent sortie solidified at the heart of the rule of Lebanon. The 1960s were a glowing period of Lebanese prosperity, for the upper and middle classes. Beneath them, with dreadful consequences to come, the poor stayed poor or became poorer and resentment grew, from the deprived south to the slums that ringed the cities. To augment this social unrest came Israel's victory over the Arabs in June 1967, another Arab catastrophe. Lebanon's brief golden days were drawing to a close. Nidal's generation of hopeful, talented and broad-minded youth were to see their country sundered as never before and to live a life of unremitting upheaval. For this famous actress, tempests of Shakespearean fury have been her off-stage accompaniment, but, true Lebanese that she is, she remains unbowed; her performance continues.

Fugitives from the Catastrophe

7

The evocative and elegant simplicity of the Martyrs' Square memorial in downtown Beirut, remembering those who died in the struggle against the Ottomans' Young Turks, is not replicated at the anonymous, mass grave in the Chatila Palestinian refugee camp, in Beirut's south-western suburbs, on the way to the airport.

There is a double iron gate leading to an enclosed field of grass, a stone, plain monument at its centre. Here lie the remains of defence-less, civilian Palestinian and Lebanese whom Christian militiamen slaughtered during a three-day period in mid-September 1982. During this atrocity, the invading Israel army held the ring and helped guide the killers towards their victims. Before independent observers could reach the scene, the Christian fighters and Israeli soldiers had time to bulldoze beneath the earth and beyond enumeration many of the dead. So it is not known how many perished. The final figure could well have been as many as 3000. Some of the Sabra–Chatila area camp's inhabitants escaped before the killers reached them; most were entrapped, surrounded by the Israeli army and their Christian collaborators.

'A Massacre Against Humanity', it says, in Arabic, over the gate. 'We Believe in God and God is Great'. One would need to believe in God to have withstood and survived the Sabra–Chatila massacre, and to continue, as so many scores of thousands do, to live on its site and among its terrible memories, in such apparently fruitless squalor. All Palestinian refugee camps are ripe for despair and hopelessness, yet are also defined by a determination on the refugees' part to survive and to go back to their homes in Palestine, or at least to acquire decent compensation, resettlement in a place of their choice and citizenship. They require a settling, in a word, of the physical and moral accounts with Israel and the 'international community' for their loss. That is what most refugees will tell you and it is the position of the Palestinian movement – the Palestinian Authority, the PLO, the different parties. Right of Return to Palestine (what is now Israel) for the Palestinians is, indeed, inalienable under the UN Charter and in relevant UN resolutions.

Nobody, however, has thought to ask the refugees themselves to set out officially – in a disinterested poll by a suitable international or Palestinian body – what it is they actually want.

These people display dignity in adversity, refusing to disappear. The legal case for their Return is unanswerable. Their status as refugees is official. Their survival and the steady increase in their numbers, as families grow, is one of the most persistent and important political factors in the whole Israel–Palestine confrontation – perhaps *the* most.

The Palestinian – and therefore the Israeli – stories are at the heart of what has happened and is happening to modern Lebanon. The seeds of a great part of Lebanon's misfortunes were sewn in 1948, only five years after Lebanese Independence, when the Palestinians began pouring across the frontier from Palestine, as it was turned into Israel, at the point of the gun. They were settled in camps across the country by the UN and the Lebanese government. But those seeds of misfortune did not flourish until after the 1967 war, when Israel seized the West Bank, all of Arab East Jerusalem, both then under Jordanian control, Gaza, then under Egyptian rule, the Egyptian Sinai Peninsula and the Syrian Golan Heights.

During this period, the mid-1960s, Palestinian resistance and nationalism was reborn; and much of it, in its military form, took root in Lebanon's refugee camps, triggering Israeli reprisals, incursions and invasions. This growing cross-border conflict between the Israelis and the Palestinians exacerbated domestic Lebanese social upheaval. The radical political thinkers and guerrillas of the Palestinian movement encouraged, enthused and eventually armed and fought alongside Muslim, leftist, Nasserite and other radical groups. The fighting in the south, near the Israel–Lebanon border, caused the flight of hundreds of thousands of mainly poor and mainly Shi'ite Muslims to the suburbs of Beirut, where the domestic tensions were focused. The result was civil war, Israeli and Syrian intervention in Lebanon, communal terror and a system's collapse.

It is easy, but would not be unjust, to hold the Palestinians solely responsible for Lebanon's plight. Their leaders made serious mistakes in the exclusion zones into which the *Nakba* – the 'Catastrophe' – of 1948 and the subsequent disaster in 1967 had forced them. Tracing the roots of blame in the recent Palestinian history of catastrophe is not a duty of this book and has been widely written about elsewhere. But the Palestinians were a catalyst in the Lebanese experiment, perhaps a crucial one, and their presence changed the country irrevocably.

It is with a sense of desolation that I retrace my steps through these passages and alleyways. Here, 25 years previously, I had been one of the first foreigners to stumble across the carnage and wreckage that three days of state-assisted murder and mayhem had wrought among a repeatedly abandoned people.

At the site of the mass grave, sad and stark in its tidy simplicity, there are billboard-size photographs of the scenes we found as we walked into the camp that Saturday, 20 September 1982. To reach the centre of the disaster, we walked past eddying waves of hysterical women, mothers and wives, widows, daughters and sisters, a few grandfathers and newly orphaned children. They were being herded away by Israeli soldiers into holding centres, traumatised by what they had experienced and terrified of what might be to come.

There are grim posters, too, portraying later massacres, of Lebanese, at Qana, for example, in 1996, and in that same village again in 2006. Over the past 40 or so years, hundreds of thousands – perhaps even a million – Lebanese have suffered death, injury, loss and displacement alongside the Palestinians in and because of their struggle with Israel and its consequences on Lebanese soil. They were caught up in this regional imbroglio and exile, and the battle over land and identity that has poisoned the region since the end of the Ottoman Empire and the arrival of the Western Powers in 1917.

Sabra–Chatila, September 1982

There are no easy or definitive places to begin this dreadful Palestinian narrative, but here I am starting with the late summer of 1982. The Israelis had invaded Lebanon during the three months from early June to the end of August, fighting and bombing their way up to the outskirts of Beirut, entering the Christian militia-held sectors of the city. In August, the Israelis and Palestinians agreed to a ceasefire, under American pressure. Lebanon had had enough and the Palestinians under their leader, Yasser Arafat, finally accepted the fact. The US envoy, Philip Habib, arranged the ceasefire with Saudi Arabian help (the Saudis could talk to the PLO, the Americans to Israel, as at that time neither the USA nor Israel recognised the PLO).

As part of this agreement, the Israelis stayed where they were and pledged not to try to move into the largely Muslim areas of Beirut's West and South, inside which were located the big Palestinian refugee camps, Bourj el Barajneh and Sabra–Chatila. These were near the Fakhani area, which had until August been the nexus of the PLO, its offices, fighting forces, armouries, hospitals, living quarters, and home of most of the PLO's constituent parts: Fateh, the Popular Front for the Liberation of Palestine (PFLP), the Democratic Front, the Arab Liberation Front, Sa'iqa and so on.

Under Arafat, these guerrilla groups had fought against heavy odds to keep Israel's air force and army at bay, but they had surrendered in August of 1982, in the face of overwhelmingly superior arms, after the American diplomatic intervention. Even the Americans, then, had only a limited appetite for allowing their Israeli allies to pursue their one-sided battle and its mounting toll of civilian death and destruction – it was estimated that some 40,000 Lebanese civilians had died during the summer campaign, and hundreds of thousands more had been injured, made homeless and displaced. The international community, under American control, had – as it was to do so many times in the coming decades – allowed a disproportionate Israeli military assault on its Arab neighbours to go on for far too long, if indeed it should have been allowed in the first place.

As August entered its final days, the Palestinian fighters, and the Syrian troops who had been stationed in central Lebanon since 1976, left Lebanon and Beirut by sea westwards and by road eastwards. They did so under the supervision of a small international peace force: American, French and Italian. Fighting had ceased, for the moment. The Israelis occupied roughly the lower third of Lebanon, including the Shouf mountains to the east of Beirut, the Beka'a Valley up to the Damascus Road that links Beirut to Syria's border, and parts of Christian east Beirut, most particularly the area near the presidential Palace in Ba'abda where they had set up their military HQ.

The Christian groups, particularly the LF under their young leader Bashir Gemayel, had co-operated with the Israelis. Though they had not been of real military use, they were a benign factor for the Israelis. Both shared the aim of ending Palestinian military and political power in Lebanon and removing their armaments. This achieved, the Maronite Christians would be restored, it was thought, to something approaching their traditional supremacy in the country. Furthermore, presidential elections were due in Lebanon, and the Israelis would have a close friend, even ally (it was assumed), in the post in the form of Bashir Gemayel. On 23 August 1982, with US oversight and orchestration, Gemayel was elected by the assembled Lebanese deputies. This time the election took place under the close eye of the Israeli army (in 1976, Elias Sarkis, his predecessor, had been elected with the help of the Syrian army).

All appeared to be going according to American–Israeli–Lebanese Christian plans. But differences were beginning to emerge between the young president-elect and the Israeli prime minister, Menachem Begin, about how close the relationship between Israel and Lebanon would be. Begin wanted an immediate peace treaty, Gemayel wanted 'normalised' relations, to be promulgated over time. Whatever the details, Gemayel was heavy-handedly alienating both the Arabs and his Israeli friends: the former, by stressing volubly that the days of Lebanon's 'Arabic' and 'Oriental' character were over; the latter, by dithering over his relations with the Jewish state and showing signs of ingratitude for Israel's having allegedly saved Lebanon's Christians from the Muslims and Palestinians.

These hostile regional reactions added fuel to the debate about who (on the night of 14 September) detonated a remote-controlled bomb under the Phalangist Party's HQ in Ashrafiyeh, in Christian east Beirut, killing Bashir Gemayel and some 60 of his supporters. This gave the Israelis the pretext to break the international pledges made in August to Lebanon and the USA and immediately launch a military takeover of Muslim west Beirut. In doing this, they secured the perimeters of the refugee camps to avert bloodshed, so they claimed.

Most Lebanese I spoke to were convinced that the Israelis had killed the young Gemayel for his reluctance to do their bidding. He had some support among Muslims, which might, it was thought, have diluted his pro-Israeli tendencies. Despite his right-wing and anti-Palestinian views, he appeared to a wide section of the community as a man of the people,

a new, youthful, tough and independent voice in the moribund, manipulated life of Lebanese politicians. My own view, later I think borne out if
not definitively proved, was that Syria was behind the assassination. The
idea of a pact between Lebanon and Israel was anathema to Syria; and
two years on, Damascus was to sabotage another Lebanon–Israeli treaty,
this one signed by Bashir Gemayel's elder brother, Amine, who almost
immediately replaced him as President.

However, all the politicking and speculation about Bashir Gemayel's
assassins was drowned out by events. Israel's so-called attempt 'to avert
bloodshed' most certainly did not do so. Rather the reverse. Israel's
Defence Minister, Ariel Sharon, had agreed with Bashir Gemayel that
the LF, the army or the Phalange, or any or all of them, should enter
the Palestinian camps and 'clean out' the hundreds of 'terrorists'
Sharon claimed were still there, despite the internationally supervised
PLO exodus of August. Bashir's sudden demise meant that in the
ensuing meltdown all diplomatic agreement could be held to be off and
the Israeli army could enter west Beirut and mastermind any Lebanese
military or militia efforts to do the job. It was impossible, then and
now, to believe that in such an event a massacre would not be
inevitable and that Israeli intelligence would not have known it.

For the Israeli military, intelligence and political establishment,
Beirut was the Forbidden City, the first Arab capital Israel had entered
by force. The Israeli Army moved in to west Beirut on 15 September,
quickly encircling the Palestinian camps and meeting spirited but little
effective military resistance from the few armed Palestinians and
Lebanese fighters who remained.

In collusion with Christian militia leaders from the Phalange and
elsewhere, Ariel Sharon and Israeli military intelligence officers
arranged for hundreds of Christian fighters to enter the camps under
the protection and guidance of the Israeli forces that now virtually
surrounded the Palestinians. The plan had been finalised on 15
September, as the Israeli forces took up their positions. This was at last
the promulgation of Sharon's planned 'clean-up of terrorists'.

Except that there were no 'terrorists'. The armed units of the PLO
had long gone. The period from 16 September, when the militiamen
went into the camps, until 18 September, when they left, constitutes
one of the most appalling chapters in recent Middle East history. Its
brutality and callousness live on in the minds of those who survived or
escaped, and those who witnessed the slaughter and its results.

For those three days, until the Saturday when the aid workers, diplomats and journalists managed finally to get into Sabra–Chatila camp, the Christian forces did their work. The Israeli army and its senior officers, including Sharon, were well able to view the action from their positions on the roof of the Kuwaiti Embassy and UN buildings that overlooked the camp from the hill of Bir Hassan, a few hundred yards from the camp's centre. It would have taken someone blindly ignorant of Middle East politics and of the murderous attitude towards Palestinians of these Christians, especially after Gemayel's death, not to know how they would behave once they were free to roam the camp with their guns, knives and axes.

The Israeli army and intelligence services were not blindly ignorant of Middle East politics and were not unaware of these Christians' view of the Palestinians as 'dangerous vermin'. I had no doubt myself within minutes of entering the camp that this was either a deliberate, planned war crime, or an act of criminal negligence unthinkable on the part of the national army of the Middle East's 'only democracy'.

For those two first days the press corps and TV cameras were unable to get to Sabra–Chatila, mainly because it was surrounded by Israeli soldiers and tanks, who were shelling and sniping at the low-lying area beneath them; but also because in districts on the perimeter the Israelis had not yet reached, handfuls of frightened young Palestinian and Lebanese men with automatic weapons were nervously firing in the air or at anyone who tried to approach. I know, because I tried, as did scores of my media colleagues, diplomats and NGOs.

A friend who was a PLO official had telephoned me from somewhere outside the camps to tell me 'something was going on' in the camps, but he either did not know or would not say what. Perhaps he felt a sense of shame at the way in which his people had been abandoned by everyone, including the PLO, to the mercies of the international community, the Israelis and the Phalangists, with him at liberty and unable to do anything. It was a shame said to be common among survivors of the Nazi death camps.

At night we could see Israeli military flares floating over the camps, making temporary daylight of the night sky; but we could not get close enough to see why. It became clear when we did enter that the Israelis had lit the Christian fighters' way to their victims.

I remember one failed attempt to get to the camp, on the Friday. The little group I was with reached the large, walled compound of the Soviet

Embassy, just off the Corniche Maasra and near the northern entrances to the camps. When we could make no further progress the Israeli soldiers invited us into the Embassy building, which they had taken over. They were keen to show us round their new billet. Perhaps some of them had Russian roots, or enjoyed tweaking the tail of a Palestinian and Syrian ally. In one large reception room an Israeli officer sat at a grand piano, playing Chopin. If we had known then what we were to find out the next day we would not have found the incident entertaining. But it must be said that many, perhaps most, of the ordinary Israeli conscripts surging around Beirut that day clearly had no idea of what their political and military bosses were plotting with Lebanese Christian help.

That was as near Sabra–Chatila as any outsiders reached on the Friday, when the killing was in its second day and at its peak.[1]

Early on Saturday morning, we finally entered. When I arrived at the camps' northern access at about eight o'clock a few aid workers and an American diplomat were already there. I walked some way in and saw one dead body, a few of the injured in the Gaza Hospital at the northern end of the camp and several Israeli officers shepherding women out of the camp towards the Camille Chamoun football stadium nearby. (Why is it that sports stadiums recur in tales of political killings?) At one point I saw the Israeli army commander, Rafael Eytan, patrolling and conferring with his officers on the outskirts of the camp. Later on, Ariel Sharon appeared at the scene.

One did not have to be a military analyst to see immediately that whatever had happened inside the camp had happened under the gaze of the Israeli Army (at that stage we could only guess at the level of complicity). I said as much in the report I sent a few hours later, to the BBC, the first news of the slaughter to reach the outside world. The Israeli Prime Minister always claimed that the 5 pm local time BBC news transmission (2 pm GMT) was the first he knew of the massacre. Subsequently that proved to have been the case: even this former terrorist was in the dark.

To my alarm, I needed to send the report revealing the massacre through the Israeli military communications system. The telephone exchange in Beirut had collapsed, not for any conspiratorial or Israeli-inspired reason, but because that was how things were in a city under intense siege for nearly three months. The oil for the system's generators had run out.

Getting to the Israeli command post at Ba'abda was the only way, therefore, to transmit radio dispatches, and thus my report would have to be vetted by the Israeli military censor in Tel Aviv. Clutching my pre-recorded cassette in the vain hope that at least the soldiers in the post would not hear me describing aloud the Israel-assisted atrocity (I would be playing it down the line, directly from recorder into the telephone), I made my way for an hour or more through scores of road-blocks, of various militias and the Israelis themselves, and through epic traffic jams. At that time, those were the joys of being a correspondent in an Arab country – you might obtain a story, but you never knew whether you would be able to send it.

I despaired of the Israelis allowing my report through. I therefore made it as circumspect as I could in the circumstances, without omitting any information or diluting my (correct) conclusion that the Israelis would have seen everything that was going on inside Sabra–Chatila. I suggested that the massacre could not and would not have happened without Israel's presence.

To my astonishment, the censor in Tel Aviv let it through without demur. Israeli censorship ruled that only information that might hinder Israel's military progress should be cut, and this was not deemed to be the case. I cursed myself ever after that I had not written and said more.

Then it was back to west Beirut and the frustration of being incommunicado. What we had all seen that day was horrifying, even for war correspondents, many of whom had been in the Middle East for years or had come there recently by way of Vietnam, Cambodia and other theatres of war. My BBC colleague in Israel, Michael Elkins, having at first tried like a good Zionist to knock my story down after its first transmission at 2 pm GMT, then hijacked it completely and wrote forcefully and eloquently all night about how disgracefully Israel had behaved, and how ashamed all right-minded Israelis were. He was in high dudgeon and won an award for his reporting. But critical as it was, his was an Israeli version of the events *as they affected Israel.* He could not know or begin to describe the horror we had witnessed close up.

Before we in Beirut could take up the story again the next morning, when the phones were reconnected to the outside world, we had plenty of time to reflect on the real meaning of the carnage we had witnessed. As I walk through Sabra–Chatila again, the images are vivid. They intensify my anger, already aroused by the fact that this unholy displacement of humanity, the descendants of the survivors, are still stuck here, inhabiting, even haunting this killing-ground of old.

On that Saturday morning, once I had entered the camp proper, a US diplomat and a young man from Save the Children had said to me 'look in there', pointing up an alleyway. They were white-faced and soon so were we all. As we pushed forward up the stinking street, we walked past (covering our mouths and noses with handkerchiefs) the bodies of women, children, old men and some young men. They lay in piles where they had been shot or cut down, filling the miserable labyrinths. Many of the bodies had been mutilated, one hoped to God after death.

Three days after the massacre began the Lebanese and Israeli bull-dozers had started hiding the evidence, but had by no means finished. The details of the killings have been described many times and the story told in great particular, from Israeli, Arab and independent perspectives. But the guilty have never faced justice, though we know who they are by name. One of those most responsible, Ariel Sharon, became Israel's prime minister.

That day I saw vivid examples of such human cruelty and bloodlust that some psychological shock temporarily blanked them from my mind, for me to recall later. I do not suppose I could have described them on air anyway. If they were too difficult for me to take in, what of the people back home? One lesson of Sabra–Chatila was how the Palestinians and Lebanese had been co-mingled in suffering, and how relentless were the Israelis in pursuing those they perceived as enemies to the ends of the earth, if necessary.

Until then, I had taken a dim view of Israel's deleterious effect on the region, but thought somewhere at the back of my mind that reason could somehow prevail. It was at about this time that mutterings of a two-state solution were heard; and the world's reaction to the Israeli invasion of Lebanon, even before Sabra–Chatila, and America's late but reasonably helpful intervention had inspired some hope that at last 'someone' would do 'something'. The international community, such as it was, and public opinion had certainly been stirred up in Europe and even in the USA by that summer of invasion, siege and mass murder.

Israel's cynical refusal to take real responsibility for this war crime brought home to me its absolute commitment to erase at any cost the Palestinian people's identity, place, future and hope. To attain this, it was prepared to ignore the sanctity of the lives of others and to imperil not only its neighbours but its own future in the region.

To walk again along Rue Sabra is to be reminded how far Israel has gone in its unremitting battle to expunge the Palestinians from history.

But it is also to see how Israel has failed. Amid this misery is some kind of spirit and backbone that cannot be removed. It is all around me as I walk through the camp along the winding central road.

Sabra Camp is one long market of vegetable sellers, peddlers of watches, CDs, videos, DVDs, clothes, tee-shirts, jeans, blouses, dresses and the incessant noise of horns as drivers push through the wandering shoppers, Lebanese as well as Palestinians. Many of the stalls are run by Syrian traders. As you turn into Chatila the density of all this intensifies as the street narrows. Behind the lines of stallholders are the broken alleyways and breezeblock two- and three-storey buildings, laced by impenetrably tangled electricity wires and cables, dark little enclaves inside which barefoot children play on mud floors running with water. Infants and adults pick among the mounds of rubbish by the roadside.

Mothers hang washing on balconies and walls, and families sit in dank courtyards watching the visitor with blank, resigned faces. Small smiles of welcome appear if you offer a greeting. In any European city Chatila would be called a slum, like most Palestinian refugee camps in Lebanon. But this is where these benighted people have had to live in increasing numbers, with no chance to extend their space, for the past 57 years. During this time circumstances forced them to turn their tents first into iron and wooden huts and then into these stark concrete blockhouses. In these awful conditions, Palestinian families, often six or seven people crammed into three rooms, manage to maintain hygiene and dignity.

The old Gaza hospital, where I first saw the wounded of the massacre on that September day, has become a dreary apartment block. In another such building, not far away, up a flight of stairs, Jamil Ismail Hamad, who is 71, sits on a couch. He is wearing socks, a pullover, slacks and a waterproof coat and is eating *foul*, a basic Arab dish, a staple of broad beans cooked in oil and spices, and drinking mint tea. The walls of his living room are patched, peeling and damp. Apart from the chairs and a low table there are only a dressing table and a mirror. Above him are three brass plates decorating the wall. That is it: three rooms for him, his daughter and his grandson.

This, and worse, is a scene replicated in the nine other camps in Lebanon and the many more in Syria, Jordan, the West Bank and Gaza. The rest of his family, says Jamil, 'Thanks be to God', have spread wide:

two more daughters in Canada and Denmark, two sons in Germany and the USA. He has a Green Card, the document that grants an immigrant the right to live and work in the USA, but he will not live there. Jamil says this is because life is different there and lonely: the familiarity and solidarity of the camp and his fellow Palestinians suit him better.

Jamil comes from the Palestinian village of Safsaf, near Safed, in Galilee in the north of what is now Israel. When he was 12 he watched as killers from the Jewish army, the Haganah, put his family to death – two of his brothers, his father, an uncle and ten more distant relatives. Jamil was spared. He was too young to warrant a bullet. He says the killers told the survivors they were welcome to stay in Safsaf. But as they prepared to leave, the Jewish fighters threw the bodies of the murdered villagers into the village well, fouling the water source.

Jamil thus set off with the womenfolk and other survivors on the trek north to Lebanon, about three miles away. It was a story repeated all over Palestine. The Palestinian fugitives took what possessions they could carry, out of Palestine, for ever, although none of them realised the finality of their journey at the time.

After that, Jamil was moved around Lebanon – 'shipped around like sheep', he says: Tyre, Tripoli, then to Chatila, in 1955. For the next 20 years he worked in a variety of jobs, ending up in a Lebanese clothes factory near the presidential palace in Christian east Beirut. But in 1973 the troubles between the PLO and the Lebanese Army began to take violent shape and he became afraid to go to Christian-controlled areas. After that, he stayed in Chatila.

Jamil's story exemplifies how the Palestinians are treated by the world as commodities rather than individuals with rights to freedom, life, work and independence. The Lebanese State is part of that careless world, regarding the Palestinians with hostility, severely limiting their ability to find proper employment, move freely or live in decent accommodation. They are not permitted to expand the areas of their camps as their families grow and need more living space, unlike, for example, the illegal half-a-million Jewish settlers in the Israeli-occupied Palestinian Territories.

The Palestinian refugees of Lebanon fare no better than most of their fellows in the Occupied Territories. (No Palestinian alive outside Israel today – about 10 million of them – is not a refugee, a displaced person or an exile. Even those who stayed in Israel in 1948, now about 1.2 million, are second- or even third-class citizens, severely restricted in the land they can purchase, and with little status or influence in civil society, business or politics. Most of them cannot or just would not join the Israeli Army, the fast-feeder route to power and esteem in Israeli society.)

In Lebanon there is no real definable political representation for the refugees: no votes, no say in the running of their lives. Jamil is one of them. His only representatives on this earth are a moribund PLO, which lost most of its power and effect when in 1993 Oslo Accords removed the Palestinians' aspirations to nationhood to the confines of the West Bank and Gaza, and made them the responsibility of the Palestinian Authority, which notionally rules over those territories. The UN Relief and Works Agency (UNRWA) has responsibility for the organisation and financing of health and education to secondary level for registered refugees, but little political muscle and ever-diminishing amounts of money from the international community. Beyond these institutions the refugees organise their own NGOs and self-help groups through what funds can be raised overseas, from European, Palestinian, Arab and other sources.

Jamil's daughter Nohad, who is in her mid-40s, runs one of these organisations, a vocational training centre for women and young people. She is a member of the Najd Association, which supports women, works to reduce domestic violence, runs kindergartens, teaches embroidery and holds classes in social education. She tells the story of what happened in 1982, when she was in her early teens.

On the evening of 14 September she and her family heard that Bashir Gemayel had been killed, but knew no more than that. Israeli planes kept breaking the sound barrier, keeping them in a state of nervous tension. By the 15th they could hear Israeli tanks rumbling around the camp periphery and could see them on the raised level of the airport road. The tanks were firing into the camp, but not into the area where they were living.

A leftist Lebanese group gave some Palestinian youths Kalashnikov rifles, but Palestinian elders told the boys to go home as their guns were as useless as air rifles against tanks. They hardly knew how to use them anyway, and their presence would only provoke the soldiers and bring trouble. On the night of the 16th the Israelis fired flares into the air and the camp was lit up like daylight, says Nohad. It was at that point that people started to come up their street saying there had been a massacre. Later on, an ammunition dump blew up and they started to see injured people running away. They fled the camp and took refuge in a public hall in a nearby Muslim working-class Lebanese area. No Lebanese would let them into their homes: 'They said, "We don't want you, the Israelis are after you, not us".'

They returned home. Seeing nothing they showered and ate breakfast. But at about 10.30 am they saw a woman covered in blood, screaming and tearing at her hair, who told them soldiers had come and killed all her children. They heard sniping. More and more people were running away. Although they did not themselves see any enemy militia-men, they finally decided to listen to their father. He had been trying for many hours, in vain, to get them out of their home; now they saw for themselves why and as the panic became tangible they at last took his advice. The family ran from the camp at its north-east corner, a remaining escape route where the Israelis had no troops or tanks and which the marauding Christian killers had not reached.

They were safe. But many of the friends and neighbours they left behind were to perish in unthinkable torment.

I ask Jamil about the Right of Return, the question at the heart of the Palestinian predicament, and of importance to the Lebanese as well. He says he would only ever go back to his own village. He says if someone told the Palestinians there was a boat for Gaza and a boat for Europe, the boat to Gaza would be empty. Palestinians want to return to their own villages, their own towns, not strange parts of their land. Failing that, it seems they would rather be financially compensated and settled elsewhere completely, inside or outside the Arab world.[2]

The Lebanese authorities, not just Christians, are also made nervous by the fact that the Palestinian movement has been fudging the Right of Return issue. They fear that perhaps Lebanon will remain the refugees' permanent home.

Nohad says her father is unpopular in the neighbourhood because he says what he thinks, cursing Arab 'terrorists' in the West (presumably the perpetrators of attacks in New York, Paris, Madrid and London), admiring European law and order: if he had (former French President Jacques) Chirac's number, he says, he would telephone to tell him to put all those Algerians and Moroccans who burned cars in France in boxes and send them home. 'They say my father is far from God,' says Nohad, smiling. But I think what he has to say about the boat to Gaza is interesting.

The Palestinians need either to go home or to find somewhere decent to settle – in a welcoming country and with financial compensation. For re-settlement in an Arab or a foreign country like Canada or Australia, or even to stay in Lebanon, they need an identity, a state, a passport. A separate Palestinian state, say its proponents, could grant the refugees these requisite artefacts – the documents of citizenship. These would enable them to move freely around the world and to apply for visas and immigrant status. But at present, none of these options is on offer, except in the unproductive mouths of diplomats and politicians.

A sad little museum

Dr Mohammed al-Khatib started his tiny museum three years ago in an alleyway in Chatila. It is dark. Water drips down the walls at times. It is very humble, but it contains the artefacts and memories of Palestine he has collected from friends and neighbours in this and other Palestinian camps. People who visit us, he says, should see that we are not just mired in poverty as victims of expulsion and war, but have a past and a culture. Dr Khatib also writes poetry and, when he retires, to a house near Sidon, he will write his memoirs. He comes from near what is now Kyriat Shmoneh, in northern Galilee, just across the border with Lebanon.

When the Israelis left Lebanon in May 2000, at the end of their 22-year occupation of the south of the country, he took his 90-year-old mother to the border for the first time in 52 years, to see where their home had been. The house is still there, lived in by Jews. His brother – who has a German passport and can enter Israel – has visited it. He told the Jewish family: 'You're in my grandfather's house.' 'Maybe,' said the Israeli, 'but we're here now.'

Dr Khatib's sad, damp and cramped museum holds many mementoes. The first item he shows me is a British Army tin rations bowl from Mandate days and the second an axe the Phalangists used in their butchery of Sabra–Chatila in 1982. It is appropriate, in this place. Then we move on to the gowns and garb of the people from his district when he was young. There are the house keys that so many Palestinians hopefully kept, thinking that when the fighting died down all would be restored to normal and they would return home. Of course, they never did. There are farm implements, old radios, kitchen pots, camel-blankets, *nargilas* (one with a picture on it of a Turkish officer), copper bracelets, a vegetable slicer, oil lamps and a framed British-Mandate Palestinian pound note.

The museum is about a lost past. But past is future for the Palestinians, right now. There is no future for them, certainly, in Lebanon. They cannot work properly outside the camp. There is little work in the camp. It is very difficult for most of them to get out of the country, and if they do, to get back in. They cannot return to their Palestine, because it only exists in their memory and in Dr Khatib's museum. If it is to be a place of the future, it is a far-distant future. They are not keen to go to the West Bank, were that ever possible, as they are not from there and they are not sure how they would fit in. So the Palestinians enter their 60th year of limbo, and for the Lebanese their presence evokes sentiments ranging from sympathy to resentment to fear to hatred. But as far as the government in Beirut is concerned, they are someone else's problem, parked in Lebanese space.

Whose problem are the Palestinians? At present they remain in limbo, the problem perhaps of that amorphous body, the International Community. This, in its many forms, pitches the Palestinian file into that so-far unclearable in-tray called the Peace Process.

I admire Dr Khatib's museum. However poor, however small, this repository of Palestinian memories is his way of keeping his country's memory alive and its existence real; there are many other Dr Khatibs.

An official of the diaspora

Soheil Natour is a long-time senior official of the Democratic Front for the Liberation of Palestine, a Marxist faction of the PLO, once influential far beyond its size. It has become less so since the Oslo Accords brought about so many splits inside the Palestinian movement, not just dividing the 'insiders' of the Occupied Territories from 'outsiders' (the diaspora in the Middle East and across the globe).

Soheil sits as he has done for the past 30 years, in his office in a little back street of the tiny Mar Elias camp, on the edge of the airport road. It is in the area known as 'UNESCO', whose building and local HQ are nearby, a typical example of how a Beiruti landmark turns into the name of a locality. He works in the camp's office of the Human Development Centre, opposite the Red Crescent Society and just along from a Norwegian-financed clinic that specialises in disabled children.

Soheil came as 'luggage', as he puts it, as a one-year-old child from Acre, with his family, in 1948. He says with the resignation which is his due by now that the refugees are inured to the fact that the return that is their right is a long way off. In the meantime all concentration has to be on improving their dreadful lot in Lebanon.

Historically, the relationship between the Palestinians and the Lebanese deteriorated from one centred on humane concerns for the refugees the Lebanese had played host to between 1948 and the Six-Day War of 1967 to one of mutual mistrust and hostility by the beginning of the 1970s. Finally it all descended into war. That is physically over, but the clash of interests that caused it remain.

This outright conflict of interests began in earnest in 1968 when Palestinian guerrillas began deploying in the Arqub, a mountainous area in the south-east of Lebanon that runs alongside the northern spur of the Galilee, in the shadow of the highest peak in the region, Mount Hermon, or Jebl Sheikh. The idea was that Palestinian fighters could penetrate Israeli Galilee, disrupting the farmers and kibbutzim there, to re-establish the Palestinian claim to the land. They would put the word 'Palestine' and the Palestinian cause back into the consciousness of the world after 20 years of obscurity. Since 1948 the Palestinian cause had been seen merely as a 'refugee' problem, the responsibility of the Arab states and the international community. These had failed the Palestinians in every way. Even before the 1967 war, young Palestinians across the region were beginning to organise and mobilise politically and militarily.

The rout during the Six-Day War made it clear to the displaced Palestinians that their fate was best kept in their own hands. The PLO would be their vehicle and Fateh, the party headed by Yasser Arafat (soon to become PLO chairman), its strongest component. The guerrilla movement eventually made its major, semi-permanent base in Lebanon.

As the guerrillas moved in, they had with them the support and sympathy of many Lebanese: leftist and Muslim parties, activists and sympathisers, and students of all sects who were tired of the elitist, sectarian and corrupt system of government in Lebanon, and were mortified by the humiliation the Arabs had suffered in 1967.

Very quickly, the Palestinian movement began to establish itself in Beirut, in the camps and outside, building the beginnings of a military and political infrastructure and solidifying alliances with the various elements of the Lebanese opposition.

The Lebanese government, meanwhile, was divided on the Palestinian issue. It was incapable of retaliating against Israeli incursions. For example, Lebanon was helpless when the Israeli air force attacked Beirut International Airport in December 1968, blowing up 13 airliners of the Lebanese carrier Middle East Airlines in response to a Palestinian attack on an El Al airliner in Athens. This was before the PLO had established itself properly across Lebanon. For Israel, which assumed or presumed that the refugee camps would have supplied the Athens attackers, Lebanon was a convenient and vulnerable address.

Matters came to a head in April 1969, when demonstrations by Lebanese opposition members and students against the government in Beirut ended in the deaths of 11 people and the wounding of scores more by army and security forces. The Egyptian President Gamal Abdel Nasser, trying unsuccessfully to recover from the wounds of the 1967 war, moved quickly to intervene in the Lebanese crisis. In November of 1969 he brought Yasser Arafat and the commander of the Lebanese Army, General Emil al-Bustani, to negotiations in Cairo.

The resulting Cairo Agreement was ostensibly intended to control the Palestinian movement in general and its guerrillas in particular inside Lebanon, and to regularise relations between the Palestinians and the state in which they found themselves. It actually did the opposite. The Palestinians had such popularity, strength, determination and general Arab support, inside and outside Lebanon, that they were able to use the Agreement to build on their 'state-within-a-state' as the 1960s moved into the 1970s. This meant in effect that the Palestinians had control over their security and activities in the camps, including the holding and deployment of heavy weapons and artillery, and had freedom of movement in much of Lebanon, including as armed units free to attack Israel.

The Agreement's proposed Lebanese controls on these privileges and freedoms went largely unobserved. When the Lebanese security forces tried to enforce them, battles resulted that the Palestinians usually won. The State was challenged and often lost. The Lebanese opposition was delighted. The Palestinian movement was a useful military and political tool to help it alter the power balance and political nature of Lebanon; Nasser and the Syrian leader, President Assad, each saw the Palestinian movement as a way of getting back at Israel. They tried to increase their own controls over the PLO at the expense of Yasser Arafat, intending to use him rather than be manipulated by him. They did not wish Palestinian actions to force them into some untimely confrontation with Israel, at a time of his rather than their choosing. They had their political ambitions in the Levant, and Arafat had his – and they were by no means identical.

Both leaders, and to some extent this was also to become true of the Saudis and the Iraqis, saw the Palestinians as both their tool and their responsibility. This meant that Lebanon was infiltrated, not just by the Palestinian movement but by a bewildering fusion of factions and competing regional interests, viewing one another down the barrels of guns.

Nowhere outside Lebanon did Palestinian fighters have such freedom. They had been expelled from Jordan; in Syria the authorities had total control, helping the Palestinians to confront Israel but not from inside Syria. Nor was Nasser going to risk even greater Israeli depredations than he was suffering already by allowing the Palestinians hot pursuit into Israel and Israeli-occupied Sinai and Gaza from his domain. Such attacks from Egypt into Israel and Nasser's perceived menace had been a part of Israel's excuse for launching the Six-Day War.

Lebanon was the only place contiguous with the Zionist state from which Palestinian attacks could be mounted. It was also the only state weak enough to have to tolerate the guerrilla presence and thus become host to the Conscience of the Arab world. As a result, between 1967 and 1975, Lebanon, and more and more of its citizens, became enmeshed in mutual suspicion and enmity towards the Palestinian refugees and fighters. It was a condition which 15 years of inconclusive civil war and the seemingly endless exile of nearly half a million Palestinians in Lebanon have done little to alleviate.

Soheil, with whom I am sitting in his small, simple office in Mar Elias, has lived with this crisis all his adult life. He is one of many Palestinian activists one can find all over Beirut, in similar offices. Many of his colleagues moved on with Yasser Arafat, first in the exile to Tunisia in 1982 and 1983, after the PLO's forced departure from Lebanon, and then to the Occupied Territories, in 1994, and to what they thought would be the rewards of Oslo and the beginnings of statehood in Palestine itself. Many of these men have become rich, far beyond the dreams or aspirations of Soheil and the faithful few that have remained with their people in the camps of Lebanon, and far more powerful. It is doubtful many of them are any less disillusioned.

Soheil is not unlike an English colonel of the old school to look at, with neat, thick white hair, matching moustache, and a cardigan under his sports jacket. He is smoking a briar pipe. Occasionally he bursts into sudden, almost hysterical laughter, seemingly at the ridiculousness of it all. I suppose if you are a Palestinian refugee, laughter is one way of dealing with hopelessness. However, I do not feel it right, as a citizen of the nation which handed the Zionists Palestine, to offer more than a sympathetic smile. There is a hollowness to his laughter, more an echo of pain than a manifestation of humour.

Soheil has never tired of retailing his people's stories to the parade of foreigners who come to his office. History is not just history for the Palestinians, something to be looked back on with interest and scholarship – it lives with them, forms their lives, and is vital to explain. Soheil has many interesting things to say about the Palestinian question, including a barbed set of criticisms of the Palestinian leadership.

As far as Lebanon is concerned, things are not good, he says. Over the past 20 years or so, he tells me, Palestinian leaders like Yasser Arafat and Mahmoud Abbas (better known as Abu Mazen, Arafat's successor as President of the Palestinian Authority) and many lower down the tree, such as Yasser Abd Rabbo and Sari Nusseibi, have indicated to the outside world that the Right of Return to Palestine of the refugees, enshrined for ever in the 1948 UN General Assembly Resolution 194, is negotiable.

The endless bargaining over the creation of a Palestinian state in the West Bank and Gaza has involved suggested compromise on this basic refugee question. This is a compromise the West is anxious to see because its clients, the Israelis, insist on it. In Western eyes, whatever Israel wishes must not be denied. Soheil says that with the marginalisation of the PLO, which used to represent all Palestinians wherever they were, and its replacement by the Palestinian Authority, which supposedly governs the fragmented West Bank and Gaza, the millions of Palestinian refugees and exiles have been virtually abandoned politically and physically. They are not properly heard, certainly not as one strong voice.

Soheil reckons that if Israel had been more generous with land and with Jerusalem in the Camp David negotiations of 2000, Arafat would have bypassed the Right of Return question. He would have made an agreement with Israel that effectively abandoned the refugees. This is a radical view, of course, and does not reflect the centrality of Palestinian thinking, but in the even more intensely suspicious world of Middle East politics that has emerged during the past 15 years or so, and with the rifts that have appeared so markedly inside the Palestinian movement itself, such views or not as rare as they might once have been and there is evidence to support them.

It was, Soheil thinks, the impasse on other substantive issues, such as the status of Palestinians in Jerusalem and responsibility for its Holy Places, and illegal Israeli settlements, which enabled Arafat to claim that 'Right of Return' was the sticking point. There have been subsequent interventions on this issue by other Palestinian leaders that have not reassured the Palestinian diaspora. One such case was the Geneva Accords, signed in 2003 by former Palestinian and Israeli political leaders. These accords appeared to compromise the Right of Return and angered many Palestinians throughout the world. There have also been the repeated but invariably unproductive meetings between Palestinian Authority leaders and Israelis and various Western representatives. These sessions indicate a relentless pursuit by Israel and its Western allies of Palestinian compromise on all serious issues.

Abandonment of the refugees' inalienable right of return has also caused the Lebanese great and growing alarm. Humanitarian or moral reasons aside, there is not a Lebanese living who does not believe that the refugee camps should be dismantled and the Palestinians removed, whether as the result of a just solution or by some other means.

Now, says Soheil, it could get grim. If the Lebanese think they will be stuck with the Palestinians for ever, they might resort as before to military tactics to get rid of them. What is worse, he says, his political antennae raised, the Lebanese know this time that it is the Palestinians themselves who have been trying quietly to ditch the refugees. It is not as before, when the Palestinians could say it was all an international or Zionist plot. This time, the Lebanese can say, this is your fault and we can take steps against you. Furthermore, it is not just Christians who might feel threatened if the Palestinian Sunni Muslims became an integral part of Lebanon; the Shi'ites would lose their leading edge, too.

For the time being the Lebanese and the Palestinians are trying to co-operate to make daily life for the Palestinians easier, to improve their conditions, perhaps to allow them more freedom to work outside the camps and to take part in a wider array of jobs. What sense is there, for example, in Lebanon importing workers from all over the world, as well as Syria, when they have a local, Arabic-speaking workforce on their doorstep?

The Palestinians also have arms to bargain with: not the heavy weapons they had when the PLO controlled Fakhani and the Arqub, in the 1970s and early 1980s, but enough to protect themselves. As the Lebanese see it, better conditions for the Palestinians might also deter them from going 'fundamentalist', as has happened in the Occupied Territories. The leftist, secular groups and the mainstream Fateh are much stronger in Lebanon vis-à-vis Hamas than they are in the Territories.

Soheil is not completely bereft of optimism. Lebanese Ministers paid an official visit to the Beirut camps in 2006, for the first time in history, he adds, and the PLO has been allowed to set up a representative office in Beirut, 24 years after the Israelis evicted it from Beirut and the south (the Syrians completed the task of expelling the PLO and Arafat from Lebanon in 1983). There is a committee for Palestinian affairs in the prime minister's office, and more money has been available from international sources to improve the camps' infrastructures. Soheil explains this process: 'There is a big difference between saying, at such political cost, "This is in reality our permanent home so let us make it as excellent as possible," and "This is in reality our home for a very long time, as long as it takes to be granted our human rights, so let us make it as liveable as possible".'

In a word, the problem was created by the Zionists working in concert with the old imperial powers. It could be solved in an afternoon by the Zionists working similarly with today's imperial power in Washington and its followers. But nobody, least of all Soheil, sees that happening in the foreseeable future.

The Hills Above the City

8

The quickest route out of the heat and noise of Beirut to the peace, quiet and evocative beauty of the Lebanese hills, the lower slopes of the Mountain, is the half-an-hour or so winding drive up towards Aley, the main town in the middle of the Druze area, amid pine forests and villages, abundant with fruit, vegetables and potential mayhem. Old men in black blouses and pantaloons watch as we drive by, their women in multi-coloured smocks hefting their bags of shopping, people sitting and noting who comes, who leaves, who passes by. It is friendly, knowledgeable, intimate, cool in the summer, yet so near the wet heat of the coast.

These hills are where so much of the history of Lebanon has been furiously forged; the centre of the principalities where dynasties emerged and fought each other and, when they were not fighting each other, turned against the visiting rulers, Mamluks, Ottomans, French and the Lebanese mixture that has followed.

We used to come this back way to Damascus during the civil war, when the main road was closed. We could hear the sound of battle echoing in the hills to the north of us as we drove towards the border. This was, before the war, a holiday paradise for Lebanese and Gulf sheikhs. Paradise was lost in 1975. For many years afterwards, along these routes, standing stark against the sky were the ruins, the broken outlines of villas and hotels, ravaged by shells, rockets and bullets, more monuments to the mayhem that set its course across Lebanon. If for the moment a tentative peace has arrived, that mayhem's causes hang in the air, making themselves known in speeches, TV and radio tirades, the press and the occasional reminder from an assassin's bomb.

My companion and driver is a Druze woman in her mid-30s who works on NGO projects in her area. She is married to a Maronite

Christian. He is a supporter not of the Phalangists, Aounists or Geageaists, the choice of most of his religion, but of the secular National Syrian Social Party. This means they are not a typical couple, though middle- and upper middle- class intermarriage between sects is not as rare as many outside the Middle East imagine. It does mean that my companion, whom I am not naming, is not considered a real Druze in religious terms. She is not popular with the local powers because she does not support – though she likes – Walid Junblatt, the hereditary clan leader and warlord whose writ runs through this part of 'Druzestan' from his stately eyrie-cum-castle in the Shouf, further up into the mountains and less accessible to alien forces. Most of her friends are Junblattis. It pays, she says, to be a Junblatti in this region.

Her husband, she tells me, is not popular with his Maronite cousins either, not so much because his wife is a Druze but because he is not with one of the traditional Maronite parties. That he is with the NSSP enhances his unpopularity with his co-religionists. He is also an atheist, which they would see as concomitant with his support of the NSSP, which is strong in this part of the Druze area, and complicates but does not undermine Walid Junblatt's rule in the region.

Walid Junblatt is a character. For me, he epitomises the individuality and almost suicidal eccentricity and determination of some Lebanese leaders: brave, crafty, egotistical, feudal, foolhardy, but always claiming Lebanon as his own and at his heart. He is the son of one of the most outstanding politicians of modern Lebanon, Kamal Junblatt. This family has been part of the history of the Mountain for hundreds of years, fighting other Druze and Christians and outside powers alike with ferocity and maintaining its ascendancy against an array of challenges. The family rules most of the Druze area, as it has done for more than 400 years. Although there is opposition from its traditional rivals in the Arslan family and there is a new 'upstart' (as he is seen by the Junblattis) called Wi'am Wahhab, who has the backing of the Shi'ites at time of writing (2007 – these things can change quickly), not much gets done around here without Mr Junblatt's permission or backing.

The Junblatts have been a power in Lebanon since the sixteenth century, with other Druze clans managing to maintain power over their own people and independence in their area despite the increasing weight and presence of the Maronite Christians and, above them, the Ottoman Empire and its designated pashas. The Ottomans gave leeway and wide responsibilities to local sheikhs, tax-collecting privileges most important among them, cracking down only when these tribal leaders went too far, which they often did. And here in the end lay the seeds of change and social eruption in the Mountain.

The emergence of the Mountain

The template for an independent Lebanon, based on the peoples of the Mountain and later to be linked to the coastal areas, was almost certainly designed under the Druze Prince Fakhr al-Din Ma'n, in the late sixteenth century. In close alliance with the powerful city state of Tuscany, he did battle with the Ottomans, widening enormously the autonomous 'Mount Lebanon' the rulers in Istanbul had put in place, and becoming the first proper ruler of the whole area. In the end he over-reached himself, threatening to secede from the Ottoman Empire altogether. The Ottomans defeated him and executed him in 1635. The Ma'n dynasty continued less dramatically, and had withered away by the close of the seventeenth century.

Broadly, though, the Emir – perhaps in a sense the founding father of modern Lebanon – had made a number of far-reaching achievements: he had established the Mountain as a political entity, which could be expanded in all directions depending on the powers of regional and foreign forces; and it was he who had introduced silk growing, the raw fabric an important export to the Italian city states and later to France. He had also demonstrated the necessity of having a foreign ally, for the supply of arms, money and foreign menace. In economic terms, the silk trade of the mainly Druze Shouf area brought work and prosperity and the movement of Christian workers and traders to the southern areas of the Mountain.

The Christians became more numerous, more important and more powerful, challenging the autocratic rulers of their own, Christian regions, but also the Druze chieftains and landowners – and therefore tax-collectors – in the traditional Druze areas they were now infiltrating, and, it has to be said, being invited into by the Druze themselves.

This mixture was to prove volatile. Over the succeeding years, there were struggles for power among the rival tribes and sects, but also social upheavals as ordinary people – mostly but not entirely Christian – challenged the tax-collecting privileges of the rulers and their apparatchiks.

From the Fakhr al-Din era onwards, the Junblatts emerged as the most powerful Druze family. The Kurdish 'Jounbelads' had originally been a power, in the sixteenth and very early seventeenth centuries, in northern Syria, running a kind of autonomous principality that took in Aleppo, Homs, Hama, Damascus and a part of Turkey itself. The Ottomans threw them out in the early 1600s, whereupon they found refuge in the Shouf hills. Soon, the Junblatts had become one of the most powerful families in the region, joining Fakhr al-Din in his struggles against the Ottomans and converting to the mystical and highly secretive Druze religion.[1]

It was a time when the Muslims and Druze between them held political sway in the Mountain, and the Druze were regarded – and certainly regarded themselves – as the aristocracy of their part of the Mountain, the *chevalier* class, at the apex of which were the Junblatts. The Maronites, their neighbours, lived with them and mostly under them as artisans, farmers, serfs and, later, factory workers. Druze power, however, was on the decline. Their numbers had been seriously depleted in a Mamluk massacre in 1585; there was much upheaval over the years as Ottoman strength waxed and waned, as local groups fought one another for land and advantage, as the Druze dominance began to peter out, and the Ma'ns faded away altogether.

A Muslim Emir, Bashir Chehab, took over in the early eighteenth century, when the Druze clans could not agree on a candidate, and his descendant, Bashir II, who ruled from 1788 to 1840, converted to Christianity. The Junblatt family stood by him, managing to widen their local possessions and power through their closeness not only to the Emir but at that stage to the Ottomans, with whom Bashir II was aligned. It is easy to see how alliances changed, evolving and shattering on grounds of self-interest and the 'enemy's enemy is my friend' basis. For example, the Junblatts had greatly helped Emir Bashir Chehab II into office. (It was Bashir II who built in the Shouf the beautifully proportioned stone palace on the promontory of Beit-eddin, which, these days, is a shrine to Kamal Junblatt.)

Bashir II in the early nineteenth century, however, was not a grateful man. As happens in Lebanon, the powerful ally became perceived as the foe. The Maronites were challenging the Druze for absolute power in the Mountain. Their numbers and their ambitions as upwardly mobile workers were growing. The Emir turned against the Druze who had helped him, persuading the Ottoman pasha of Sidon, who had overall local responsibilities, to hang the leader of the Junblatt family, also a Bashir. The Junblattis were outraged but subdued. They waited for the cycle of Lebanese history to take its course, which it duly did when the Emir finally overreached himself in the eyes of the Sublime Porte and was exiled to Istanbul. He died there in 1851.

Through all these upheavals, the Druze warlords had managed to maintain the loyalties of their own people in the face of Christian opposition and attempted domination and held sway over the Christians living in Druze areas. In 1858, dissident Christians rose up against the Druze overlords, with terrible results. The Druze crushed them, in a series of massacres, events which helped the Western Powers make yet further inroads into the region, the French helping their old friends the Roman Catholic-aligned Maronites; the British their new associates among the Druze. A colourful and graphic mural in one of Walid Junblatt's reception rooms shows this intervention, with warships toting *Tricoleurs* or Union Jacks arriving at Lebanon's shore and foreign troops marching across the landscape and among the locals.

It was during this period that the sectarian basis of Lebanese political rivalries was confirmed. The Druze survived as a coherent and powerful force, but basically mainly on their own turf. Elsewhere, the Christians dominated. Social rebellion had done for Druze power over the wider Mountain, as the Christians, among other matters, objected to the tax-collecting and tax-evading privileges the Druze had acquired under the Ottomans by dint of their Muslim status and their aristocratic and warrior-like profile. The Christians, as 'people of the book' only, did the work, had the skills and paid the money. Revolts and disturbances had been breaking out all over the area since the end of the eighteenth century, in the end exploding to a level, in the late 1850s, that required foreign intervention to help the Ottomans retain and impose their authority.

By the middle of the nineteenth century, after some 20 years of appalling civil strife, the Mountain-as-Emirate had disappeared. At first the Ottomans had tried to divide it into two districts, north and south, each with a council of 12 members of each religion: Maronites, Druze, Greek Orthodox, Greek Catholic, Sunni and Shi'a. It was in a sense an early version of the national sectarian 'balance' that would inform the National Pact at independence, and enshrined the concept in the Lebanese political order. It did not work out. Rebellions and riots persisted, with the Christians particularly disturbed by the fact that their majority status was not adequately recognised in the ruling bodies.

In the end, after much negotiation and foreign involvement, the Mountain came under the rule of a non-Arab Christian Ottoman administrator, the system known as the *Mutassarifate*. The Druze won the battles, but lost the peace to the Christians in terms of authority and influence.

The uncanny echoes of the past in modern Lebanon can be heard in a final and failed attempt by the Christians, in 1866, to overthrow the Ottoman ruler of the Mountain. The Christians' leader, Yusuf Karam, a former eminence who had been exiled for a while after he overstepped his limits, but who had returned to Lebanon in rebellious mood, was surrounded by Ottoman forces at the town of Bikfaya, north-east of Beirut. On the point of his defeat, the French intervened and persuaded the Ottomans to spare him (of all the foreigners, the French were playing the hardest and most intrusive tactics). They were duly allowed to extricate him and take him to France aboard a gunship. Much the same process took place almost a-century-and-a-quarter later, in 1990, when the French Ambassador, with Syrian compliance, spirited General Michel Aoun away from his besieged bunker at the presidential Palace at Ba'abda, into a 15-year exile.

In the last half of the nineteenth century and into the twentieth, the Mountain's fortunes or otherwise were characterised more by economic upturns and downturns, by famine, by emigration, and by the steadily rising appetite among all the Lebanese, of whatever religious persuasion, for freedom from the enfeebled and erratic Ottoman Empire, than by internecine conflict.

But whatever its nature, the Mountain had become a separate political entity, with proven potential for expansion to the littoral and the south and east. The coast, except for Beirut, Sidon and Tripoli, had come under the aegis of the Mountain under the Ottomans, but now the Mountain would expand to absorb these cities and commercially essential lifelines into a Greater Lebanon. Throughout all these upheavals, and despite the end of Druze supremacy in Mount Lebanon, the Junblatts remained pre-eminent among their people and a prime force in the Lebanese arena.

Revolution plotted from Moukhtara

It was Walid's father, Kamal, who in the late 1940s tried to form a party with a national rather than sectarian following. This stated aim, like similarly stated aims by Antoun Sa'adeh and Pierre Gemayel, ended in failure, but his journey towards reform of the Lebanese system came nearer fruition, and it is as dramatic a tale of this region's murderous history as any chronicler could wish for.

Kamal Junblatt, who was born in 1917, grew up nursing a strong resentment against the Maronites and their ethos, which he viewed – with some individual and historic exceptions – as isolationist, sectarian, separatist, anti-Arab and nurtured by their helpers and protectors the French. He saw the Maronites as exemplifying what he termed 'the spirit of the Phoenicians' ... 'a kingdom ruled by a mad, grasping and greedy mercantilism'. Junblatt was scathing about much that was Lebanese and Arab, excoriating 'the junk in the bazaar of Oriental politics': the corrupt application, though not the concept, of Arab nationalism, Islamism, the duplicity of the Arab states, their futile quarrels and treachery against one another, their disastrous lack of unity against outsiders, the West, Israel.

As a self-styled socialist and democrat, he railed against states like Syria and Iraq who pretended socialism and democracy, but abjured these systems at every level. The Maronites, in his view, were like the Zionists: trying to create a religious state under the aegis of a powerful protector – in the former case France; in the latter, Britain. He was contemptuous of the feudal base of Lebanese politics, though it is undeniable that he was certainly part of it, a reluctant part, perhaps, but still very much dependent on his core support among the Druze, his HQ his castle-like residence at Moukhtara, towering unapproachable and inviolate above the forests and rivers of the Shouf. Junblatt, for all this Druze loyalty and sense of pride and honour, shrouded in a mystique outsiders could not comprehend, renounced the abuse of wealth he saw among his rivals and even allies and presented to the public an aura of asceticism and integrity that was rare if not unique among the region's notables.

He came to prominence after World War II as a young man, an MP for his area, leading the opposition to the economic domination of wealthy, newly independent Lebanon by the French and a claque of Lebanese leaders and businessmen whose enterprises had been granted concessions first by the Ottomans and later by the French Mandatory authorities. He also fought to change the system of religious quotas that had informed the selection of members of the legislature following the acceptance of the unwritten National Pact at independence in 1943.

Junblatt wanted a secular political system for Lebanon. But his motives were mixed. He was disguising behind the ideals of modernism and secularity his ambition of cutting down to size the Maronite ascendancy. As a politician, he could widen his base and his appeal by reaching out to the many others, most but by no means all Muslims, who shared this aim.

Using the mechanism of his Progressive Socialist Party (PSP) in alliance with other leftist, Nasserite or Muslim groups as seemed appropriate, he campaigned for land reform, the re-parcelling of estates in the grip of the clergy and various vested interests; for rent reform and fixed rents, in the cities; and for more political power for the Muslims, whose accelerated population growth and concomitant muscle and manpower was not reflected in a system in which the Christians had the numerical edge in parliament, army, cabinet and senior civil service posts.

In practical terms he came to international attention when he formed a major part of the military and political alliance against President Camille Chamoun, who acceded to power in 1952 and immediately set about trying to involve Lebanon in military pacts with the West and against alleged Communist threats in the face of much regional Arab and local Lebanese opposition. Chamoun, another but lesser clan leader, had been a British Intelligence 'asset' during World War II and saw Lebanon continuing as a Western rather than an Arab entity. He was also perhaps the most corrupt of all Lebanon's chief leaders, a not inconsiderable feat. Junblatt was a key part of the forces, his own PSP, Druze militia, and Nasserite and other Muslim groups, that stalemated Chamoun in the civil war of 1958, which was fought very much on the basis of all these issues (most of which remain today), and denied him a second term in office.

In the two presidencies that followed, Junblatt held government posts, including Minister of the Interior, in which latter role he tried to ameliorate the growing and violent tension between the Palestinian movement and its fighters and the State and its conservative and Christian supporters, an attempt to conciliate between two sides who both were making dreadful errors of judgment and behaviour. In this he failed, but so did everyone else.

Junblatt believed in radical reform rather than revolution. The latter came, in the end, but, as the first stage of the civil war drew to a close with Syrian intervention in 1976, he was to regret that, in his view, his programme of reforms in the Lebanese system were on the edge of success, a victory which he claimed would have stopped well short of trying to subdue totally the Christians and their forces.

Kamal Junblatt's plans for Lebanon were aimed at changing and secularising the whole political and social structure. His alliance in the 1970s with the Palestinian movement and Lebanese opposition forces would have been a formidable one had Syria not entered the lists, at American instigation in Junblatt's view. He had made startling headway. But the Syrians subdued his National Movement, rescued the Maronites and the traditional Lebanese confessional way of doing things, and began their long programme of trying to co-opt the PLO.

But the question Junblatt posed remains: Could even his powerful alliance have 'secularised' the whole system? It is unlikely. While many Muslims saw reduced Christian power through this mechanism, they would have balked at the idea of secularising the social aspects of the system. Muslims in Lebanon had their own Shari'a law, administered by Islamic Courts, when it came to private and family matters (though not criminal and civil). The Christians and Druze had their own systems. The loyalties obtained in business, political patronage and military matters were based on sectarian connections. They were endemic. As the great Lebanese historian Kamal Salibi put it, even if the political secularisation of Lebanon had gone out through the door, it would have reappeared through the window in other forms. Syria's intervention saved Lebanon from trying to put any of this to the test.

Syria saw other dangers in Junblatt. It has been a continuing Syrian motif of its hegemony, or watchful eye, over Lebanon that leaders who defy or appear to defy or even *think* about defying Damascus must not long survive or prosper. Largely, they do not. The Syrians' view is that any substantial change in Lebanon's systems should not take place without their approval, indeed inspiration. In accordance with this article of faith, in March 1977, during a lull in the civil war, Kamal Junblatt was assassinated as he rode in convoy in the Druze hills. It needs no assiduous analyst of the Near East to figure out at whose hand he was dispatched.[2]

His son Walid was a controversial young man in the 1960s and 1970s, something of a playboy, with the not unpredictable yen of a dynastic heir for fast cars, motorbikes, women, *boites,* booze, exotic substances, leather jackets and flares, the tastes and uniforms of the young of that age and to a large extent this. He was thus popular in Beirut among the youthful and the journalists, local and foreign, who were themselves of an age with Walid.

Insofar as he is more restricted these days in his movements, Walid Junblatt is still a sociable and generous figure. Even today, he gives the impression of being slightly zany, but is articulate, amusing and good company. Walid is ready at a moment's notice to show visitors round his well-protected palace in the beautiful mountain-side forests of Moukhtara, and his collection of Soviet artefacts, armaments, pamphlets, journals, books, paintings – a splendid one of Marshal Zhukov on his white horse at the victory parade in Red Square in 1945 (which so angered Stalin).

On his father's death, this Prince Hal put his somewhat misspent youth behind him. He quickly emerged as a national political figure and much more aloof politician – as befitted his position – when he inherited power, taking over as feudal chief, landowner, clan, militia and area leader, with a strong following and a major political party, the PSP. He took to life in national politics in a big way under the various stages of Syrian overlordship of Lebanon after 1976, gaining ministerial posts and co-operating with the Syrians until the middle of the 2000s. Views of him differed wildly as to year of assessment and political taste. Walid is nothing if not erratic and enigmatic. (As Lebanon appeared to stabilise in 2008 and 2009, Walid appeared to be having something of a rapprochement with Hezbollah, whom he had bitterly opposed in the preceeding years as a scion of the March 14 movement.) But he could never be dismissed as insignificant or uncontroversial.

In these fertile historical hills where I find myself today, for all the turns in his allegiances and fortunes, Walid remains governor of all he surveys. Nationally, however, his reach has been circumscribed by the division of Lebanon into the forces of March 14, which forms (in mid-2007) the existing if paralysed government at this stage of the nation's dismal fortunes, and of which he is a member; and of the opposition, which is made up of a strong Christian party, the supporters of General Aoun, and Hezbollah, which is close to Iran and Syria. Walid had fallen out *con brio* with Syria by the middle of 2007, using eye-wateringly colourful language about the Syrian nation and its leader (it is not usually done to be personal in political abuse in these parts unless one is prepared to face personal consequences), and offering his powerful neighbours – Syria and Hezbollah – undiluted defiance.

Given the high-risk nature of this approach and its often fatal consequences, Walid Junblatt moves under exceedingly close protection and is usually to be found either in his Moukhtara redoubt or in his well-guarded villa in west Beirut.

More history looms up as I negotiate a bendy road near Bchamoun. Bchamoun is known as the Village of Independence. It was here, in 1943, that a young man from the NSSP (then the PPS), Sa'id Fakhreddine, threw a bomb at a French patrol and found himself a posthumous place in Lebanese folklore. He made the attack because General Charles de Gaulle, who had with Allied, mainly British, help taken back control of French-mandated Lebanon from Vichy, was perceived by the Lebanese to be dragging his feet on independence. It was the French way in those days, whichever French system was in power.

To make his point, Sa'id hid behind a tree in the village of Ain Anoub and lobbed his explosive device at the French soldiers. None of them was hurt, but he was shot dead. The memorial to him and the credit for all this go to Bchamoun because that was where Sa'id was born. It was here soon after the incident that a group of Lebanese leaders of all faiths and factions – Mir Majid Arslan (rival to the Junblatts), Sabri Hamadi, a Shi'ite from Baalbek, Sa'ab Salam, a Sunni and prime minister-to-be, Camille Chamoun, a Maronite Christian and president-to-be, and Hamid Franjieh, another Maronite – signed their names on a Lebanese flag as an earnest of their belief in an independent Lebanon.

All of these men, in the turbulent post-independence future, were to find themselves at one time or another fighting or machinating together or on opposite sides, depending on the shifting winds and patterns of Lebanese politics and advantage.

Warriors, villains and survivors

Ain Anoub, where that little episode of nationalist history happened, is typical of the mixed villages of the Druze area, within and outside the

Shouf. In the foothills we peer dizzily down on Beirut like gods in a gallery. The ferment below, the haze of the city's fumes shrouding it, seems a long way off. Above us, towards the Beka'a Valley and Syria, is the Shouf, the Druze mountain stronghold. Yet it is a mistake to be deceived by this physical elevation into thinking it is a spiritual one; to think that these scented forests, quaint and friendly villages, cascading waterfalls and sweeping vistas lift us above turmoil. Here is where that familiar and familial slaughter so often broke out.

During the past 1000 years or so, with violent intervals, Christians here did share villages and towns with the Druze. In fact, until the beginning of the nineteenth century, Ottoman reforms, social and industrial changes, and foreign intervention, the sectarian aspect of Lebanon had been much less pronounced than the hierarchical. At the top were the Muslims – next tier down, the various Lebanese emirs and sheikhs, who could be of any and all sects.

As the Ottomans' grip loosened, lower-class rebels rose against their betters, who were ruling under Ottoman remit, and used sectarian loyalties as their engine. Even after the civil troubles and massacres of the mid-nineteenth century, until the mid-1970s, when the civil war started, there was peaceful co-existence, on the whole; there was as much intra-clan feuding and fighting as there was between the main sects of the Maronites and Druze.

The civil war split these sects. Kamal Junblatt's fighters and their Palestinian allies emptied many villages and districts of their Christian populations. The main Damascus highway became, for about a year, impassable. It was another front line between the two warring divisions. Lebanese who wished to travel to Syria had either to go – if they were on the Christian side – via a northern route until they reached the relative safety of the Syrian-controlled Beka'a Valley; or – if they were on what was known as the 'leftist-Muslim' side – were required to snake up through the hills to the south of the main road, until they could rejoin it at Syrian lines at the mountain town of Bhamdoun.

Calm settled to a degree in 1976, when the first act of the civil war ended. Some Christians and Druze remained in the same towns, villages and areas, but for the most part remained apart and mutually fearful after the bloodshed of the previous year. Hostility continued between the Druze leaders; first Kamal then his son Walid, from early 1977, and the Christians, the Gemayel and Chamoun families most particularly. But this hostility was embalmed in relative peace under the auspices of what was effectively an occupying Syrian army and accompanying security attachments, and a Syrian-produced government under Elias Sarkis.

The lid remained shakily on for some six years. Then came June 1982, and the massive Israeli onslaught on Lebanon, the comprehensive defeat of the Syrians and the PLO battalions, and the latter organisation's political and military demise in Lebanon in August of that year, depriving the Lebanese opposition and assorted leftist, Muslim and other opposition forces of their muscular backing.

The Israeli occupation army remained in the Druze hills after the fighting ended, bringing vengeful Christian militiamen, from the LF, into the Druze areas to run roadblocks and generally act as their local policemen. They made life deeply uncomfortable for the Druze, under this protective Israeli shell. When the Israelis pulled out in 1984, consolidating their occupation in Lebanon's south, away from most of the Mountain and Beirut, the Druze set upon the Christians that remained, in mixed and Christian-only areas, slaughtering many hundreds of people. The Christians that survived fled. By 1990, when peace came, many Christians from the area had started new lives, in Lebanon and abroad, it having been 15 years since there had really been any proper semblance of normality or co-existence for the two sects.

Walid Junblatt and the Maronite Patriarch Boutros Sfeir finally met to publicly patch the two communities notionally together in 2000. Walid Junblatt announced that Christians were welcome back and would be safe. By the mid-2000s that ostensible communal guarantee had been consolidated by the political pact between the leader of the Christian LF party, Samir Geagea, and Walid Junblatt, who formed part of the backbone of the March 14 movement and was a minister in the government of the time.

The Lebanese Christians are wily enough to know that nothing is forever. They have trickled back. In some areas the Christian mayors of mixed villages visit their parishes once a week or even less. Many come just in the summer or for weekends, or to tend their houses or gardens. My guide and driver reckons that in her village some have returned. But when we walk around the Christian part of Ain Anoub it looks deserted. The church is used only for the occasional mass. I see a lone Virgin Mary statuette with a glowing light behind it standing forlornly in the window of an empty house.

This area is run by Walid Junblatt and was, like the whole Druze region, under him and pro-Junblatti town councils from 1976 to 1990.

They provided their own services: water, electricity, health, schools and – naturally – defence. In the 1980s, as the stand-off with the Christian forces continued and battles broke out across the hills, they built a road called the *Tariq al Karami*, loosely 'the Road of Dignity', which linked their area with Syria, the south and Beirut, snaking around hostile regions of Christians and Shi'ites.

Since the civil war ended, Junblatti rule has continued. Any Christian who wishes to return knows it. But it is not only politics that keeps the Christians away. They not only have poisonous experiences, they have settled elsewhere. A new generation that does not remember 1975 or 1980 or even 1985 has grown up, adults who have little memory or practice of living with others of different faiths and loyalties, except perhaps in the much broader and more chaotic urban atmosphere of Beirut, or overseas. Most of them have grown up, been educated and found work in Christian areas or abroad. Their old villages, largely, have little more than sentimental value. It is only in some solidly Christian villages dotted about the Shouf and on its fringes that Christians have come back in numbers.

There are many empty houses, a considerable number showing the marks of war – wrecked homes, walls with the dents and chips of 50-calibre shells. One beautiful old palace stands crumbling by the side of one of the roads on the edge of Ain Anoub. This belongs to the Junblatti clan's main rivals, the Arslan family, but they do not seem to be interested in either selling it or restoring it.

With its yellowing stone, arched windows and rafters, this Ottoman-era pile would make a fantastic hotel. I have a momentary vision of Sidney Greenstreet in a tarbouche, Peter Lorre simpering behind him with a linen napkin on his arm, welcoming guests across the threshold of the Ain Anoub Hotel Splendide, showing them the view of the coast and Beirut and plotting diabolical frauds and murders among the pines, thickets of shrubbery, breezy terraces and red roofs. There would be arak on the balcony, then a guided tour, possibly in an open Stutz Bearcat, of the sites of massacres, with more villainy gestating in the proprietors' devious minds.

My informant says Christians rarely had membership of their own political parties here. If they did support Chamoun or Gemayel they kept quiet about it. Some Druze supported Chamoun because they hated Junblatt. Now Christians make up about 5 per cent of her village. She says the people of the area are split between Arslan and

Junblatt, but the latter is the more powerful. To complicate matters there is a new would-be *za'im* in the area as I visit. He is called Wi'am Wahhab, who was a fighter with Junblatt during the war. He is now backed by the Shi'ite-led opposition as an opponent to the all-powerful Walid.

Junblatt's supporters refer to him as 'the man who used to close the door when Junblatti meetings were over', writing him off as a concierge-figure, a nobody. Junblatt himself never refers to him. Presumably to irritate Junblatt, President Lahoud (the pro-Syrian leader who left office in November 2007, and became more and more at odds with his own government) briefly made Wahhab a minister, leaving Junblatt out in the ministerial cold. But it is all play. The Druze community would never vote in any numbers for such a man – he was a small-time stringer in the area for various Beirut newspapers – because he does not come from a distinguished family.

The Lebanese Druze are irredeemable snobs. Alone among the sects they have retained their preference for rule by the 'good families', of whom the Junblatts and Arslans remain the cream. Even the Christians now have working-class, self-made leaders, like Samir Geagea, on one side, and Aoun on the other; the Hariris themselves are essentially 'new' money, and to many of Beirut's older families regarded as vulgar. The pedestrian Hariri mosque downtown – like the high-rises that dwarf it – has not impressed Beiruti arbiters of good taste and fine architecture.

This is not to imply that life is easy for Junblatt. His area is a fortress and his own palace within it seems impregnable. But nobody would be surprised if he were assassinated, like his father. There are troubles too with the NSSP. As I visit in 2007, there are fights and beatings. The area is nervous. No one has a grip on Lebanon. There is a grand stalemate. What if America or Israel or both bomb Iran? Will the Shi'ites erupt? What if the people accused of Hariri's murder do go on trial and it emerges that the orders for his assassination did come from the Kasr el Moha'ajareen', the Assad Palace that Hariri himself had built for the ruling dynasty on the hills above Damascus? What about the Sunni Islamic extremists, the Salafis, and others who have been bringing al-Qaeda-linked cells, ideas and violence into the mixture in the mid-2000s?

People do not know the answers to these questions, which are constantly being posed. At other times there would be different but equally nerve-wracking questions to keep the Lebanese off-balance. These are a people who have always lived geographically and politically on the edge. Another pressing current question is: Are the Israelis coming back for a second crack at Hezbollah, having failed so dramatically and humiliatingly to crush them in the summer of 2006? Israel does not like to lose. Its military reputation has been sliding in recent decades: the Arabs gave Israel a withering blow in 1973; it took Israel's army and air force months to subdue the PLO in Lebanon, despite its brutal, shock and awe tactics in 1982; the resistance in Lebanon finally sapped Israel's will in 2000 and the occupation ended, having done Israel no perceivable good. Israel has been reduced to exerting its military muscle on the largely helpless population of the Occupied Palestinian Territories ever since, apart from its Lebanese fiasco in 2006.

Even in its devastating attack on Gaza between Christmas 2008 and late January 2009, Israel failed to subdue Hamas or much reduce its strength and miscalculated Hezbollah's response at that time, diverting troops to a border alert in the false expectation that Hezbollah would join the fighting to try to migitate the onslaught on Hamas and Gaza. Syria and Lebanon are in Israel's sights all the time.

Very much Walid's parish

Aley has been a summer resort, cool air and soothing mists 2500 feet above the wet summer murk of Beirut, since the end of the nineteenth century. It has always been a favourite for Gulf Arabs, many of whom own villas along the hillsides. They swarmed here in the 1950s, 1960s and early 1970s, deserting it when the civil war broke out in late 1975.

The summer of 1975 was Aley's last opportunity to greet and take money from the Gulf cousins until the 1990s. It was in the front line during the early stages of the civil war, when the Christians and Muslims were at each others throats across the territory, and sank into redoubled strife when the Israelis occupied the region between 1982 and 1984. The Israelis deliberately left mayhem behind them, promising both Christians and Druze that they could each fill the security vacuum when Israel left.

Even when that fighting ended, in 1985, there was no relief. By the end of that decade the Syrians and the Christians were fighting each other, and pro-Aoun units of the Lebanese Army were under siege in the mountains near Aley, which remained in the front line. Other areas of Lebanon remained torn, troubled and without authority beyond that of the militias, but Beirut, Aley and the Shouf took it hardest up to the autumn of 1990.

Now Aley has a population of 45,000, mostly Druze, though I can see a Maronite Church, with its campanile and delicate architecture of soft sandy stone, through the municipality window. Churches everywhere illustrate how mixed this area once was but may never be again.

In the summer if tourists are coming, and few are, with the tensions at new heights just short of war, the population can become as high as 90,000. This summer, of 2007, the townspeople are waiting to see what damage last year's war and this year's uncertainty have done to its fortunes. I later discover that their worst fears were recognised. It is the worst of luck. Lebanon at the moment is good value, food and drink and travel being roughly half the rates of Western Europe, perhaps even less as the Euro and Sterling gain strength.

During Aley's period of isolation and trial, which lasted 15 years, the locals ran their own affairs as if the civil administration of normal times still functioned. Students took proper exams, water, electricity and fuel were delivered and billed, the municipality ordered matters, there was internal law and order as the shells and rockets crashed in. Hospitals were improved, new ones erected and organised; Druze doctors returned from outside. When the war ended, it was relatively easy for the region to pick up peacetime conditions where they had left off, though there was the massive job, still not complete, of restoring the infrastructure and rebuilding. Like everywhere else in Lebanon, this has been done with help from Druze abroad and local initiative, not by the government, which even at the best of times gains little respect or trust.

Standing in the town hall and talking to officials and watching the energetic scurrying of officials and townsfolk, I am reminded of any busy town hall in any small English town, the same atmosphere of sometimes earnest, sometimes bored, sometimes self-important people applying themselves to the necessary but almost always dreary tasks of running a municipality. As I might see in Salisbury or Chester or Truro, there are posters for concerts and exhibitions, situations wanted, people for hire. Unlike Salisbury and the like, worthy citizens of the Ottoman and French-run past stare down at their successors, from under tarbouches and over bushy moustaches.

I suppose even to remark all this is to invite charges of 'orientalism'. What after all is so remarkable about a Lebanese town hall replicating one in Europe? But it needs to be remarked because of the prevailing view in an unobservant and inward-looking West that this part of the world is somehow odd, untamed and preternaturally *different*. With that view comes inexorably the consideration that these people are 'not like us', and with *that* comes the political arrogance and carelessness that informs Western attitudes to all Arabs.

Our post-1980s leaders should hold this country in awe not contempt, admiration not despair. What makes Lebanon, here in the land of the Druze religion and across the nation, is know-how, initiative and private enterprise. It is the land of *laissez-faire*. Mrs Thatcher could have been born and raised here and taken her ideas and irrepressibility from these people. It is a place of enterprise.

For example, at the start of the civil war the Druze tore down all the electricity pylons and poles, before they were pulverised in the fighting, and cannibalised them to make a greater number of whole ones when the war was over. Under fire and siege they built the road, enabling them to bring in supplies and to connect with the world beyond them, in Beirut, in the south, in Syria. The Israelis, in 1982–4, had offered to provide them with convoys along the original roads, but they preferred to do it themselves. The Druze were smart enough to know that being the recipients of Israeli goodwill might not be the guarantee of a quiet life after the Israelis had left; but it was also a question of honour, of dignity, of pride, all qualities that go into the meaning of the '*karami*', the name of their new highway.

Over it all hangs the ubiquitous image of Walid Junblatt. There may be elections and the trappings of democracy and rivalry from other Druze factions and other, small parties, but the face on the municipal hall and the power inside it is in his hands. The key to his power is arms and the men, another basic necessity for survival and success in this land of enterprise.

Walid's Christian mayor

I drive that glorious route up through the mountains and towards the Beka'a Valley, past streams and waterfalls, through one-street deep villages, turning down the inner edge of the Beka'a, not far short of the

Syrian border, to the Christian village of Ain Zhalta. Over the next rise, the great Rift Valley sweeps south (on its way to East Africa) from Syria towards Palestine, containing in its vast confine all manner of agricultural produce, from wheat to hashish to vines. Here in this mix of Christians and Shi'ite Muslims, there is everything: wine, marijuana, Roman ruins, an Armenian city, Hezbollah and Palestinian fighters, the Lebanese Army. This great vale of abundance fed the Roman Empire. If Lebanon were left alone to develop it could be the centre of a great Levantine revival.

Under Syrian occupation for most of the civil war years, the Beka'a saw plenty of fighting at different stages. In the middle of the valley, on the Beirut–Damascus road, is Shtaura, a favourite stopover for travellers, a *caravanserai* where everyone making the journey between the capitals pauses for *manouche* or eggs or *foul* for breakfast, shish kebab and houmous for lunch, arak, wine, beer, coffee, sweets, *baklava*, *mamoul* and fruit. The Lebanese rest here, a last taste of ease and jokes, before crossing the Syrian border, which for many of them is a nervous experience. An Arab, especially a Lebanese or a Palestinian, never quite knows how he will spend the rest of his Syrian visit when he hands his ID or his car papers to the Syrian officials and secret service men who swarm over the border posts.

Shtaura is the last-chance saloon. It was in Syria's possession effectively for nearly 30 years, becoming virtually a Syrian town. When I visited in the 1980s and 1990s there were more Syrian number plates than Lebanese. Syrians flocked across the frontier at Masna'a to shop, eat and drink in the little Lebanese resort in the middle of this great sweep, this rolling plain. Nearby, exquisite Lebanese wines were being grown, bottled and shipped within a rifle shot of Hezbollah training camps and roaming radical Palestinian guerrillas. (The vineyards missed just one year of production between 1975 and 1990.)

Today, I turn off short of this cornucopia, south to Ain Zhalta. This is where I think I have arranged to meet its Christian mayor, Eddie Moughabghab. (If you want to try to say this in English, just substitute the guttural French 'r' sound for each 'gh'. It is not easy.) I drive along the Damascus Road until I reach the Dar el Baida bridge, which the Israelis severed. I can get part of the way across, but at the eastern end they destroyed the whole eastbound lane and about four 40-metre-high supporting pillars, all of which a year on remain to be rebuilt and replaced. There is a diversion, the sort Lebanese are negotiating all over their countryside after Israel's assault on its roads, communications, bridges, factories, farms and people. I drive down the eastern side of the mountains to the west of the Beka'a, through more or less dead Christian villages – probably more to do with the early spring season than the political situation – until we get to Ain Zhalta.

But Eddie is not there. The place is shut; a ghost town. There has been a misunderstanding. The mayor is in his office in Mkalles in east Beirut, not far from a triumphal statue of Phalangist fighters and heroes (it was in this district that the Phalangists and other Christians fought a long battle with the Palestinians in the refugee camp of Tel al-Za'atar, the Hill of Thyme, an operation which, like Sabra–Chatila eight years later, ended in a bloody massacre of the refugee inhabitants).

There and back, Beirut to Ain Zhalta, was an exhilarating drive though, triggering more memories and riding across so much history. At least I saw Eddie's village.

Eddie Moughabghab says his family have been in the Beka'a/Shouf region for 500 years. A British (probably Scottish) missionary came to the village in about 1865 and built an evangelical school there which is still going strong with a British teacher, Mrs Nicola Alexander, although the Christians who have learned and do learn there will be mostly if not entirely Maronite Catholics. At one stage, the Ottoman authorities tried to close the school, fearing proselytisation and conversion. (Unlike the Greek Orthodox, Maronite, Greek Catholic and other Eastern church Arabs, including Armenians, Roman Catholic and Protestant Arabs are very largely converts from the nineteenth century onwards, and those often from other, older Christian sects. The Sunni Ottomans, possessors and guardians of the Caliphate, had reason to be nervous of the missionaries, despite the improvements in education they brought.)

The story is, however, that when an Ottoman envoy visited Queen Victoria she intervened on the school's behalf and it was reopened. Those were the days when the Ottomans were trying to placate the bristling and expansionist Christian powers of the West.

Mayor Eddie himself went to a Protestant school in Beirut, even though his family, he and his brothers and sisters were Roman Catholics (not Maronites). He attended the Protestant British School for Boys in Mousseitbeh, which has since moved to Jamhour. This was a feeder school for the AUB, the most distinguished university of the

Arab world, itself an American, Protestant, Missionary foundation which has, along with its output of statesmen, engineers, doctors, writers and businessmen, produced a notorious tranche of Arab radicals over the past century. Eddie says that such was the reputation of his school in the 1940s, 1950s and 1960s that the AUB accepted its graduate boys and girls without an exam.

He says most of the Christians left Ain Zhaltah in 1975. The Druze took it over, occupied the houses and made a mess of the village. In the early 1990s, Walid Junblatt decided that the Christians should be welcomed back. He ordered his Druze subjects immediately to deliver the keys of houses back to their original owners. Some Christians returned in 1992 to see the ruins. Eddie says everything had been stolen, gardens were wrecked and uncared for, incredibly, for this is an area famous for fruit: peaches, apples, pears, cherries, figs. Ain Zhaltah is quite high up, gets enough but not too much sun and has plenty of water.

The key moment in the tentative rapprochement between Druze and Christians seems to have come in 2000 with the visit of the Maronite Patriarch to Walid Junblatt. The Syrians were irritated by this meeting, says Eddie, but the agreement Junblatt made with the Patriarch is still valid. Eddie says the Druze cannot live without the Christians, because they are so smart and rich and skilled. I wonder about sectarian claims like this, however, because everywhere I go in Lebanon I find extraordinary levels of knowledge, industry and dexterity, despite the wars and tension. Eddie's claim would certainly have been true in the years before World War I, when the Christians were better educated and could bring skills and professionalism to the other peoples of the Mountain.

There may, however, remain *elements* of truth in this. Christians are to some extent better off and better organised than many Muslims, even now. It is easier for them to travel or live abroad. It is easier for them to get visas for Western countries. They have, proportionately, more foreign family contacts, in Europe, in the USA, Australia, Canada and South America. So perhaps more of them have more experience in certain fields of work and the professions, especially the modern ones of IT and computer technology.

On the whole the Christians are, as a group, better off than the Druze, with their historical connections to the Western world and the Gulf, and their larger numbers and presence throughout the nation.

They therefore *do* things and they employ people. They do not have to live in to do this. But despite all this, the gap between the different Lebanese sects has narrowed as more and more have travelled, have been forced to travel, far from their homeland in search of education and employment.

Judging from what I see in the Druze areas, effectively denuded of Christians for the best part of 30 years as I write, they do not need many if any lessons or help in capability, agriculture, business or the arts.

Eddie says that, whereas his village was originally half Christian and half Druze, now it is only 35 per cent Christian (probably less). Many have made lives elsewhere. They come back for visits, a story much repeated throughout the area by people on all sides.

He says some Christians do not want to go back. The living and eating and social habits of all these people are identical. By no means are all the Druze conversant with or practising their own mysterious religion, and neither side is trying to convert the other or is deeply offended by the other's habits or way of life. It is tribalism and sectarianism. For some 200 years now these 'isms', it seems, have never been totally suppressed. When the surface is calm and the native population restless, all it takes is a rigorous tremor to shatter the glass. What is different at this stage in Lebanon's fortunes is that many Christians are on the same side, politically, as Walid Junblatt, who now is fiercely opposed to Syria and any Syrian interference in or even say in Lebanon's affairs. This was not always the case. (However, this new alignment of Christians, Sunnis and Druze in the feeble government of Lebanon could easily change – no pacts are written in stone here.)

The resentments of the people in the mountains are deep-seated, long-term, measured in lines of blood, but more often than not stifled by pragmatism and *Lubnaniyat*, rather than any overwhelming sense of nationality. As the Arab American scholar Usama Makdisi has put it so succinctly, sectarianism is an intrinsic part of modern, political Lebanon, 'but works against the very idea of a transcendent national identity'. Walid Junblatt exemplifies Lebanon's style of political leadership.

Walid, says Eddie, who is a reasonable and jolly man, on the surface I see anyway, has done much to improve Druze relations with the Christians, but it is not easy. In some ways they (the Junblattis) feel they are the bosses: 'We have to be friendly with Junblatt. If someone ran against him he would have no chance.' Junblatt insisted that the mayor of the village of Ain Zhalta should be from the Moughabghab family, so the Christian owes his appointment to Junblatt. The gift was his and is in his interests. Eddie may be Ain Zhalta's mayor, but he is Walid's mayor, too.

The South: Under Enemy Eyes

Sharzad and Ferial, two Persian women who live in Lebanon; Mariam, an office manager in Beirut, a Lebanese Shi'ite, whose mother lives by the Israeli border; Hossein, a Kurd, whose van we are in; and I travel south through Sidon and over the broken bridges, now largely repaired since last summer, which fracture the main highway and the smaller roads that branch out to the towns and villages of the area.

I have travelled this route, these routes, hundreds of times as the south has run its terrible gauntlet of change, war, occupation, social upheaval, migration, flight and decay over the past 40 years: to the bombed camps of the Palestinian refugees, the wrecked villages of the Lebanese after the two major Israeli invasions and countless more attacks since, the most costly in deaths and property in 1996 and 2006; the years of Israeli occupation, between 1978 and 2000; the chaos of the civil war years as Lebanon broke up into mini-states controlled by militias, the south a conflicted mess of Hezbollah, Nasserite, Amal, Palestinian, Christian and Israeli zones of command. Much of the local population, largely Shi'ite, moved north, a process in train now for more than 30 years. Often they moved back only to have to move out again after some new atrocity or eruption.

My first trips south, in the summer of 1974, were idyllic, up to a point. The old road south from Beirut led through Christian villages such as Damour and Jiyeh and Na'ameh, with old hotels and fish restaurants along the Mediterranean on the way to Sidon and Tyre. It was a peaceful way of spending Sunday. Plates of *sultan brahim* and a steadily building pile of little bottles of arak and Lebanese beer complemented the view of the sparkling Mediterranean and the lap of waves on the beach. We would sit on some shaded balcony and feel the breeze and the glow of the food and drink. All seemed well with the world. I was too new to sense what trouble was brewing around us.

Once, an American journalist, Phil Caputo, later to be invalided out of Beirut with a bullet wound in his ankle, brought the irony of our Sunday lunch home to me with a quip I never forgot. 'Just look out there,' I had said, looking seawards and sipping Chateau Musar. 'The sea, the food, the calm. This is near to Paradise.' 'Yes,' he said. 'Nothing out there but a couple of fishing boats dynamiting their catch and a few Israeli frogmen.'

A few days later the Lebanese Army took us to a different south. As we neared a Shi'ite village in convoy we heard shelling, Israeli shelling. As we entered the village its inhabitants, mainly women, rushed out and shrieked at the soldiers, begging them to do something, anything, to protect them. The Lebanese Army had been shamed into making this visit and taking journalists with them. They had to confront their shame with us watching, filming and taking notes. I felt sorry for these soldiers. What could they do? A Lebanese politician had once boasted that Lebanon's 'weakness is our strength'. The Lebanese Army was far too small and under-powered to fight any outside force; was geared to look after internal difficulties. Thus, this man meant, there was never a reason for anyone to attack this unthreatening Lebanon. But they were attacking it now. There was a threat to Israel, if not from Lebanon itself, from on its soil. It was the problem at the heart of almost every-thing that has happened since.

1974 was probably Lebanon's most prosperous year, as oil price rises worked their magic in the region and most ordinary people were trying to turn a blind eye to the internal contradictions that were shak-ing the country.

In the south, the villagers were jammed on their home turf amongst the Palestinian fighters in and around the half-dozen refugee camps in the region. These had been given – or perhaps more correctly had seized – Lebanese-Arab state leave to attack Israel as and when they liked without interference from Lebanon's security system, such as it was (under the so-called Cairo Agreements). Over the way, as it were, was the might of the Israeli army and air force who sought to defend their state by shelling the whole area, terrifying ordinary people and trusting that removing them would yield Israeli aircraft and artillery a clearer Palestinian target. This was augmented by regular air raids on the refugee camps, mostly killing and injuring civilians and doing little to deter the guerrillas.

The Lebanese Army was the internal security force that might have disciplined the guerrillas – but the Cairo Accords had more or less tied its hands, and the Palestinians were becoming stronger, better-armed and freer to move and manoeuvre than the state's army.

It was in Sidon, which we are passing through today, that the civil war lines of battle formed to reflect the social dimension of the struggle. Sidon in the mid-1970s was primarily a Sunni Muslim city with strong Nasserite tendencies forged in the 1950s. Its former deputy, its current mayor and *za'im*, was Marouf Sa'ad. He had been a prominent opponent of the pro-Western president Camille Chamoun in 1958 when the country almost broke apart. Then it was under the strains of an opposition supporting Gamal Abdel Nasser and his United Arab Republic with Syria, and a government bent on allying itself with the West and the anti-Communist, anti-Nasserite Baghdad Pact (a sort of Middle Eastern NATO that brought Turkey, the Shah's Iran, Royal Iraq and pro-Western Pakistan into an Anglo-American defence pact). A similar East–West push-me pull-you contest, this time between the USA and its friends on one side and Iran, Syria and theirs on the other, helps destabilise Lebanon in the first decade of the twenty-first century.

In February 1975, the fishermen of the Sidon region went on strike in protest against a major deep-sea fishing franchise that the Lebanese government had granted a Japanese company. In this company, Protein, the former president, Camille Chamoun, had a major interest, which intensified Sidonese resentment. The fishermen were concerned that the concession would severely damage their interests. At the same time, the whole of the south was taking part in a general strike because of the government's inability to do anything to stop the low-grade but debilitating war between the Palestinians and Israelis.

The Lebanese Army was probably as embarrassed by its own impotence as it was by the protests themselves. For their part, the strikers, the Muslims of Sidon, the fishermen, the workers, saw any attempts by the army to restrain them as the interventions not of a national security force, but of an arm of the dominant Christian Maronites, among whom Chamoun was prominent. On 26 February, units or a member of the army, or perhaps even an *agent provocateur*, fired on a protest march led by Marouf Sa'ad. He was fatally wounded. Clashes ensued between the Lebanese Army and the Nasserites, local supporters and Palestinian guerrillas. The two sides in the long war to come were taking shape.

Sidon became a Palestinian-leftist stronghold throughout the early stages of the war, until the Israelis reached the city and occupied it, briefly, in 1982. The Sidonese and the Palestinians first had to defend Sidon against the Syrians when they tried to exert control over it, in 1976. For a long time one of the visitor attractions in the city, pointed out gleefully by locals and Palestinians alike, was the top of a Syrian tank and its gun barrel sticking out of the upper reaches of an office building, a position to which it had been elevated by a Palestinian anti-tank squad. It was an undignified reminder to the Syrians, and to others, of the Syrian army's failure to make headway in the south and of the destructive skills of the Palestinian resistance. It foreshadowed the vulnerability of the Israelis during their stay in the south, many of their armoured vehicles meeting similar fates at the hands of Hezbollah.

Sidon is a big city, one of the three main cities of Lebanon, half Shi'ite, half Sunni, bustling and busy, still with the massive and rancorous Palestinian camp of Ain el-Hilweh at its eastern edges. The camp has a population of some 40,000. It is surrounded by the Lebanese Army. Within it, Palestinian factions struggle for dominance and Islamist fighters for a foothold and base. Sidon is a proud city, one of the Levantine coast's ancient city states, with the traditions that come with such historical status and experience; but it is not a wealthy city: unemployment is high and prospects are low.

As on our many trips south to monitor the wars, camps, invasions and occupations, Sidon today is a convenient place to stop to visit one of the city's sweet and bakery emporiums, where, come shells, bullets, tempest or foreign soldier, the bakers turn out the most splendiferous arrays of cakes, desserts, confectioneries, *mamoul, baklava, knaffee,* chocolates, dates, figs, marzipan and assorted bonbons, all carefully, immaculately and elegantly displayed in tiers of trays on marble-topped counters.

No dieter should even look in the window of these establishments. Only the most assiduous weight-watcher could leave empty-handed. Hossein, a legendary trencherman who uses these expeditions to fill his van with Lebanon's regional food and drink – if you can call Johnny Walker Black Label a regional drink – is in heaven; we all are. It is the paradisiacal interval on a journey which has so often been to and from a kind of hell.

As we go further south and turn inland, it is quickly evident that seven months after the Israeli bombardment and brutalisation of

Lebanon, of which the south took the fullest weight, the signs of war and its detritus are very much there. Every bridge of any size was smashed from the air. Most have now been repaired, either permanently or temporarily, often with Iranian or Gulf money. Qatar in particular has been pouring in money to help people rebuild houses. The Qataris do it in a clever and encouraging way, feeding in the money slowly and monitoring the progress of each individual house or building to see that the finances are properly spent.

In one shattered town, all the roads are up. We bounce and skid along pot-holed bypasses, noticing signs, with the Lebanese and Iranian flag intermingled, announcing that an Iranian Committee for Reconstruction in Lebanon is rebuilding the roads here. There are messages of thanks from the Lebanese government. Everyone we speak to complains that the Lebanese government has so far done little or nothing to help people get back on their feet.

In Nabatiyeh, the main town of the deeper South, the local deputy, Abu Latif Zein, says people are still waiting for money pledged by the government for destruction delivered by the Israelis in their infamous Grapes of Wrath onslaught 11 years previously. Some money arrived, a first tranche of about US$10,000 for each ruined house, but that was it. And Mr Zein, going on past performance of a variety of Lebanese governments, is by no means confident now that a newly configured government – say, one with more Shi'ite representation and a more Hezbollaesque tinge in the parliament – would necessarily be different. He seems a gloomy man, difficult to bring out, as he greets his retainers and deputations of townsfolk at a mini-*diwan* (public gathering in the presence of a sheikh or other notable). I suspect he is one of the more well-meaning traditional leaders in the south, caught now between the non-existent government in Beirut and the corruption that has marked central government and local dealings with it, and the new phenomenon of Hezbollah and the remarkable power it is exercising in his area.

A frontier incident

We motor on through the war-damaged landscape to the place where it all began in July 2006, the latest explosion in Lebanon's 59 years with Israel, to Aita al Shaab, another 'ordinary' little spot on the Lebanese map buried in myth, legend and lie.

Prisoners in this part of the world, for both sides, even dead ones, are hostages. They are bargaining chips. The Israelis play this game here and in the Occupied Territories as avidly as, and with far greater resources than, the Arabs. When Israel seizes people it does it in bulk, in scores, hundreds, more in the Occupied Territories. The Arabs have to be content with the odd one or two, which is why to the untutored eye these prisoner exchanges seem so uneven.

The day I was down here the most recent exchange of Lebanese prisoners in Israel and Israelis held in Lebanon had been brokered by the Germans in 2004, when Ariel Sharon was Israel's prime minister (more were to take place in 2008).

Hezbollah units, with this in mind, and possibly acting on their own initiative rather than on the direct instructions of the leadership of Sheikh Nasrallah in Beirut (who might well have been cagey at that stage about provoking Israel), went either very near or more probably across the Israeli–Lebanese border, up a hill about a half-mile or so from Aita al Shaab. We stand in the rubble at the south-western edge of the village and look up towards that border and the field of that engagement. The Hezbollah fighters grabbed two Israeli soldiers – captured or kidnapped, depending on how you choose your words. I like 'captured', for after all this was a clash between military men. In the melee, they killed others. Hezbollah were operating under a set of rules laid down with UN mediation, in 1996, after the murderous Israeli Operation Grapes of Wrath, as to how the ongoing battles were to be conducted and who could do what to whom and what levels of response were acceptable.

Under these rules, which had functioned reasonably efficiently, given the circumstances of occupation and resistance, since 1996, and after the occupation ended in 2000 turned into mutual loathing and exchanges across the frontier, the Israeli response would have been expected to be hot pursuit, seizure of Lebanese citizens and bombing raids confined to Hezbollah positions in the south. Hezbollah would have replied with a limited salvo of Katyusha rockets into northern Israel. In other words, retaliation and responses would have been proportionate. Perhaps there is no Hebrew word for proportionate. The Israeli response was not delivered under made-to-measure, punishment-fits-the-crime, UN rules. It was an all-out, long-planned, month-long bombardment of Lebanon from north to south and east to west.

That day, here in Khalet Wardeh, the Valley of the Rose, where we can see the Israeli line and their watchtowers, electronic surveillance masts and dishes, the Israelis responded to the Hezbollah capture/ kidnap by sending tanks across the frontier to try to retrieve their soldiers. They were soon in the midst of a Hezbollah minefield. Several men were blown up. Some eight Israelis were killed. Then it got really nasty.

The houses whose sites we are standing on, surrounded by calm but helpful onlookers, were demolished deliberately, blown up by Israeli sappers as a punishment, rather than just damaged by shells or air power. These demolitions are widely used in the West Bank and Gaza as a form of collective punishment the Israelis learned from the British during their rule of Mandate Palestine. The British detonated homes during the Palestinian uprising of the mid-1930s, a technique invented by the deranged Orde Wingate, a British special forces officer with Zionist and fundamentalist Christian beliefs who was let loose during the Palestinian uprising against the British Mandate in the mid- to late-1930s. An Israeli twist to the British scheme has been to blow up the houses with the people still in them, but that did not happen in Aita al-Shaab.

How familiar this scene is. I saw it in the 1970s, 1980s and 1990s and see it again well into the twenty-first century – the Lebanese recycle war, or someone recycles it for them, but they rise from the ashes quickly and indomitably. This little town, like so many others we see, is now more scarred than crushed. Nearby is a Christian Maronite town, Rmeiche. Atallah Marina, a 64-year-old teacher, says that Hezbollah fighters came into the town during the early days of the Israeli invasion, but the Christians asked them to leave as they did not want to invite Israeli attack or shells. The fighters left as requested. Israeli troops entered Rmeiche but peacefully, though it is only a ten-minute drive from Aita al-Shaab.

The Christians say Hezbollah discipline is good and they have no interference from the Party of God. Little that is reported from the south these days contradicts this, though given the power and ubiquity of Hezbollah it might be considered unlikely for any local person, of whatever religion, to voice dissent to a stranger – and in all such circumstances self-restraint is always advisable. But as elsewhere in the south, there are no young males roaming with guns and no overt sign of military or militia, other than the occasional UN post or patrol. Certainly there is no Islamic ban on the sale of liquor in Rmeiche. At the little shop where our driver has stopped, Hossein stocks up with

Black Label, to add to the piles of food, shoes and other supplies in the chaotic rear of his people-carrier. As a veteran of war trips round Lebanon he will never be caught short for supplies. He is a man incapable of buying less than five kilos of any commodity.

The Rmeiche teacher, who studied law and teaches Arabic among other things, says neighbouring Aita al-Shaab was a Christian village until trouble in the mid-1890s. Some Christians killed a Shi'ite man who wanted to marry a Christian woman. The Christians were evicted. Not all Christian villages avoided the Israeli invasion like Rmeiche. Ein Ebel, another Christian village, with three churches and the French flags that seem to give some Maronites so much reassurance, did not escape Israeli firepower: Hezbollah fighters and Israeli troops did fight here, and 120 houses were destroyed. Ein Ebel, higher up than Rmeiche and on an important route into the south, was of more strategic importance to both sides.

As the broken bridges and bombed factories in the north and east showed us, being Christian is no guaranteed advantage if the Israelis are on the move.

In Bint Jbeil, the centre of which was obliterated, the Qataris have already rebuilt just a year on two brand new buildings, a school and an office bloc with a cinema. Work is going on all around, though much damage remains. At Aitaroun, nearer the border, which was badly bombed by the Israelis and where the fighting was intense, a gleaming new Israeli tank, polished by local people, sits on a plinth, a trophy of war. A poster over it shows Sheikh Nasrallah brandishing a Kalashnikov. There are quite a few of these monuments displayed near the Israeli border, some close enough for Israeli soldiers to see from their blockhouses along the frontier. My favourite is a tank with a cardboard statue of Ayatollah Khomeini standing over it. (These be-robed, black, bearded, turbaned figures distributed throughout southern Lebanon's gentle landscape are almost other-worldly, metaphysical creatures of either reassuring or menacing aura, depending on whose side you are on.)

Such reminders of military success, like our statues in Whitehall, or Waterloo Station and Trafalgar Square, and of Israeli failure are important to the citizens of Lebanon's south. Although Israel's fighting performances become less overwhelmingly successful with each conflict in the Middle East, its seemingly indestructible dominance of Middle Eastern destinies, its magical grasp of American vitals and its endless capacity for making mischief and worse among its neighbours, mean that for these Lebanese even such a wounding experience as July 2006 can be hailed as a famous victory. This time, blows were landed on Israel and Israeli soil, whereas until 2006 Israel had fought its wars on other peoples' lands.

Luncheon with the sheikh

Aitaroun sits under the hills of Maroun al Ras. Once the Israelis were on the ridge, it was simple for them to pepper the town with shot and shell.

The house we are in, with Mariam, in her 50s, and her mother, Leila, in her 70s, was right in the line of fire. Cluster bombs lurk in the fields around, making picking tobacco and olives a hazardous enterprise. They will do so for some time. A large donkey wanders around in an olive grove. The local sheikh, who is lunching with us and I reckon is a Hezbollah man, says most of the victims nowadays are sheep and goats and cattle. How much more a detonated donkey would alarm *Sun* readers than a dead or maimed human.

Mariam's mother stuck the war out in her house for two days, elsewhere in the village for ten days, then for two weeks in another frontline village called Tibnine. She finally took a taxi to Beirut and relative safety, for US$500 (the normal price for a *servis* to Beirut would be about $10).

Leila tells me she has been to the Holy Shi'ite cities of Qom and Mashad, in Iran, and loves it there. She says she is Lebanese first and Arab second, but after 30 years of invasions would much rather live in Iran than Lebanon. I doubt this is really true, but it illustrates how deep and how spiritual is the connection between the Shi'ites of Lebanon and those of Iran, though there were Shi'ites in Lebanon 500 or 600 years before Iran adopted Shi'ism as its official religion. I think she is making a point, if a valid one. In Iran she would also be a lot further away from the Israelis, who occupied her village for 22 years and have just attacked it again, with much damage and loss of life.

Mariam's mother seemed a little morose at first and was suspicious of a foreigner with a notebook. Any Lebanese might well be suspicious of a foreigner with a notebook, but surprisingly few of them are. Her daughter tried to convince her that her stories were not going to appear on the AP wire or Al-Jazeera TV news, but she remained intractable and listless. Then, lunch approached, the smell of lamb cooking and garlic filled the air, *houmous* and beans and *tabbouli* and *babbaganoush* appeared, the tables outside in the big garden were laid, spring was in the air and the sun came out. Leila sat on a rug near a wall between her house and the meadow littered with cluster bombs, laughing and joking with her guests. Her objections to talking to reporters and writers vanished in the breeze that whisked down from the hilltops of Maroun al Ras, the Israeli border just beyond.

We were to picnic with the sheikh. I had expected a portly, gowned figure in a turban to emerge at the bottom of the garden path, possibly stepping from a black Mercedes, escorted by a couple of large young men in dark suits and white shirts with shaved heads and neat beards. But it is nothing like that. A very slight man in green shirt, green dungarees, a woollen car coat and those sturdy brown walking shoes you see in catalogues appears at the gate and walks up to meet us. He is bareheaded. He is affable, smiles at me, shakes my hand, depositing his walkie-talkie in a coat pocket before he does so, but bows to the women and places his hand across his chest in greeting and acknowledgement instead of shaking their hands.

The sheikh, Qassem Hamadi, also has a mobile telephone. He is well in touch with his people.

Ferial has put a pretty scarf round her head, loosely, as a mark of respect to the sheikh, but Mariam and Sharzad do not cover their heads, which does not appear to bother him. When he is not filling us in on Lebanon and the Shi'ites, he talks on his mobile.

Mariam's mother tells us all, the sheikh included, her people's story. They have been in southern Lebanon since time immemorial. In the Middle East that is a long time. Many Lebanese in this area, she says, still have land in Israel because of the way the frontier was drawn between the two mandated territories in the 1920s, between British Palestine and French Lebanon. We in the West began arbitrarily sectioning the lands around here in our own interests in the early 1920s.

The people whose homes were damaged and livelihoods shattered in 2006 have received nothing from the Lebanese government, she says. She is distraught again. She produces four plastic bags filled with medications. A lot of people here are, unsurprisingly, unwell and depressed; taking various pills and potions. For these older generations life has been one of continuous assault, threat or occupation for the past 40 years. It was not easy even before that, the south always dirt-poor – farmers struggling to make a living from landowners and the tobacco co-operative.

Even the most energetic and hardy Lebanese wonder if it can ever end. Unlike the Palestinians, the Lebanese are on their own land, just about; and it is beautiful, fertile land, where a simple but pleasant and adequate living can be made. Lebanon has water, a commodity the Israelis are greatly in need of and have spent much effort in lifting from under the lands of others – in the West Bank, in Gaza, on the Syrian Golan Heights (whose water is the main reason the Israelis have annexed them). They actually sell Golan water abroad, to Britain among others, as bottled spring water. The Lebanese are convinced that Israel's ambitions in Lebanon include guaranteed and eternal access to its waters, and indeed the early Zionists, David Ben-Gurion included, Israel's leader and iconic founding father, coveted the Lebanese springs and rivers.

For everyone here the past has been grim, the present precarious and the future threateningly unknowable, with Israel across the wire and a President in the White House, at that stage George W. Bush, whose Middle East policy seemed to consist largely of menacing or bombing people who did not toe the line as it is perceived on the banks of the Potomac or from the broad acres of Texas. Neither is there any concrete sign yet that his successor will be able to reverse the US policy of more or less open-ended and uncritical support for Israel, whatever it does. And yet for all this, every home I visit is immaculate, the hospitality unfailingly generous, the people at ease with outsiders and pleased to see us, the children healthy and playful but well-disciplined.

The sheikh is very thin, with bright sparkling brown eyes under a high-domed forehead. He smokes incessantly. Unlike many of his compatriots he is not feeding *misbaha*, worry beads, through nerveless fingers. His mobile, perhaps, stands in for them, and he is forever trying to organise cluster bomb victims for our fellow reporter Sharzad to interview, or checking his parishioners.

This is Hezbollah territory. The yellow flags and pictures of 20 years of martyrs and their leaders and gurus, Nasrallah, Khomeini, Ayatollah Khamenei (the Iranian leader), *inter alia*, prove it. Amal, the first proper Lebanese Shi'ite party, formed in the mid-1970s, often in the past at war with its replacement as the main party of the Shi'ites, Hezbollah, does fly its flags in the villages in which it holds sway.

Amal's first and most famous martyr, his picture now fading, Bilal Fahs, the first suicide bomber to attack the Israelis, in 1983, is up there as you enter Nabatiyeh – he is called the 'Bridegroom of the South'.

Hezbollah tolerates Amal; it exists, but Hezbollah does the fighting, organising and inspiring. Amal is very much the junior partner. So I take it that Sheikh Qassem is Hezbollah, but he will say only that he 'supports' them. In my travels in Lebanon, here and elsewhere, I have not seen anyone with a gun outside of the Internal Security Force, the Army or the various UN battalions. I would be naive to think the guns are not there. The fact that they are kept out of sight and not used as swagger sticks by the young men who run these towns and villages is yet another example of how disciplined is Hezbollah when compared with any of the other militias and the Palestinian guerrillas.

The sheikh says the Israelis bombarded Aitaroun but never entered the town. He says Hezbollah fighters were not in the town either, fighting from the mountains and the countryside.

He takes me through the region's past, saying the Israeli problems really began for them in 1967, when Palestinian resistance was beginning in the south and the Israelis were shelling the area routinely. Their idea (similar to the one that aims at making the Gazans so miserable they will switch their support to more 'moderate' Palestinians, that is, those, if they can be found, who will do Israel's and the West's bidding) was to put pressure on the people to get the government to clamp down on the *fedayeen*. It did not work then; it does not work now.

In 1969, he says, Israeli commandos came into the town and destroyed 15 homes and took back with them a number of people. He says they tied up one 40-year-old and shot him dead. Until 1974, during which time the Palestinian forces in southern Lebanon were given Arab guarantees of freedom of movement and cross-border attack in and from inside Lebanon, life in the town became untenable, with shelling, Israeli military incursions, no protection from the Lebanese Army, work in the fields difficult and many homes destroyed.

The sheikh says a whole generation lost their education because schools were closed, and a generation of young women were denied marriage because the men left the area.

On 1 April 1972, the Israelis came up to 25 miles inside Lebanon and stayed for a month. In March 1978, they came in strength, bombarding and destroying towns and villages and pushing back the Palestinian guerrillas. They stopped on passage of UN Security Council Resolution 425, which called for full Israeli withdrawal, but they never fully withdrew, instead seizing a wide strip of territory all along the border and several miles deep inside Lebanon, leaving in charge their sidekick Saad Haddad and his Israeli proxy Army of Free Lebanon. The sheikh tells me all this straight, and I can verify what he says is because I was there.

1978 was the beginning of a de facto Israeli occupation that was greatly widened as a result of the full-scale invasion of Lebanon up to Beirut and the Shouf mountains in 1982, and lasted until the year 2000.[1] The Israelis, therefore, have been heavily around, about and in the south, with a highly aggressive posture, very nearly for as long as they have occupied the Palestinian West Bank and Gaza, Jerusalem and the Golan Heights, some 40 years, 22 of those years being actual occupation (Israel defied Resolution 425 for 22 years).

We have eaten well: *mezze*, lamb *kofta*, *foul*, beans, potatoes, omelette, piles of bread; now we are on the fresh strawberries and oranges, and endless cups of strong coffee. Aitaroun, where we sit, was occupied for the 22 years. 'We were safe here,' says the sheikh. 'There was no war here. But the problem was occupation. The Israelis and their allies in the South Lebanon Army [as the AFL became, taken over in 1984 after the demise of Sa'ad Haddad by another Israeli collaborator, the Lebanese Army General Antoine Lahad] watched everything we did, heard everything we said. And we were totally cut off from the rest of Lebanon. We were in a vacuum here. We could only get out to Lebanon with Israeli permission, which was not easy to get, and we could not go in to Israel. It was as if we were in detention.'

People could not marry anyone from outside the area. They could not sell their day-to-day produce of olives, lentils and fruit in Lebanon, though they could sell their tobacco. Young people were cut off from books and information; there were no mobile phones or, later on, Internet. Land lines existed but were bugged: 'We lost a generation.' Travel even within the zone was limited and difficult because the Israelis and the South Lebanon Army (SLA) wanted to know where you were going and why. Only the collaborators and the unconcerned could leave, to go to Israel to work or shop or get medical treatment, or to Lebanon in special circumstances, such as to visit bereaved relatives or attend family functions.

The sheikh says the occupiers encouraged drink, drugs and gambling, but I wonder about this. It seems on the face of it uncharacteristic for a simple, rural, devout people. But it is quite usual that people isolated, bored and without hope of tomorrow turn to these supposed stimuli; we know it is happening in the wretched confines of the Palestinian camps, here in Lebanon and inside Palestine. If it is correct that the Israelis and the SLA did succeed with the Shi'ites of the south, then it is another sign of the adversity into which Israel has plunged its neighbours in its endless quest for unchallenged security and eternal supremacy.

Sheikh Qassem says Hezbollah has such support because it liberated the people from the Israelis: at last those living in the south, almost trapped in the south, even after the 2000 occupation ended, felt that someone was providing them with security and was representing them to the outside world, making demands on their behalf. He says they now provide services, computer and language courses, trips to other parts of Lebanon, even to the Christian areas of the north. There are doctors, clinics, medicine and assistance for the poor. But the main support stems from and is inspired by that knowledge that the south Lebanese have a guardian against the intruder.

As for the idea that Hezbollah is the creature of Iran or Syria, he denies it (as, many Lebanese would say, he would), saying the people do not accept being subjected to killing or displacement by anyone, from anywhere, including Syria or Iran: 'It is we who determine our interests. It is we who decide.' He may be right that Hezbollah is not Iran's 'creature', in that it is a Lebanese institution founded on Lebanese soil. It is, however, very much an original Iranian concept and was inspirited and initially constructed by Lebanese activists with vital Iranian Revolutionary Guard advice and help (it is widely believed Revolutionary Guard officers even now hold many posts in the Hezbollah military set-up). Iran provides arms, training, weapons and finance; Syria, as conduit for Iran's supplies and absentee overseer of Lebanon's affairs, is a close ally of Iran's and Hezbollah's.

People who question this arrangement might also, then, ask who arms and finances Israel and who twists whose tail? If Iran benefits from its strength in Lebanon through Hezbollah, then the reverse is true; just as the argument goes endlessly on as to whether the USA benefits as much from Israel as Israel from the USA. The more pressing question for non-Hezbollah Lebanese is whether the party and through it Iran wish to 'control' Lebanon.

The people's loyalty to Hezbollah, says the sheikh, drawing on his zillionth cigarette, is the same as loyalty to Lebanon – it is the only

Lebanon they know, the only power they can sense as the state cannot defend its people from Israel. He points out that Hezbollah was born out of Israeli occupation, not vice versa, and that even before the Palestinians were a strength in Lebanon the Israelis had carried out attacks on the Lebanese. Here he is wrong on the detail, but right from the historical perspective.

The Making
of the Border 10

The sheikh is implying that between the creation of Israel in 1948 and the arrival of the Palestinian guerrillas in the mid-1960s, Israel had kept up its attacks and interventions across the border. This is not so. There were border disputes as Israeli settlers pushed their acreage here and there into Lebanon; there were adjustments to anomalies along the frontier as the Israeli border patrols and defenders found that militarily, a hill here, a *wadi* there, a fold in the landscape, a strategic view, the line drawn on the map in 1949 (when the armistice agreement between Israel and Lebanon was signed) did not suit their purposes.

But until the mid-1960s the border remained much as it has been since it evolved after World War I; was violated between 1978 and 2000, the years of Israeli occupation; but is now again much where it has been for the past 90 or so years.

From the little Mediterranean border post of Ras Naqoura-Rosh Hanikra it heads due east for about 12 miles, past the spot about six or seven miles in from where Hezbollah captured the Israeli soldiers in 2006, an undulating landscape of hills and valleys, olive groves, apple, tobacco and banana plantations, and sheep; some fertile land, some rocky. Villages of simple one- and two-storey houses and stores with the pointed fingers of mosques rising against the clear blue air stand near the border, and often, just outside and above them, are the palatial villas of the emigrant wealthy.

These are mostly Shi'ite traders from West Africa who have returned to build their ostentatious family homes in the middle of this troubled frontier area, regardless. These are not just grand, pink and ochre villas, architectural extravaganzas many of them, with their elaborated facades and red-tiled roofs and swimming pools, tucked into the sides of the stony hills, their TV dishes and antennae bringing the residents news from Al-Jazeera and al-Manar, BBC and CNN, rolling reminders of the trouble they are in right where they sit. The money invested in these grandiose piles of brick and ceramic are statements of intent and determination. Many of these little palaces have been abandoned, cut off, occupied or shelled during the past 30 years, but still the Lebanese of the region come back to build, and settle and reclaim their home-land. Their persistence has paid off. The Israelis have gone, even if they are just over the rise and continue to visit in person or by bomb, shell and over-flight. The land is wholly Lebanese again.

After this 12-mile eastern course, the border turns sharply north-north-east near the point where I have been talking with the sheikh near Aitaroun, running up for about 15 miles to the area opposite the northernmost Israeli Galilee town of Metullah. Along this route the mountain, the Jebl Amal, becomes tougher, even more impenetrable, the rough, craggy gulches ideal for guerrilla warfare. Sometimes the Lebanese road runs right alongside the Israeli military posts, close enough for conversation, were it advisable, between people on each side, though barbed wire, mines, tank routes and the latest technology in electronic observation mark every inch of the way. This is a frontier rather than a border. Each side has unfinished business. Every now and then a massive billboard that in another country might be adver-tising petrol or jeans or four-wheel drives plays host to the Shi'ite icons of the day, Nasrallah, Khomeini, Khamenei, Imam Musa Sadr, from where they stare grimly and implacably down into the Israeli farmland.

The Lebanese government traditionally was not all that concerned about this border. In fact, after Israel was created it welcomed rigid enforcement of the Armistice Line because while it did not particularly care that Shi'ite farmers could no longer visit, do business in or graze cattle or plant tobacco in Palestine/Israel as they had traditionally done down the centuries, Lebanon did not wish to see Arabs wandering into Israel and possibly provoking Israeli reprisals (as was to happen later on such a devastating scale). The Lebanese were so keen on keeping the Israelis sweet that on one occasion, soon after the setting up in 1949 of joint Lebanese–Israeli armistice teams to police the border, Lebanese police helped the Israelis send back to Lebanon several hun-dred Palestinian refugees who had managed to return to their homes in Palestine-now-Israel.

Israeli patrols came into Lebanon briefly during the Lebanese civil war of 1958, when there were (false) reports of an imminent Syrian invasion of south-eastern Lebanon; and there was a border clash in April 1960, between the Lebanese Army and the Israeli forces – four Israeli soldiers were captured and later released. In August 1965, about the time Palestinian guerrillas were beginning to cross the Israeli border, but with nothing like the strength they were to acquire later, Israeli soldiers came into Lebanon and blew up two houses and three water towers. One woman was killed.

But essentially, between 1949 and 1967, the border remained closed and the area quiet and untroubled, except for the economic consequences for the people of southern Lebanon, who could no longer treat with their markets and relatives and friends inside Palestine.

Where the sheikh, and many Lebanese, have a point is that from the inception of Zionism as a force to be reckoned with, from the beginning of British Mandatory rule in Palestine in 1923, and even back to the British takeover of Palestine in 1917, it was evident that the Zionist movement had territorial ambitions in the country. Zionist policy was to destabilise Lebanon, build a shaky confessional state and take as much of the south as possible. All this succeeded to a point, certainly the idea of a shaky confessional state.

After World War I and the defeat of the Ottomans came the consequent French–British carve-up of the Levant. This was most impertinently characterised in the Declaration by the British Foreign Secretary, Arthur J. Balfour, in November 1917, in a letter to the Zionist financier Lord Rothschild: that the British government was in favour 'of the establishment in Palestine of a national home for the Jewish people'. The Zionists, if not perhaps Mr Balfour himself, saw in these few words a pledge by Britain to create a Jewish state in Palestinian Arab territory; to magnify and solidify the boundaries of such a state they openly sought a northern border that would take in the waters of the Lebanese river, the Litani (or *Qassimiyeh* in local usage). Depending on which plan one read, the border would go as far as just south of Beirut, or be as generous merely to include everything from the Litani southwards, including the large port of Tyre.

The Zionists wanted this – and other Arab water sources in Jordan and Syria – both for irrigation and for hydro-electric power. Various schemes would have seen the waters of the Litani, the Jordan and the Yarmuk, and other headwaters of the Golan Heights, combined for the benefit of Israel-to-be. There was, it was thought, no other way to sustain the massive numbers of Jews who would be emigrating to Palestine in the coming years, a phenomenon the Zionists were confident of as early as 1919. These ideas were being fed into the receptive minds of the British government even as peace terms in the Middle East were inchoate, four years before the League of Nations presented the British the Mandates for Palestine, Transjordan and Iraq in 1923. The Jews were rightly confident that the British government of the day would go along with their plans for the border with Lebanon. And this was at a time when the Jewish population of Palestine was barely 10 per cent of the whole.

They need have had few worries about British compliance. The British were keen to expand their territory at the expense of the French, who had the Mandatory rule of Lebanon and Syria. The Lebanese themselves, under the French, were not concerned about what happened in the south. When Jewish settlers tried to move into Lebanon, it was the French who resisted them, though there were already Jewish settlements in northern Galilee – the eastern 'finger' that prods up into Lebanon, and whose irregular extension, disfiguring the East–West line, was a product of the existence of settlements at towns like Metullah and Tel Hai (where there was an Arab massacre of Jewish settlers in 1920).

It was not just the water the Zionists coveted. They also knew that a line north of the Litani, running east from just north of Tyre, would be more defensible in this area of criss-cross valleys, mountains and rivers than the one that eventually came into being. It would also be more convenient in the event of any northward assault, or punitive expedition or action, as has been shown during the past 30 years.

In February 1919, the Zionist Organisation proposed to the Paris Peace Conference: 'inclusion within Palestine of the Litani river and the headwaters of Mount Hermon [the second highest peak in the region, now shared by Syria, the UN and Israeli occupying forces but officially all part of Syrian territory].' Under this plan, the Lebanese border would have run due east from Sidon, to the point where the Litani hooks north, then down into the Golan Heights. That would have given Palestine/Israel a goodly quarter of all Lebanese territory.

The British were happy with this. David Lloyd George, wartime prime minister and in 1919 leader of the British delegation to the peace talks, was enveloped in that cloud of woolly biblical myth that pervaded so many of the pro-Zionist, low-church Protestants in the British government and among its officialdom, emphasising the central role of Israel and the Israelites in the Christian epic. Lloyd George had an ill-conceived plan inside his head, an obsession almost, that saw the Israeli/Palestinian Mandate border drawn from 'the Dan to Beersheba', a line which, whatever it was, was not a political starter. The chapel-goers (A.J. Balfour was one as well) were in the hands of the Zionists. The French, however, were not chapel-goers. Neither were they keen to see their more powerful ally-cum-rival, Britain, increase its territory at France's expense. In the end, the French idea of the border prevailed.

The Lebanese establishment – another early indicator of its carelessness about the south – was not itself that concerned, and nor were most of the country's citizens who lived in the central and northern regions, that is, most of the nation. They regarded the south as a distant place of which they knew or cared little; 'working' Lebanon for them was the Mountain and the coastal cities from Sidon to Tripoli, including the fast-growing capital, Beirut, and its hinterland. Here, the Sunnis and the Maronites and the Greek Orthodox made the money and did the business. The Christians had a further reason for not wishing to include the south in Lebanon: the large Shi'ite Muslim population there, and its high birth-rate, was a threat to the then Christian plurality in Lebanon.

The people of the south looked to *their* south. Trade, family ties, friendships, cross-border land, plantations and grazing tended largely to be with and in Palestine, not with the north; towns like Acre, Haifa and Safed were the southern people's magnet, for business, kinship and pleasure, not Beirut and Sidon. For most of the period from 1922 to 1948, the line established between Lebanon and Palestine, very roughly where it is today, was an open one.

Had it not been for the French, that notional line would have been drawn along the Litani river, with little local opposition. The French put their foot down and in 1924 the line was drawn, officially, where they wanted it, except for the obtrusion of Galilee north-east.

The Zionists never gave up, a lesson not all Lebanese appear to have digested, apart from the Shi'a of the south and some of the more politically astute in the rest of the country. In 1937, David Ben-Gurion took the view that 'Eretz' (Greater) Israel was not to be limited to the territories that had been under the British Mandate (remember, this is 11 years before the state actually existed). General Yigal Allon, who commanded the Jewish forces that established Israel in 1948 and became commander of the Israeli Army, later criticised Ben-Gurion for having accepted a ceasefire too early and at a time when the Israelis could easily have commandeered both banks of the Litani, in 1949.

In fact, the Israeli forces captured the 'elbow' of the Litani, in the east of Lebanon, where its southern flow turns west to the sea. But Ben-Gurion ordered them to withdraw, reckoning that Lebanon, which had played a minor role in the war of 1948–9, would sign a peace treaty with Israel and agree to share the Litani's waters with its new neighbour. Unfortunately for Ben-Gurion, and Israel, Arab anger at the creation of the Jewish state and the plight of the Palestinian refugees was such that Lebanon could make no such treaty and hope to survive the repercussions at home and abroad.

It was not just politics and the influx of Palestinian refugees that overwhelmed and distorted the south in 1948. Economics mattered, too.

From 1926, the French and British Mandatory authorities had set in official stone the easy-going nature of the border between Lebanon and Palestine. People each side were free to move across, buying, selling, socialising and even owning land that stretched either side of the frontier. There were no passports, taxes or customs dues involved for people travelling or dealing between the two Mandatory states. The connections that had existed for centuries between the inhabitants of northern Palestine and southern Lebanon survived the creation of two nations-in-the-making, a new and very European imposition on the area.

The only interruption in the progress of the 'soft' border came between 1936 and 1939, when the Palestinian Arabs rebelled against the British Mandate over increasing Jewish immigration and plans by the British to partition the state (disproportionately) between Jews and Arabs when independence should finally come. The Arab Revolt was bloody and shook the British so much that they resorted to brutal tactics against the resident population. They deployed Orde Wingate, the model for the crazed Brigadier Ritchie-Hook in Evelyn Waugh's *Sword of Honour*, to deliver what mayhem he could both sides of the border. There was plenty of it. Orde enjoyed his work. The British hanged rebel leaders and people suspected of armed resistance. They used methods such as collective punishment – blowing up homes, razing villages and destroying crops and produce, practices the

Israelis employ to this day. The British brought in the notorious security expert Sir Charles Tegart, whose name lives on in the fortress, block-house style police stations that still mar the Palestinian landscape and have been passed on as bastions of intrusive field security in Palestine from the British, to the Jordanians, to the Israelis and to the Palestinian Authority.

But the British found that whatever strength, type or depth of security fence they introduced to try to stop Arab guerrillas taking refuge in and reappearing from southern Lebanon, it did not work for long. However barbed the wire or close together the pillboxes, the fighters penetrated the system. All that this reinforced frontier achieved was to antagonise civilian Arabs on both sides. Their progress back and forth was interrupted. This increased opposition to the British and to the French, who in the later stages tried to help the British crush the rebellion, not wanting instability in their mandated territories, in which they were seriously overstretched militarily.

In the end, what finished the Arab Revolt were not the field security measures but the brutal reprisals, the hangings of offenders, the promise that Jewish immigration would seriously be slowed and the Palestinian Arabs' lack of organisation, leadership, military experience and political cohesion. The latter was a fundamental set of weaknesses for them in 1948 and the years running up to it. These weaknesses were and are perhaps not altogether unforgivable in the face of such insuperable odds.

The Zionists learned that 'ethnic homogeneity', that is, Arabs, in large numbers and in close proximity each side of the Lebanese border was not to be tolerated. It was, to a Jewish state, a source of danger and instability that would be almost impossible to police or control. Thus there was an added reason, apart from the sheer demographic one that encouraged the Jewish underground army, Haganah, and its associate terrorist groups, Irgun Zwei Leumi and Lehi, or the Stern Gang, to throw the Palestinian Arab citizens out of their state and denude Galilee of its Arab population to as great an extent as possible. By 1949, the Arab problem, such as it was, was beyond Israel's borders – for the time being.

The French also made mistakes that were to resonate in the south of Lebanon for decades to come. One serious one was made as early as 1925, when the Druze of Syria rebelled against them. The Druze insurgents occupied a couple of Christian towns inside southern

Lebanon. The exiguous French forces armed Christian villagers in their own defence, setting a pattern by which the often beleaguered or frightened Christians of the region turned to outsiders for help against their Muslim or Druze, and, later, Palestinian neighbours. After 1967, those outsiders tended largely to be the Israelis.

The Jewish fighters of what was to become the Israeli Army were already familiar with Lebanon by the time it became a problem again in the late 1960s. In 1941, after France had fallen and the Vichy French had taken command of France's colonies and possessions, the Allies, in the form largely of two Australian brigades, attacked Lebanon and Syria with the aim of replacing a French system sympathetic to the Nazis with Charles de Gaulle's Free French. Part of this eventually successful invasion force was a Jewish Brigade, including a young officer named Moshe Dayan. (It was in combat in this campaign that Dayan lost his left eye.)

The experience was invaluable. It proved to the Jewish fighters how difficult and impenetrable southern Lebanon was – the Australians had to attack Beirut and Damascus using essentially the same and only usable axes south-to-north that the Israelis were to use in the summer of 1982: up the coast and up the eastern side, through the Beka'a Valley, between the Lebanese Mountains and the Syrian Anti-Lebanon range. It was this knowledge, in 1949, when the Armistice Agreements between Lebanon and Israel were drawn up under UN aegis that informed Israel's successful insistence that the agreements stipulate that only 1500 Lebanese soldiers would be stationed south of the River Litani. Thus feebly defended, Lebanon would be easy for the Israelis to penetrate, if and when such intrusion became necessary, as the Israelis, with their usual prescience, knew it would.

The Lebanese of the south, and those mainstream politicians and thinkers who retained some concern for the integrity and future survival of this small, vulnerable, virtually indefensible but uniquely constituted state, remained uneasy about their powerful neighbour. They knew Israel was peeved that it had been, as Israel saw it, cheated out of Lebanon's waters by the confirmation of the 1924 line of divide in 1949, and by its failure to seize the Litani river when it had the chance while fighting continued and Lebanon and the Jewish state were at war. They knew also that Israel must see southern Lebanon as an irritatingly dangerous strategic area peering down at its new, neat European-style northern settlements and its well-tended, meticulously laid-out fields and crops.

The Lebanese were right to be concerned, although none of them could have known it at the time. In late 1948, David Ben-Gurion had written in his diary: 'Muslim supremacy in [Lebanon] is artificial and can easily be overthrown. A Christian state ought to be set up there, with its southern front on the River Litani. We would sign a treaty of alliance with this state.' In 1954, in a letter to the prime minister, Moshe Sharett, Ben-Gurion repeated the idea. Moshe Dayan, then Israeli Chief of Staff, in the same year, made an uncannily prophetic observation along identical lines: his aim, he wrote, was 'to find an officer, be it only a simple major, whose sympathies we could either gain or buy, and so incite him to proclaim himself the saviour of the Maronites'.

It is here that one has to sympathise with what outsiders so often see as a peculiarly Middle Eastern predilection for plots and prophecies, usually those of powerful strangers. Twenty or so years after Moshe Dayan had posited his simple Christian major, such a man was found. He was Major Sa'ad Haddad, a renegade Greek Catholic major in the Lebanese Army, who grasped the hand of Israel in defending his southern Christian enclaves against Palestinians and assorted leftists and Muslims, and with their assistance created the Army of Free Lebanon, known in those days by the UN peacekeeping force as the 'De Facto Forces'. Ultimately, after Israel invaded in 1978, Haddad's mostly but not entirely Christian band was put in charge of a zone some 5–7 miles deep inside Lebanon, all along the border. This defied UN Security Resolution 425, which required Israel and its cohorts to vacate Lebanon entirely. The zone was hugely expanded and solidified after the devastating Israeli invasion of 1982.

It is this history, Israel's invasions and possessions, destructions and occupations, manipulations and menaces, and territorial ambitions, going back 90 years, that informs our Lebanese sheikh and Hezbollah's determination to survive as the only capable armed resistance to Israel. It is Hezbollah's southern constituency – an area of 2000 square miles and a population of up to a million – that is in the firing line. Many Lebanese outside this zone were glad enough of Hezbollah's success in liberating the south, finally, in 2000 and resisting so manfully – the first time the Arabs properly carried a battle into Israel itself – when Israel assaulted the whole country in the summer of 2006. Memories, however, are short in much of Lebanon. Israel's potential for aggression, if not forgotten, was soon overtaken in many people's minds by the perceived threat from the internal political and military force that Hezbollah represented, a destabilising presence, as it was seen, in Lebanon's sensitive sectarian system.

There are other anomalies along the border. To the outsider they may seem trivial. However, this is an area where yards of turf matter, both for reasons of strategy and economics and as questions of pride. It is an area where the politicians loathe each other, are historical, tribal rivals who make a series of unstable and temporary alliances of convenience – but also have serious doubts about the Jewish State's legitimacy.

In this little patch, much land has been stolen, and kept. Syria's peace negotiations with Israel have been held up for nearly 20 years now, over – ostensibly – a few hundred metres near Lake Galilee on the Golan Heights. Not far away from the Golan, on the western slopes of Mount Hermon, are the Sheba'a Farms. This is an area of about 25 square kilometres of fertile land, most of it orchards.

The Israelis occupying this say this is part of Syrian territory, and therefore any departure has to be negotiated as part of a peace treaty with Syria. The Syrians, and therefore the Lebanese, argue – with no proof or sustaining maps so far produced for international consumption – that the Farms are in Lebanese territory and should have been vacated by the Israelis in 2000, under Resolution 425, when they left the rest of southern Lebanon. Well founded or not, this enables Hezbollah to say it is justified in harassing the Israelis inside the area. It is also regarded by many Lebanese and the Western powers who support the forces of March 14 as a spurious excuse for the Syrians, Iran and Hezbollah and its friends to maintain their armed men and armaments on a scale denied to any other grouping in Lebanon, including the army itself.

In Hezbollah's defence, when the easternmost sector of the Palestinian–Lebanese border was drawn (in the early 1920s), and where it all connects with the Syrian border, there were five kilometres that were left vague, badly marked or not marked at all.[1]

The Lebanese, in 1999, also claimed, under the then prime minister Selim al-Hoss, a respected national figure, possession of seven villages that were incorporated into Palestine during the French Mandate. These villages, all Shi'a originally, are also not covered by Resolution 425, but would presumably have to be part of any negotiations that may come when Syria and Lebanon – this will have to be a joint effort – meet Israel across the table.

As we have seen, apart from the period from 1936 to 1939, the south Lebanese and Palestinian Arabs had been able to trade freely. With the creation of Israel, all that stopped. Palestinian refugees flooded into southern Lebanon. They were welcomed and taken in, but inevitably their arrival and the new, firm border caused a poor regional economic strain and upheaval (this was long before the Palestinians were able to organise themselves into any kind of coherent armed threat to Israel or to anyone else).

The Lebanese of the south were suddenly cut off from their natural hinterland by a militarily enforced international border (it remains to this day an Armistice Line, though Israel ceased to recognise it as such after 1967). This meant that they were forced to turn for trade and sustenance to a largely unsympathetic central Lebanon, which exploited them as cheap labour and as a source of low-cost primary produce – bananas, tobacco, olives, fruit, fish – but offered them little in return in welfare, resources or protection. The rich Shi'ites, who had made fortunes in West Africa or the Gulf, or were traditional landowners, were often unhelpful, joining in the general exploitation.

This was when migration north began, and slowly but surely during the coming 20 years underpaid, under-privileged but angry young Shi'ites began to join leftist parties (as their *confreres* had in Iraq). They started to learn radical lessons of politics, of displacement, exploitation and Israeli aggression and the crimes of Western Imperialism and division-and-rule, from their better-educated Palestinian and Lebanese fellow-activists, mostly in and around Beirut, but also in Tyre and Sidon and even abroad. It was these young men, now in their 50s and 60s, who were the seedbed of Shi'ite political power, first felt through the Communist Party, then the Amal movement, and later and most powerfully through Hezbollah.

They also took lessons from how the PLO's power as a virtual state-within-a-state inside Lebanon could be used to manipulate that weak state, where *Lubnaniyat* was so much more evident than any sense of real national identity or a real nation state. They eventually came to organise against the Palestinians' power and authority in the land and were pleased at first when Israel and Syria between them reduced Palestinian dominance in the early 1980s. They watched also as the Maronite Christians organised themselves and their allies into yet another state-within-a-state, for a time (1975–88), before that too fell apart under internal and external strains and contradictions. Out of this, with much help from Syria and Iran, but also with their own internal guidance, faith and determination forged from bitter experience, they began to make a party and a resistance that they hoped would outlast the temporary nature of the other groups' and even the state's flimsy grasps on power.

It was a slow lesson but it stuck. If the Lebanese of the March 14 movement and many others, understandably afraid of this phenomenon, argue as they do that Hezbollah is financed and armed by Iran and is therefore Iran's stooge in the area, they must acknowledge that, if true, this is not a process unique to Hezbollah; further, it is arguable whether Hezbollah is anyone's stooge.

Most forces involved in and around Lebanon are financed or enabled to a greater or lesser extent by outside forces, Arab and otherwise. March 14 itself is made up of many leaders and supporters who were happy to co-operate to the fullest degree with the Syrians between 1975 and 2005, Christians, Druze and Sunni Muslims among them. Rafiq Hariri and Walid Junblatt were very close to Syria, as were the Sunnis of Tripoli and the Christian Franjieh family. They were not alone. Lebanon was replete with Lebanese who worked with and for the Syrian secret services, the *mukhabarrat,* and it probably still is. Many businessmen and leaders made fortunes out of illegal trading, smuggling and financial deals with their powerful neighbour.

Now the Syrians have left, as overt controllers, money has poured in from the West and the Gulf to help arm March 14's supporters (so far to no great effect) and to sustain a pro-Western government, however unpopular and/or paralysed. There is nothing unusual about this, but it is unfair to claim that only one side can rely on foreign finance or that such foreign finance implies puppet status.

Recent books by US academics, politicians and a former president show that there is growing unease about what ordinary Americans are at last recognising is Israel's virtual stranglehold on US Middle East policy, as the flow of money, in the form of massive influence-buying and penetration, goes flooding into the USA and many of its institutions.

The Maronite experiment was also armed and advised from many sources abroad, including Israel, and later Iraq, mainly for the purpose of aggravating Syria.

In this century, the West's intervention in Lebanese affairs has become cruder as the European states have swung more and more solidly behind US policy in the region, the UN Security Council in 2004 passing a resolution (1559) that was seen by many critics in the West as well as in the Arab world as interference in a nation's internal affairs, at the expense of the Syrians – not so much to aid the Lebanese as to embarrass and weaken a state that was standing against Israel and a vital source of help to Hezbollah. It was this resolution that contributed to Syrian paranoia, which, added to Syria's increasingly heavy-handed and dismissive approach to the Lebanese, helped turn into a hurricane the tide of Lebanese feeling that had built up against Syria over the years, culminating in the climactic events of 2005 and beyond.

It is all this that sits so firmly in the mind of my lunchtime guest, the sheikh, and his many friends, co-religionists and supporters.

Hezbollah is not a threat to Israel in the sense that the PLO was or was seen to be, or chose to be seen to be. The Palestinians wanted their land back and were prepared to use military as well as diplomatic and political means to try to get it. Hezbollah supports the Palestinians' cause, but does not claim Israel's territory. If it argues that Palestine should be Arab or Islamic or both, this is no different in essence from Israel's argument that the whole of Palestine, and perhaps more, including part of Lebanon, should be under the control of the Jewish state. Conversely, Israel is a threat to Lebanon's territory in general and Hezbollah's constituencies in particular. The history of the years since 1978, and the clearly stated and yet to be discarded claims of the Zionists over the past century or so, from the beginning of the end of the Ottoman Empire, bear that out in an indelible tracery of threat and active aggression.

The Sheikh
Makes His Point

11

Lunch is continuing with the sheikh, the sun beginning to sink towards the sea, behind my head, but still lighting up his narrow, amused face. Coming from the cynical world of Western politics, it is easy, or would be easy, to infer from that wry look that he is taking a rise out of me, a gullible foreigner. I do not believe everything he says, but I believe a lot of it. Or should I say, I believe he believes a lot if it, and has good reason to.

'The Israelis want psychological control over us,' he says. 'They are not people like us. They kill children in schools, they destroy homes over people's heads, they attack ambulances. These people are like a virus which poses a danger to our humankind.'

He retells again what happened in 1978, in 1982, in 1996, here, and then again in 2006, and brings in what has been happening with increasing severity over the past 40 years in Jerusalem, the West Bank and Gaza. I look up to the hills of Maroun el Ras, to our south and east, and I visualise what Miriam's mother saw as a young woman in 1948: hordes of terrified Palestinian refugees, on foot, shambling hungry and in rags over the frontier into Lebanon, leaving behind their homes and their dead – for good.

His complaint is about what Israel is doing and has done, repeatedly, to its Arab neighbours: spreading internal damage among them, infecting them like a virus, as he puts it. The Lebanese, he repeats, are constantly under attack. History is with him. The sheikh points out that Israel does what it likes and none of the powerful states of the West gainsays it. Either these states cannot or, more likely, they will not. This is also true. To note these facts of modern-day existence in the Middle East is exactly that, to note these facts. Those countries or leaders with any ability to bring peace to the region and to these poor people rarely do 'take note', or, if they do, act as a result of them, whether in North America, Europe or most of the Arab world. To register what the sheikh is saying does not mean that the Arabs wish to throw the Jews into the sea, though the worse this all gets the more many of my inter-locutors in the Arab world may begin to wish it. Certainly there is not an Arab living that does not wish either the disappearance of the Zionist state *as* a Zionist state, or at least what seems to be at this stage in our history an unthinkable alteration in its attitude towards and acceptance as equals of its Arab neighbours.

All this flashes through my mind as I sit with the sheikh, my friends and the elderly mama in the sun and in the shadow of Israel. I look at the sheikh, with his mobile. What about Hezbollah? Is it not a state within a state? Is it not over-reaching itself in its retention of arms and its current efforts to change the Lebanese government years before elections are due?

'If 10 million people in Britain asked for a share in government, would you deny them?' asks the sheikh.

'Yes,' I say, 'that's exactly what happens. Most of us opposed the war with Iraq but it didn't make a damn bit of difference and still doesn't.'

This does not floor him: 'Sixty per cent of Lebanese are asking for a share of government, and forty per cent are denying it them. They do not want to share power.'

There is something in this. There were indeed elections in 2005 and now Hezbollah does not like the results and is arguing for a new poll. (It has gained a bigger say in Lebanon's affairs in subsequent years, though at time of writing in 2009 these arguments continue.) On the face of it this is not democratic, except, says the sheikh, that the basis on which the parliament was formed has changed, with new and ever-shifting alliances changing inside the Lebanese political matrix. The Hezbollah cabinet ministers have resigned their posts, and so, he argues, without the balanced confessional government make-up their presence ensured, that government is no longer valid, no longer in line with the old National Pact that makes such balance essential. (It is arguable and remains much argued over.) The Hariri assassination and the abrupt and humiliating exit of the Syrians, their spooks, placemen, controllers and army complicated the issue.

With the Syrians gone (though only just over the hills) Hezbollah has to fight that much harder for a significant role in the Lebanese political power balance, to resist the blandishments of the Americans, the West and their Israeli clients. In fact, Hezbollah is replacing Syria as representative of Arab interests and watchfulness against Israel in the Lebanese system.

The problem as the sheikh sees it is that the USA and Israel are trying to manipulate Lebanon, and Hezbollah does not accept the domination of an outside state. But Hezbollah's relationship with Iran and Syria is what worries the government's supporters, who know about outside influences here down the centuries and know also that people who pay billions of dollars to help their friends and allies and spiritual brothers in another country do not do so out of altruism.

The sheikh insists that *marjahs*, spiritual leaders, are simply to do with religion and not politics: the *marjah* in Lebanon would be Sheikh Fadlallah or the spiritual master of most of the Shi'ites in Iraq, Ayatollah Sistani, neither of whom believe in *velayat al faqih*, the Khomeini doctrine introduced after the Iranian Revolution of 1979, the rule of the spiritual jurisprudence. The people here in the south follow, spiritually, Sheikh Fadlallah, whose message goes out from his mosque in the Beirut southern suburbs every Friday Prayers and is not, by the way, remotely apolitical. It is not possible to separate the spiritual from the political.

But the sheikh in our little garden insists that there is a difference. Sheikh Nasrallah is our 'political' *marjah*, he says. Iran's supreme leader Ayatollah Khamenei, is a symbol for the Lebanese: he gives opinions but not orders.[1]

Despite these debates, there is a certainty about Hezbollah, a prime moving purpose, however it is explained. Lebanon as a whole, viewed as a separate entity from down here near the Israeli border, seems in some ways in more of a mess than ever because of uncertainty, a singular lack of any outside authority, such as the Syrians, to exert control, for better or for worse, and an international climate of the gravest danger. President Bush is in the White House as I write, in 2007. He is fixated on enforcing democracy worldwide and obsessed with the fear of 'Islamic terror'. There is an Israeli Army suffering the indignity of failure in Lebanon in 2006, and no doubt anxious to redeem its reputation with another, this time decisive, crack at Lebanon, no doubt encouraged by the unease and divisions in the country. There is Iraq in a mire of blood and partition. And there is Iran, many of whose political elements are deeply unpleasant and ambitious, taunting America with its rapid strides towards nuclear power and, possibly, a bomb.

It is a strange situation. Since the spring of 2005, it has been the first time for 30 years that Lebanon has not been under the direct control or aegis of a neighbourly power: the Syrians ran the country to varying degrees between 1976 and 2005.

Though the Lebanese complained and, certainly, Syria often behaved ineptly and just plain badly, under Syrian hegemony there were boundaries beyond which no one could go. This gave shape to the country. Ghazi Knaan, the Syrian pro-consul who during the 1980s and 1990s ran Lebanon from the Beau Rivage complex over-looking the southern beaches of Beirut, got on well with Hariri and no doubt profited handsomely from the friendship. When he left, in the early 2000s, the relationship between Lebanese and Syrians deteriorated.

Left to themselves, the Lebanese fell even more easily into the trap of being played off against one another by outside powers. This present crisis ought to be one that is solved without outside influences, but it seems no one is here to protect the Lebanese from themselves. Might they not be better off with Syria as arbiter than an undue influence on their government by the USA and its all-embracing, uncritical love for their most powerful, aggressive and acquisitive neighbour?

If asked, most ordinary Lebanese would say 'no' to any outsiders. At the same time, their leaders cannot resist trying to use them and thus being used by them as they are tossed in this Levantine pool at whose centre swims the largest shark in the Middle East. The problem seems to be that everyone is suspicious – in this game of sectarian checks and balances, the slightest perceived gain by group X is seen as a massive intrusion or gain at the expense of group Y and vice versa. Given that loyalties are almost always to the clan and the group, this is the way forward. Rational people have hoped the system might be tempered by common sense and a secular method evolve: many Lebanese have suggested it. But sectarianism is entrenched in modern Lebanon and would always emerge at some point in the political order.

This is why Hezbollah is important. It is a massive entity, substituting in a way for the divided state, taking on its responsibilities. It could well be argued that Hezbollah holds Lebanon together, with some sort of dignity in adversity, rather than tears it apart. The problem is, the other clans do not appreciate it; their state-as-manipulative-plaything is gone; the Americans and Israelis do not like challenges of this seminal kind either. And the arch-enemy of the region, as perceived in Israel and the USA, Iran, is the most stalwart challenge to Western power in the Middle East, its militant expression here defined by Hezbollah.

The sheikh remains unconcerned by these dangerous eddies about him. And he has found us some cluster-bomb victims.

A sad young victim

We are spared the most harrowing sights of the victims of cluster bombs, for they are dead. Israel showered these deadly and deliberately child-attracting weapons over southern Lebanon in the last days of the 2006 conflict as George Bush and Tony Blair delayed imposition of the inevitable UN Security Council ceasefire. They were giving Israel time to make up some of its losses against 'the terrorists'. Many of these, perhaps most of them, remain less than a year after the fighting ceased.

These devices vary in size and design, but their essential task is to spray the area around them with tiny 'bomblets' which in turn explode and pepper anyone near with lethal shrapnel. Some explode in the air or on impact, but many do not – lying there like mines (now banned) and just as lethal. The UN has put posters in Arabic all over walls inside and outside public places and in the streets throughout the south, showing the different models and giving stern warnings to people not to go near them. But people, especially children, are curious and careless.

The two homes we visit are full of children, dignity and calm. In the first, a view of Mount Hermon, Jebl Sheikh, and the occupied Golan Heights visible to the east from the balcony, a young mother and her five children sit quietly and talk to us. The small boy who discovered a 'bomblet' is almost recovered and seems untroubled now. There are some scars on his leg, well short of serious disfigurement or disablement. (I think to myself that the very sight of a Briton should drive them into a towering and avenging rage. It would certainly be hazardous for an Arab whose country had connived in the littering of dangerous explosive devices across London to visit a home in, say, Camden Town. Instead, as ever, I am offered sweet tea, fruit gums, chocolate and biscuits and open conversation.)

It is almost as if this wicked hazard of cluster bombs is just another facet of life in the south, as we in London or Birmingham or Bristol might be irritated by a new set of speed bumps or a quarter per cent rise in the Bank Rate: it is all ultimately ridden with calm, adjusted to as part of the historical pattern of life and death. The Blitz in 1940–1 wartime Britain lasted less than a year; the doodlebug bombs and V-2 rockets that came at the end, in 1944 and 1945, were devastating but brief in duration, and for those under them at least the end was known to be in sight.

Here, the war is endless: sometimes it is up-tempo war, as it were, as in 1978, 1982, 1996 and 2006; sometimes it is 'routine' shelling and air raids; sometimes it has been occupation and incursions; sometimes, most of the time now, it is animated suspension as everyone wonders when the next round will begin and in which category of aggression. It has been like this for 40 years. Yet the people are stoic.

It is slightly different at the house of the next victim. Again, this is a big family living in plain circumstances inside a walled interior. We gather round a table in the little area as tea and sweets are brought. The mothers and aunts sit with us, the men stand and watch, and the children play around our feet. A young boy, Hassan, eventually emerges with his mother, a studious boy of perhaps 13, but seeming in his gravity and grace much more mature than those years might imply. It quickly becomes evident that he is a thinker and a reader in the making, way ahead of his peers intellectually and destined for great things in Beirut or beyond if he ever has the chance; but there is no arrogance or aloofness with Hassan. It is clear that all his family admire and love him for himself.

It is surprising he can bring so measured and thoughtful a manner to the proceedings. In fact, it is deceptive. His mother describes how some children found the device a few doors down the street and, playing with it, exploded it, so that the force of it struck down Hassan but left them unscathed. Hassan, still disabled but not without hope eventually of full recovery and perhaps proper completion of his education, listens quietly to a story he knows well. Then I see tears in his big eyes; quiet tears. He wipes them away. Sharzad is crying as well. I am tempted.

Her tears and my incipient ones are not tears of anger or regret, or of sadness, but of bitter frustration. Why did they send a cluster bomb for Hassan, and all the other Hassans? Hassan's tears are of sadness.

He is too young yet to wonder at the injustice, but old enough to know his life has been put at risk by something beyond his comprehension. That must make him sad. As he grows up, and perhaps goes on to university, he might overcome his sadness; but on the other hand, in the mind of an intelligent young man the memory of what happened to him, of how nearly he was brought low, and how others like him were killed or brutally maimed, might channel today's tears of sadness into a more constructive – or destructive – anger. Who could be surprised at that?

We make our apologies and shake hands with Hassan, who smiles, and limps back indoors as we drive off into the approaching dusk and the darkening, rocky hills of the Arqub. After half an hour or so travelling parallel with the Israeli border, Galilee just over the minefields, tank paths, razor wire, watchtowers and electronic warnings, and the UN patrols gliding up and down between the two sides, we stop to look up at what is left of the battlements of Beaufort Castle, built by the Crusaders in the twelfth century. Like Hezbollah, the Palestinians, the UN soldiers so far from home and ourselves, it too peers down into Galilee, where nothing much seems to be happening but where menace sits like an animal among the pines and fir trees. When I first arrived in Lebanon in 1974 the PLO's guerrillas held the indomitable and, it appeared, impregnable Beaufort ruins, from where they could, and did, lob missiles into Israel and maintain a hawk's eye view of Israelis – soldiers, farmers, kibbutzniks – going about their business.

The Israelis hurled the Palestinians out in the invasion of 1982, a heroic military enterprise that meant commandos scaling the sheer cliffs, a sheer hundred metres or so, while above the Israeli air force reduced the standing remains to rubble. No one is there now. There is nothing to be in, only the ruins, the detritus of a once-magnificent Norman castle. These days there are more sophisticated ways of looking into Israel.

The People's Republic of Tyre

12

Foreigners are supposed to get government and Army permission to travel south of Sidon. It is for their own safety, it is said. This may be so. All writers and journalists must obtain passes on a daily basis to visit the many Palestinian camps in the south, the large Rashidiyeh Camp near Tyre, for example, and the very biggest, Ain el-Hilweh, which is a large and troublesome district of Sidon, on the edge of the city centre. I want to go to Tyre, which is about 30 miles south of Sidon, and some 20 miles north of the Israeli border.

Thus, my driver and I are in an army barracks on the edge of Ain el-Hilweh camp, waiting in line with scores of workers, many of them Syrian, seeking work in and around the south, mostly on the many reconstruction projects that are being mounted in the wake of last year's Israeli invason. Others are seeking to visit relatives or friends inside the camp itself, which is perpetually surrounded and guarded at its various exit points by the Lebanese Army. The heyday of the Palestinians in southern Lebanon, where the Cairo Accords of 1969 made them free to roam where they like, armed or otherwise, are long over. The PLO was relieved of its heavy weapons in 1991, after the end of the civil war, treated as just any other Lebanese militia, though all the camps are awash with small arms and explosives.

In the barracks I note, as ever in the Arab world, that as a foreigner I am treated with relative deference (I am also over 60, which helps in a region where respect for the ageing has not yet been expunged), unlike the poor, shabby workers lining up for their passes to commit hard labour on roads, bridges and building sites. They are examined by the panel of officers behind their desk with – if they are lucky – careless scepticism. As we walk downstairs with our day passes (which we are never asked subsequently to produce), I see a man sitting on a bench, next to a police officer, who has obviously had a beating. He looks resigned, as if he not only expected it to happen but would not be all that surprised if it happened again. Whether it is the military police who beat him or rescued him it is impossible to say.

My guess is that he is a Syrian or more likely a Palestinian who found himself in the wrong place at the wrong time, an easy qualification to meet in southern Lebanon. Especially now. The army and the security forces are particularly alert (it is late June 2007) as there is fighting in its fourth week at a Palestinian camp in the north, between the army and Palestinian and Sunni Muslim extremists who have taken refuge there. Some of the insurgents may have come from Ain el-Hilweh, where Sunni Islamic extremists, Salafists, Wahhabis, Al-Qaeda enthusiasts and the like are trying to establish themselves. There is also perennial trouble in Ain el-Hilweh between the Palestinian factions, including the two main political parties, Hamas and Fateh, who had a serious confrontation in Gaza in the first half of 2007. Hamas won, leaving Palestine in even greater chaos and uncertainty than ever. The rivalries spill into the Lebanese Palestinian camps, but here Fateh is probably the stronger faction, unlike in Gaza.

We motor down on the new highway, turning right on to the old road to Tyre after about half an hour. We cross the Litani, that river so much a focus of Israeli attentions, and stop briefly at the army checkpoint that guards the bridge. It occurs to me that if anyone well armed really wanted to take or destroy the bridge, as the Israelis did in 2006, or as Hezbollah might in some notional future civil strife, the army checkpoint would be wise to disappear before it was disappeared. As in so many aspects of Lebanese life, the Army patrols cautiously and does so where and when it can with the consent of the people. In the north, in 2007, the Army was able to use its firepower against the militants of Nahr el Bared, the Palestinian refugee camp north of Tripoli, because they were outsiders, or seen as such. (The Army was fighting bravely. The bad news was that at this stage it was not making much progress and was losing too many lives; the good news is that it was winning enormous popular respect across the population. In the end, its victory over the dissidents in late 2007 helped Michel Suleiman enormously, as army commander, in exerting his authority and popular appeal and winning the 2008 election.)

Tyre is a unique entity in Lebanon – an ancient port, a Canaanite city state, a place of sea-faring and mercantile trade for millennia, a seat of the Phoenicians (birthplace of the fabled Dido) with their possessions in Carthage and their debts to the Persians, Greeks and Romans, all of whom seized it. Essentially, though – for the past 2000 years or so anyway – the people of Tyre and its hinterland have been of west-Arabian stock. (The Phoenicians may have taken their name from the eponymous bird that burns itself to death then rises from its own ashes, as Tyre has done so many times in its long years of alternating prosperity and conquest.)

Greater Tyre, with about 40,000 people, is largely Shi'a, unlike the other coastal city states – Sidon, Beirut, Byblos, Tripoli – and Shi'a numbers have grown steadily in modern times. People returned from wealthy ventures abroad, mainly in West Africa, in the mid-1970s, awash with money after the oil price boom; people also fled to this relatively safe enclave from the troubled areas around Beirut, where the civil war was at its most consistently severe, and from nearer the Israeli border, where there had been a strong Palestinian guerrilla presence and concomitant Israeli shelling and air raids.

The city was not so safe later on, during the second Israeli invasion of 1982, when Tyre was bombed and then occupied until 1985. The Israelis did not include this area and the Palestinian camps nearby for the whole period their long-term 'security zone', from 1978–2000. In the south, only from 1982 to 1985, did they occupy Lebanon from the frontier with Israel to the Awali river, north of Sidon, thus including Tyre.

The old city, around the port, is home to about 7000 people, half of whom are Shi'a and a quarter Christians of different sects. The others are mostly Sunni. The Christian district is a dense one of narrow alleyways and ancient houses, at the south-western end of the harbour. This is all protected now by UNESCO diktat – nothing can be pulled down or changed unless it reflects the existing character of the old town – and it is dotted with churches and shrines, Maronite, Catholic and Greek Orthodox. Sitting by the quay fishermen repair nets, fix bait and drink coffee after their overnight sojourns in the bay. Sailboats bob in the harbour and motor boats chug in and out and past the long sandy bay. Out there is the wide world of the Mediterranean and beyond, which these people's forefathers explored, traded with and emigrated to, founding empires, settling and returning, as Lebanese when they returned as the day they left, but with more knowledge of the outside and the other. Now Israeli patrol boats lurk. Trade is minimal. This world has been turned in on itself.

The large Christian minority of Tyre means that beer, wine and arak accompany the fish and *mezze* in the bars and cafes around the harbour. To the east of the Christian area runs a narrow road connecting the harbour, near the government House, or Serail, to the promenade that runs south west then eastwards around Tyre. On the west side of the road are Christians, on the east, Muslims. It is known, jokingly, as the 'Green Line', but this is a Green Line no one has fired across.

A friend, a local man, tells me that, although Hezbollah is becoming more powerful in Tyre, many local Shi'ites, like himself, are secular, not particularly enamoured of Hezbollah. So far, he says, the easy-going way of life in and around the port, the availability of drink, mixed bathing, women in bikinis on the beaches and at the pools and in normal western dress in the streets, continues uninterrupted. Tyre, if easier days were ever to come for Lebanon, would benefit mostly from tourism, from elsewhere in Lebanon and abroad, for not only is the atmosphere welcoming and free, but the beaches are endless and unspoiled and, at present, sparsely populated.

My friend and guide cheerily tells me, 'Here in Tyre you can still have cold beer and hot women.' We opt for the former and lunch in a secluded restaurant in an old walled house overlooking the bay, the odd ferry or fishing boat gliding by glimpsed through the palms, an ancient lighthouse just beyond the *belvedere* in the gardens outside, tipping down to the shore. It is idyllic, a scent of Durrell's Alexandria or the Jaffa of the 1930s and early 1940s.

No one else is here but us two, the driver and the small staff. We sip beer and snack on *mezze* and grilled red mullet. The upstairs room is wide and cool, with long windows looking out to sea. In the big open room downstairs the driver chooses to eat away from us, chatting with the patron. There are six of us, including chef and waiter, in a famous establishment that can easily hold 200.

The economic outlook is not healthy. The fishing boats that lie moored here dare not venture far out to sea for fear of the Israeli navy, which more or less blockades the south Lebanon coast permanently. The little Lebanese fleet is not equipped for deep-sea fishing. Overfishing, including old habits like fishing with dynamite (banned since the 1990s but still happening) and newer ones, as in too-finely meshed nets and pollution, have depleted the stocks of this part of the eastern Mediterranean. Tyre has been rescued to some extent by the local battalion of the UNIFIL force, the Italians, who buy their produce locally instead of importing it, as do their colleagues in the other national units. The port is still the conduit for the import of cars. This goes back to the days when Beirut port was shut off for so long, and somehow the concession has stayed local. But in general, the pickings are thin. I would not know it from my guide, a wiry middle-aged man in slacks and shirtsleeves who looks ahead to the days when all this is over and Tyre flourishes again, with trippers, tourists, guided tours of the ruins and more bikinis.

Tyre has always had a raffish quality. It was something of a haven during the civil war, run by an alliance of leftists and Palestinians, hence the name it acquired, being well beyond any one group's or state control, of 'the People's Republic of Tyre'. The Palestinians and the leftists did not always get on. Two wrecks in the harbour, one just visible, were the results of quarrels in the late 1970s between different factions, probably Palestinian, over incoming cargoes and who was to benefit from the 'port duties', or *baksheesh* – in one case arms and ammunition, the other wheat. When the disputes were not resolved satisfactorily, the aggrieved party onshore shelled the vessels and sank them. In the case of the arms, the Tyre fishermen profited from the exchange by hiring themselves out as divers to retrieve what weapons they could.

No arms arrive these days. The Israeli patrol boats pay close attention to what they see steaming towards Tyre.

Jobs in Tyre are few, opportunities for the young, small. Fishermen cannot any longer afford to educate their children as they used to, fitting them for better things, in the way Welsh miners were once so determined to do for their children. The fishing industry is too depleted for the children to find much future there. Many youngsters leave to find jobs and opportunities in and around Beirut or further afield. Hezbollah, with its wealth and organisation, has increased its influence in the city by employing people, but the leader of Tyre, I am told, is a popular Amal man. Amal retains some influence in the city. There appears to be a balance of interests.

Tyre has in the past 50 years acquired and retained a leftist flavour. There is little regard here for the capital and the men in suits who, in the local view, run matters for their own benefit. Tyre was much radicalised by the presence, from 1948, of the three Palestinian refugee camps nearby. It was in Tyre that the Arab National Movement, led by Dr George Habash, a Palestinian physician and Marxist who had studied at the AUB (the Middle East's London School of Economics in political terms), came into being in the 1950s. His movement later evolved into the small but powerful and militant PFLP, which was leftist, secular and mixed intellectual vigour with guerrilla tactics and occasional terror operations inside and outside the region in the late 1960s and 1970s. (The PFLP is much depleted now, but retains influence far beyond that which its numbers would imply.) Until 1958, Tyre had been run by conservatives, mostly from one family, but they were turfed out of power after they backed the pro-Western and venal government of Camille Chamoun in the brief civil war of that year.

Maybe it is because it is early summer when I am there, but a cheery atmosphere seems to prevail. Work is under way to restore damaged buildings going back to the Israeli invasion of 1982, on mosques, churches, go-downs, a museum and on one Greco-Roman site in the middle of the town, not far from the port, where two columns now prone in the dust are to be re-erected. 'These pillars had managed to stay upright for 2000 years, then the Israelis came,' says my friend.

The UNESCO rules about restoration mean that expanding living accommodation in the port is impossible, which disproportionately affects the Christians. Unlike the Shi'a majority, the Christians do not possess property in the hinterland around Tyre – they are townspeople; so they cannot move into the suburbs or nearby villages as their families grow. To solve this, a Lebanese NGO, headed by Yusuf al-Khalil, a highly intelligent and forward-looking denizen of a Tyre family, who is a senior official in the Lebanese Central Bank (and who has filled me in expertly on Tyre, though if there are errors they are mine, not his), is building a block of flats in the city that will eventually house 60 Christian families, which I suppose would mean some 300 people.

Tyre's separateness is emphasised in that once it was an island, but now juts out to sea as a little peninsula. The most impressive Greco-Roman ruins sit at the south-eastern edge of the city. Alexander's Gate is here and the remains of the causeway he had built so that he could capture Tyre. Next to it is the vast hippodrome on one side, and on the other the graves of Greek soldiers with the names and tributes in Cyrillic script still visible. Beyond this, there is the bay to the south, making a deep sweep more than halfway down to the Israeli frontier, at its northern edge a base for the UN soldiers and their vehicles.

During the 2006 invasion, Tyre was largely spared and became a relatively safe and intact base from where the press corps could venture into the war zone. One building destroyed, with Israeli accuracy (this time), was the Nabil Kaouk edifice, right in the centre of the town, not far from the main street that runs from the port towards the outskirts and where Tyre does its marketing. The building is in one of the little roads and alleyways that shoot off the high street.

Sheikh Nabil Kaouk is Hezbollah's chief operative in the south. He and his aides had left the building long before the raid came, as did Hezbollah officials and leaders almost everywhere. They well knew that their offices had been located and would be targets. Lebanon has eyes everywhere. There could have been few people in the city who did not know where Hezbollah's HQ was. That meant Israel knew. Its new HQ is equally easily spotted and pointed out. If I know where it is, so does Mossad (and it was not I who told them).

The only death in the raid was an old man who lived next door and was in his garden when it happened. It is a miracle in a way. This part of Tyre seethes with people, shopping, meeting, haggling; women in black chadors (gowns that cover them completely, showing all the face but not the hair) and *hijab* chattering with young women in short skirts and jeans and gaily printed blouses and sweaters; men as ever idly watching the world go buy, drinking coffee, flogging cheap clothes with unlikely fashion-house tags, tampering with cars, sitting astride scooters, careless of the fatal landscape they inhabit.

Another building, near the biggest ancient site, on the southern edge of Tyre, was victim to a less accurate enterprise. The Israelis put one of their 'smart' bombs through the roof, piercing the roof and all the floors without exploding – until it reached the basement, where it was detonated, killing ten people in a shelter. The bomb may have been smart, but not its aimers, unless they did not care particularly. This was not a Hezbollah lair but a Lebanese Civil Defence office. The people killed were non-combatants. Local suspicion is that the Israelis saw a lorry carrying digging equipment and pipes near the building and mistook it for some sort of anti-aircraft device or mobile rocket-launcher.

For all their military skills and superb technology, it is surprising how often the Israelis mistake cameramen for gunners, civilians for terrorists and ambulances for armoured personnel carriers.

Other than this, there was an Israeli raid on a Lebanese Army post just outside Tyre, which killed one Lebanese soldier and destroyed a tank and two buildings. This was apparently a failed kidnap attempt. And inevitably the Litani river bridge was targeted, presumably to stop Hezbollah forces moving about. This enterprise failed as well. The only people and vehicles seriously inconvenienced were civilians in cars, buses, taxis and trucks, and ambulances and heavy-lifting rescue equipment.

It is dreadful to reflect in this way, but war and isolation have preserved Tyre and its sites and personality, saving it from the depredations of tourism and development that have happened further north and 100 miles or so across the sea in Cyprus. Tyre reminds me a little of Kyrenia, in northern Cyprus, in that one can see how it once was – except that in Kyrenia what I call 'the Paphos effect' is working: the loveliness, the quiet Mediterranean ease of the place, the stillness of the sea and the gentle to-and-froing of fishing boats are beginning to be swamped by the onrush of hotels, holiday flats, stores of tat and cheap restaurants and bars, and the trippers, not to say the men with concrete, only too ready to accommodate them, and the politicians with the permits in their turn always willing to co-operate, at a price. In a permanently peaceful Middle East, Tyre would go the same way of so many of its overdeveloped Mediterranean neighbours.

I like Tyre as it is; but it is a selfish attitude. I take solace from the knowledge that I will be dead before it changes much. A 'permanently peaceful Middle East' is some way off.

The Imam's sister

At the south-eastern tip of Tyre and at the north-western edge of the long stretch of sand sits what looks like a modern, elegant, white-stone university campus, its sides dotted with palm trees. This is the Imam Sadr Foundation, an iconic institution in the south, now spreading over some 30,000 square metres, founded in 1962 by the man who awakened the Shi'ites of Lebanon to political activity and self-realisation after centuries of neglect, impoverishment and exploitation. He was, and many like to believe still is, Imam Musa Sadr.

To the writers of news and history, but not to his devotees and family, who are legion, he is the *late* Imam Musa Sadr. His sister, Rabab, a handsome middle-aged mother of four young men, is president of his foundation, an area of peace, study and reflection. She carries the torch for her brother and has done so ever since he disappeared in Libya in 1978. The official foundation booklet says simply that the Imam 'was forcefully disappeared in August 1978 during an official visit to Libya'. Those who do know what happened to him or were responsible, inside or outside Libya, have never revealed the facts to the wider world. It is more of a mystery than who killed Hariri.

Characteristically, Colonel Gaddafi, now apparently a much-admired statesman in the West since he agreed to go quietly and confess to his country's alleged involvement in the Lockerbie Pan Am bombing in 1988, has never revealed all he must know about the Imam's final hours, and he keeps changing the stories he does tell: Imam Musa Sadr was never in Libya; he was, but was captured by Palestinians; he was a good man; he was a bad man; and so on. Anyone familiar with the Colonel's electrifying meanderings will not be surprised by this, but it all adds to the nearly 30 years of grief felt by Mrs Rabab Sadr Charafeddine and the rest of his surviving family and millions of admirers.

Many still expect him one day to reappear, another missing Imam, another messiah awaited. And, naturally, to all Shi'ites and many others he is another martyr – a leading one in Lebanon's pantheon, up there with Rashid el Sol, Kamal Junblatt, Bashir Gemayel and Rafiq Hariri – his eminence as a revered holy figure lending the Imam added tribute.

Rabab wears a patterned *hijab*. All the women working in and flitting silently and gracefully about her offices are in Muslim modest dress and headscarves. My Persian friend Sharzad does not cover her head. No one takes any notice.

Rabab's and the Imam's great-grandfather lived in Lebanon, a religious scholar, a Sayyed, a descendant of the Prophet, doing good works and preaching his religion, but in the end the Ottomans denied him permits for his various ventures. They threw him into Acre jail (later on the British would incarcerate Zionist terrorists in the same calaboose). He escaped, probably because the guards took pity on a good and holy man and left the gate open. He then headed for Iraq, home of the great Shi'ite Holy Shrines of Najaf, Kerbala and Qadamiyeh (in Baghdad). Different elements of the Sadr family went in different directions, spreading the word, seeking knowledge, as Rabab puts it. Eventually the father of Rabab and the late Imam,

Sayyed Sadreddin al Sadr, found himself in Iran, where he married Safiyeh, the daughter of a *Mushtaheed*, a man so religiously learned that he is qualified to teach, in the eastern holy city of Mashad. They produced ten children, of whom six are still alive.

This story of family, religious journey, jail and exile well illustrates the close and complicated historical connections between the Shi'ites of Lebanon, Iraq and Iran, the intermingling of Arab and Persian, a fusion our leaders in the West seem incapable of understanding or unravelling intelligently, or perhaps unwilling to recognise, preferring to measure it all in the calibrations of power-bloc politics, laced with 'Islamism' and spiced by the 'War on Terror'.

When the chief Imam in Lebanon met Sayyed Musa Sadr in the mid-1950s, he invited him to come to take over after his death, which is exactly what happened, in 1959. His sister Rabab followed him in 1962, and they set about what would nowadays be called raising consciousness among the deeply oppressed and ignored Shi'ites of south Lebanon and the Beka'a Valley; not only that, but organising and helping them and persuading wealthy Shi'ite landowners and businessmen to fund schools and scholarships for the young, making the people aware that they had the same rights as the Christians and Sunnis who ran Lebanon but, essentially, ignored the Shi'ites as if they were of, even in, another country.

To the very religious Sunnis, the Shi'ite Lebanese were not only poor but apostate, a continuing and increasing source of friction in the twenty-first century as Islamic extremism, Wahhabism, Salafi'ism, resurge across the Arab world, funded by Saudis, spreading out of Saudi Arabia into Iraq, Pakistan, Afghanistan, Lebanon and beyond, inspired by the failure of Arab states and institutions and the ascendancy of an aggressive and intrusive West. As for most of the Christians, the Shi'ites were poor Muslims taking their rightfully apportioned and deserved place at the bottom of the heap, and out of sight or mind.

Despite these prevailing attitudes and prejudices, the Imam did manage by the force of his personality, brain, energy, enthusiasm and religious inspiration, allied to his pragmatism, to persuade the more outgoing and outward-looking members of other sects to join forces with him and to work with the Supreme Shi'a Council he formed in the 1960s. Here he brought professional men together and organised a census to demonstrate just how large the Shi'ite population was in comparison with what was thought (there has been no official census in Lebanon since 1932; it is considered too hazardous in terms of what the sectarian balance might really be shown to be). Essentially, he tried to funnel money from the few wealthy to the many poor.

This was not popular in some circles, but he persisted; and he always insisted that all Shi'ite activities come under the umbrella of the state. He also formed a committee of all the faiths, members from all the professions and intellectuals. Out of this came his Committee for the Dispossessed, which was supposed to help *all* Lebanese overtaken by poverty. Gradually, his activities became more and more political and eventually he created his Amal movement.

I recall a senior British diplomat calling me up one day, sometime in mid-1976, at the height of the civil war. I was quite excited, expecting over drinks at a deserted Captain's Cabin in Ras Beirut some epochal, even scoop-providing revelation about the fighting. In my ignorance and in my obsession with the immediacy of the war and journalism I was disappointed. 'Watch out for the Shi'ites,' was the burden of the diplomat's lunchtime message, and he went on to explain about the new power that was beginning to burgeon in the land. I had very little idea what he was getting at. All most of us foreign journalists could digest in those heady and violent days were the five or six main fac-tions of PLO fighters, their allies among the Muslims, Druze and some Christians, and the two or three Maronite parties and various militias fighting against the Palestinian alliance.

Except as victims of Christian ethnic cleansing in east Beirut, the Shi'ites did not appear to figure, though many were fighting alongside the Palestinians and the National Movement (the alliance of the Muslim–Druze–'Left').

The British diplomat was right. We were only two years away from the Islamic Revolution in Iran, the emergence of Amal on to the Lebanese landscape as a serious political party and active militia, and more, much more to come as Shi'ite politics and the Iranian model transformed the region. By the end of the 1970s the Shi'ites were claiming the attention of the Lebanese in particular and the Arabs in general, and the Americans were working hard for their suppression. In the meantime, in Lebanon, Imam Musa Sadr had, to a large extent posthumously, brought shape and political articulation to his people, beginning the long struggle to lift them out of misery and subjection, though the form it was all ultimately to take in Lebanon, as Hezbollah, was unforeseen by him and probably most others.

In the years leading up to the civil war he had organised peaceful demonstrations to bring attention to his people's plight. As the civil war approached and its portents began to appear, he struggled to avert the war, begging the different leaders not to get into a fight that could (and did) end in disaster. Imam Musa Sadr was more aware than most of the dangers, representing as he did a constituency that had lived close to and suffered at the hands of the Israelis since 1948, all of it increasing in intensity from the late 1960s onwards.

He knew that chaos in Lebanon would be bound one way or the other to involve Israel. As it turned out, Israel became involved one way *and* the other. Not only did it help at different times and in different ways Christian fighters opposed to the Palestinians, but it began forming the bases of its own raft of quislings and military support on Lebanese soil. Imam Musa Sadr failed to halt the civil war, but as its first phase gentled down with the entry of a largely Syrian Arab peace force in late 1976, his Amal movement gained strength.

Alas, someone, somewhere, was not happy about this. Many people were not happy about the Imam, and this was just before the firestorm of Islamic Revolution devoured Iran and Arab and Western peace of mind alike.

In 1978, Imam Musa Sadr began a tour of Arab states, trying to convince the different leaders that they should stop their indiscriminate support of their chosen Lebanese factions and, instead, throw their weight behind the government, the country. He was well received, for example, in Algeria, where President Boumedienne advised him to go to Libya. The Algerian telephoned Colonel Muammar Gaddafi to say he should receive the Imam. The visit was arranged. The Imam duly went. Since then, there has been no news of him.

Rabab, his sister, sitting in her modern office in the hexagonal HQ of the Imam Sadr Foundation, surrounded by telephones and computers, all the appurtenances of a flourishing enterprise, cannot bring herself to believe that he is dead. She says she cannot believe something bad has happened to her brother, especially living as everyone does in a miasma of unknowing and bewilderment. 'In this matter,' she says, 'I have to let my heart rule my head. We are still waiting for him to come back.'

She says that, although he was a man who hoped for peaceful solutions, he believed in force when necessary and would thoroughly have approved of Hezbollah and the resistance. These words are carefully and clearly stated by a dignified woman of late middle age who is careful not to become involved in Lebanese politics or speak publicly about them, despite many requests for her to lend her name and authority to various political lists and causes.

A drive through any Shi'ite area, south Beirut, the Beka'a Valley to the east, near Syria, or the south of the country, reveals the Imam as one of a trinity of Shi'ite leaders, icons, if I can use the word, on the posters of the revered: himself, Ayatollah Khamenei, Sheikh Nasrallah. Occasionally, Sheikh Nasrallah – he is always there, the constant visage – appears alongside Ayatollah Khomeini, who as father and progenitor of the Iranian Islamic revolution is thus the ultimate founder of Hezbollah itself.

The existing and intensifying factionalism in Lebanon concerns Rabab, especially the growing divide between Shi'a and Sunni, not only in Lebanon but across the region, fuelled and encouraged by short-sighted Arab leaders, in Jordan and in Saudi Arabia, for example, who do all they can to demonise Iran, its Shi'ite followers and Shi'ism in general. They are also concerned at the growing power of their old foes the Persians, Iran's integral role in Iraq, especially in the oil-rich south, its influence in the Gulf in general and with the Palestinians, its rumoured acquisition in the not-too-far-distant future of a nuclear weapon, or the ability to develop one, and its already formidable array of long-range missiles. At another level is religious conflict. This is not difficult to create and then exacerbate. Many ordinary Sunnis regard the Shi'ites in much the same way as, say, a devout Roman Catholic might a Methodist or Presbyterian, not perhaps *in extremis* as apostates or enemies, but as 'other' and outside true Islam.

In troubled times it is not difficult to parlay this disdain into deeper suspicion and even dislike and so enmity, raising the spectre of apostasy. The antics and diatribes of the President of Iran, Ahmedinejad, much exaggerated and emphasised by the Western media but crude and aggressive nevertheless, are a populist and aggravational response.

All this was what the Imam tried so hard to avoid, says Rabab. If the USA would revoke its declaration of war on the real Middle East and get over its paranoid obsession with Iran, this Shi'a–Sunni divide would fade back into the ideological deliberations and arguments of sheikhs in seminaries, and avert holy war between the two main branches of Islam.

I suppose that in the West the image of southern Lebanon and Shi'ites that most readily springs to mind, thanks to the simplicities of television and the shallow, skittish coverage of most of the media, is of black-cloaked mullahs inciting unruly rabbles of the shrieking impoverished into battle against the forces of law and order, at close hand the masked and bandana-wearing youth of Islamic militia-men, Hezbollah, Amal, Hamas, Al-Qaeda, all brandishing Kalashnikovs and grenade launchers, all mutating into some incoherent vision of Muslim outrage and anger aimed in a comprehensive and soon-to-be launched global jihad against Israel in particular, and the West and Christianity in general.

Here, on the rolling shores of Tyre, the Imam Musa Sadr Foundation presents a different and more accurate picture, a model of a co-operative, altruistic and orderly institution, now 46 years old, and much enlarged on the Imam's early efforts. From this neatly laid out, airy collection of buildings, the Foundation works with Lebanese government Ministries, such as Health and Education, UN bodies and other NGOs, on a variety of social, health and educational projects worth some US$5 million a year.

It provides teachers and schools for some 70 children with special needs and from underprivileged backgrounds, including the many orphans and other victims of war. It trains young women as nurses and social workers. It runs orphanages, looking after about 300 parentless children. It is working on improving nutrition, especially for children, and provides health care for tens of thousands of Lebanese, via clinics, medical centres and school health programmes.

Pertinently, for this is southern Lebanon, it has worked closely with the Lebanese government and the UN Development Programme on rehabilitating some 1300 detainees released from Israeli custody. The Foundation represents in tangible form some of the principled work stemming from the new thinking, the philosophical reform and renaissance inside Islam that many of the progenitors of the Islamic Revolution, especially in Iran and among the Shi'ite clergy and in Iranian academies, have been engendering during the past 25–30 years.

It is financed by international organisations, private donors, school and clinic fees, where applicable, fund-raising dinners at religious feast-times – '*iftars*' – literally break-fasts, and by government contracts. It is nothing to do with Hezbollah *per se*, and yet it is impossible that such an institution could operate across the south without protection from and co-operation with the resistance; and the Israelis did not spare Foundation sites in 2006 at a time when, for obvious reasons, the clinics, health care and hospital services were under intense strain and the ability of Foundation members and workers to function or travel was severely restricted.

Tyre itself, however, and the Foundation HQ were not badly hit, as were nearby villages, the southern suburbs of Beirut and, indeed, myriad sites that had nothing to do with Shi'ites, the resistance or Hezbollah. A year after the invasion the institution appeared to be functioning as before. The attitude was calmly and determinedly that as described in the Foundation's annual report, in 2000–1, after Israel ended its 22-year occupation: 'The south knows its infrastructure is dismembered and it is rigged with 130,000 ready-to-explode crimes [mines, cluster bombs etc], and its institutional and social bodies are badly marginalised ... but it is OK!' If anything, the summer of 2006 reinforced both that situation report and the eternal optimism and determination behind it. A year after that war the Foundation's activities were back to normal, or what passes for normal.

In Tyre, my driver Abdullah, himself a Shi'ite, with family, friends and roots in the south, and I went for lunch in a popular and crowded downtown cafe: four shawerma chicken sandwiches, *houmous*, bread, two pepsis and a large bottle of water for two of us, at US$10 the lot. Oddly – this is Tyre, a port, a haunt of UN soldiers – you do not often see this even in the smarter quarters of Beirut: a young couple in the corner are kissing, quite energetically.

Is this a family restaurant? Not this lunchtime. The girl's midriff is bare and she is wearing very tight jeans. The man, almost certainly a UNIFIL soldier in civvies, looks extremely pleased with himself, and why not? She is a good-looking young woman, though without making intrusive enquiries it is not easy to discern whether she is local or imported, possibly from the former Soviet bloc, which exports energy to Europe and prostitutes to the Middle East.

I mention it only because, despite its colourful past, Tyre remains a mainly Muslim city and we are constantly reminded that we live in devout, modest and even censorious days, especially where Islam is concerned. Public shows of affection between the sexes have never, anyway, been a feature of Arab life. The horizontal amorousness that used to be a feature of English life in the austere and buttoned-up 1950s, even hand-holding, was rarely tried or tolerated in the Middle East.

Perhaps the fact the man is of the UN and she is, possibly, a working girl, puts them into a separate category. There is after all money to be made from the UN force, and there is not much else to finance the Lebanese these days. There are uniformed UN soldiers in the restaurant as well, all of them Italian. Down here the Italians are by far the most popular of the UN battalions, as they were of the international force that came in 1982. They have a Mediterranean way and style that puts the Lebanese at ease. So perhaps eyes are deliberately averted from this very rare display of public affection, or love for sale.

This is, after all, the People's Republic of Tyre, a hint of anarchy always in the air and a pattern of behaviour and people special to this port city, with its classical ruins and easily mixed population. I always liked it here, a place of escape and, as I have seen today, down the road, a place of hope.

The place of two crimes

In Qana, 11 miles southeast of Tyre, we are in 'the town of two crimes'. Even by the rigorous standards of southern Lebanon's sufferings during the past four decades, mostly at the hands of the Israelis, two incidents take the breath away. They were phenomenally barbaric, deliberate and cynical.

In August 1996, the Israeli artillery (closer then, being inside Lebanon) fired shells into a UN Interim Force compound in which local civilians had taken refuge during one of Israel's major attacks on Lebanon from the occupied zone in the south. It was impossible that the Israeli gunners did not know their target. The UN barracks had been there for the best part of 20 years, was well marked and Israel had early on, probably well before 1978, mapped every square centimetre of Lebanon's landscape with the most sophisticated spyware the USA could provide and pay for. One hundred and eleven civilians, almost all of them women, children and old men – we read the relevant birth dates on the tombstones laid out over the common grave in the centre of town – were slaughtered, as were 13 soldiers of the Fiji Battalion of the UN force. Inside the memorial centre there are gruesome pictures. We are not spared. In one coloured frame a Fijian soldier holds a severed leg up to the camera. The curator of this macabre but necessary museum tells us that few bodies could be pieced together, hence the common burial ground.

My dominant feeling in the midst of this gloom and depicted carnage is one of claustrophobic depression. I want to rush out into the sunlight and fresh air. But I stay and look and remind myself that I do not live here as the Lebanese around me do and wonder if they can be inured to the possibility – probability? – that it could all happen again. These people cannot rush out into the light.

After the first devastating barrage in 1996, Qana became a symbol of national suffering alongside Sabra–Chatila and the Martyrs of 1916 – yet its agony was by no means over. It was a twice-accursed place: ten years on it suffered a similar atrocity. In July 2006, the Israelis attacked from the air, bombing a building where, as before, families were seeking safety.

The building was about 50 metres from the little site where Christ is said to have turned wine into water. Broken sandstone urns lie inside the wire netting that surrounds this anonymous space, the locals saying these artefacts have survived from biblical times. Down the hill is the cave where Mary Magdalene is said to have waited for Jesus – the Roman road from Jerusalem to Tyre ran through here, but it was not safe for a Jew to enter a pagan town like Tyre.

In 2006, the Jews/Israelis did not enter or indict Tyre to that great an extent either. But in this raid on Qana they killed 29 people: among these were 17 children under ten, two young mothers, two young fathers, a grandfather and a grandmother. There were no fighters among them. Pictures of the deceased are set in rows in a vast coloured placard like a macabre family or team photograph overlooking the individual tombstones: this time, unlike ten years earlier, the separate bodies could be retrieved. The graves are laid out in neat white marble rectangles, the names and various dates of birth, but only one repeated date of death, on their surfaces, all on a lightish beige–pink parquet flooring. A black flag flies at half-mast. Nearby are the ruins of an old mosque the Israelis also bombed.

It is very quiet here. As a citizen of a country whose leader helped delay a ceasefire in this conflict and which is a close ally of the patron of the aggressor state and unfailingly supportive of the state itself, I do not feel easy in myself in this town. I am appalled by the careless cynicism that helped prolong Lebanon's agony and bring these innocent people's lives to an end; but everyone is helpful, calm and welcoming.

A little while later we are sitting on the patio of a family home, watching the children play and drinking hot sweet tea. I am staring over the head of a young mother and her four children, another on the way – 'we have big families, to man the resistance', she laughs. I am not so sure it is a joke. The landscape of Galilee is some nine miles across the *wadis*. When will Israel be back, and how? My hosts show no signs of worry. After 60 years of living next door to Israel perhaps they have become resigned. At least they have Hezbollah.

Abdullah and I journey back towards Beirut. Above Sidon, in the Christian village of Magdouche, is the church of the Lady of Mantura, perched high on a crest with its twin *campanile* standing guard by the central dome and its cross below which is a fine, painted fresco of a biblical scene. Below us is a panoramic vista of the city of Sidon and Ain el-Hilweh Palestinian camp.

In this Maronite-Catholic enclave, with its grotto, a new church rising and its gardens and chapels and a high statue of the Virgin Mary and child, the religious aura is only slightly marred by an armoured personnel carrier, a sandbagged military position looking down on the camp and a few desultory soldiers wandering about.

It is an ideal eyrie from which to espy the coast, Sidon and its Palestinians, and the route north-to-south. A priest in black robes, a good-looking man in early middle age, is sitting under a tree with six parishioners, all men, reading from and discussing a religious book – I cannot make out whether it is a New Testament or a prayer book. I am invited to join the group, but neither my French nor my Christian credentials are adequate for me to make a worthwhile contribution and I decline. It was gracious of him to ask. The Lebanese are so open and natural, yet so vulnerable. A few Lebanese visitors are wandering around the holy places and a woman prays in one of the chapels. The candles flicker in the darkness, around the sacrificial images and statues, as we peer tentatively in from the afternoon sun.

Suddenly, in the stillness, from the minarets of Ain el-Hilweh's many mosques, rise faintly up to us in our Christian habitat the calls of the afternoon prayer. Out in the Mediterranean, a few miles offshore, floats a German destroyer, part of a UN flotilla put in place since July 2006. What it is actually doing there, why it is there, except to make the international community feel better, no one has much idea. It is certainly not preventing any arms shipments arriving for the locals, as they do not acquire the bulk of their weapons by sea these days. The Israelis have seen to that. I hope the sailors are getting a tan. Germans relish the sun. And at least they can get a drink and a decent meal in

Tyre or Beirut – I am not so sure about Sidon, which is a city of mainly Muslim custom. It could have been much worse for the sailors. They could have been assigned the Persian Gulf.

Magdouche has been much fought over, its eagle-eye view of Sidon and all that city's complications and armed camps and strategic position on the route south making it a military prize. The Phalange held it first, but were evicted after the Israelis reduced their occupational depth in 1984. The Amal Shi'ite militia fought the Palestinians for it: later Hezbollah kicked out Amal. Now the hilltop town, after having been almost perpetually fought over between 1975 and 1990, is peaceful, a commanding position for the Lebanese Army.

But as we drive down the hill to return to Beirut we pass Ain el-Hilweh, on our right. Although we see and hear nothing as we travel past, when we arrive home we hear on the radio that a man was killed this day in a bomb explosion in the camp. It is just routine.

An Interrupted Afternoon

13

One of the most antagonising manifestations of the opposition for many Lebanese during the mid-2000 period was the vast tented camp in the middle of Beirut's elegant, if slightly overblown, downtown area, a mixture of fancy, *haute couture* shops, smart restaurants, soaring apartment blocks, new office complexes and wide boulevards, but also home to the parliament building and the renovated Serail, the Ottoman-built seat of government that sits slightly up the hill surveying it all.

The camp inserted itself among all this modernity in late 2006, a reminder of a simpler, angrier, underprivileged Lebanon. It took the form of Hezbollah members and supporters and, in a separate enclave, Christian backers of the maverick Maronite ex-general, Michel Aoun, who had made himself an ally of Hezbollah in the broad-based opposition. Not much was happening in the camp when I visited it in June 2007, some six months after it was planted there: flags waved, people sat and chatted, slogans were brandished, often the whole site seemed virtually empty.

I am meeting a member of the Hezbollah politburo, Mahmoud Kotami. It is mid-afternoon. My friend Sharzad and I walk through the rolls of barbed and razor wire and security and military checkpoints, past the armoured cars and soldiers and police and internal security paramilitaries, to 'Tent City',which is to continue for 11 more months. At the centre of the scene, but just beyond the tents, is the statue of Riad el-Solh, Lebanon's first prime minister, in his eponymous square and leading from it his eponymous banking street.

Just beyond him, and the tents, stretches towards the sea the brave new downtown that Rafiq Hariri built, at great expense and amid much opposition after the civil war. Its practical use has yet to be demonstrated, but the area has brought back a feeling of pride and achievement to the city, even if its beneficial effects are limited to tourists, should there ever be any, businessmen and the extremely wealthy. Because of its central location between east and west Beirut and the enormous security that encloses Tent City, shutting many access roads, it causes acute disruption to those wishing to go to these fancy areas and is a blight on Beirut's new image of itself. Whether the mass sit-in has contributed that substantially to Beirut's economic woes is arguable: any deleterious economic effects are minimal compared with the debts Hariri incurred rebuilding Beirut (and Lebanon); the damage the Israelis inflicted with their savage assault on the country in the summer of 2006; and the national stasis that has obtained ever since. It seems to me that Tent City is a symptom of Lebanon's problems rather than a cause of it. It is a symbol of the political stand-off between a Western-supported government and a Western-opposed opposition, and of the argument about how Lebanon should be governed and by whom.

As we walk to the temporary hut where we are to meet Mahmoud Kotami, we are greeted cheerily by a group of middle-aged men sitting on plastic chairs under a shade and chatting among themselves. We say hello, and one of them asks us if we are Jewish. This is always a difficult question to answer in the Arab Middle East, not because of any danger involved if one says 'Yes', but because to say 'No' seems in some way even to a non-Jew to play a game of denial.

'I am Welsh,' I say.

'We had some Jews here last week,' says one of the men. He seems non-committal, at ease about it, so I put the best gloss I can on this and assume that either some Western journalists who were Jewish or some delegation from a liberal Jewish group had dropped in for an approved look-round. (I had felt a lot more uneasy being asked this Jewish question in the offices of Sa'iqa, an extremely unpleasant, Syrian-created branch of the PLO in their offices in Fakhani, the PLO's sprawling stamping-ground, in 1976, and remember then explaining at length that I was Welsh, and what and where Wales was. This baffled the guerrillas and gave me breathing space.)

When Mahmoud arrives in his black Mercedes we shake hands and move to a great covered area, and more plastic chairs are produced as his two bodyguards hover. One of them goes off for tea and soft drinks.

Mahmoud is a neat, good-looking 47-year-old with short, greying hair and a close-cropped beard. He is in a black suit and buttoned-up white shirt, with no tie, which I take to be the Hezbollah version of New Labour's dark blue suit and red tie. He is No. 2 in the party's politburo and does a lot of the talking for them.

I point out to him that as nothing much is happening here in Tent City, it has all the tension of a quiet afternoon in Regents Park, what is the point? Are you not just upsetting everyone for no particular reason?

'This is as close as the political opposition can get to the Serail,' he says, pointing up towards government house, which the Ottomans may have built with all their subtlety and elegance, but Hariri's architects tampered with to no great effect.

'But there is no one here.'

'At any moment, if we gave the order,' he says, 'we could fill the square.' The tents will remain, Mahmoud adds, until there is a national government, that is, one that includes the opposition.

The opposition believes the existing, if fractious, Lebanese government to be exercising America's will here insofar as it can and therefore sees Syria and Iran as ideal supporters. This is the situation now (2007), though by the time this book is published there may have been a compromise. (As the book went towards publication in late 2009, a government had still not been formed, despite the election of a president in the spring of 2008, and particularly elections in early sommer 2009. The wrangling over the distribution of power described here continued.) Mr Kotami does not think all-out civil war is likely, not least because the Americans do not want it. Hezbollah knows also that no Lebanese coalition of forces alone could or would wish to take on Hezbollah. A long period of stalemate, attrition and low-level violence is underway.

I get the impression that Mahmoud is generally trying to be optimistic, perhaps because I am a Westerner. He laughs a lot and chats easily, puffing on a *nargeela*. He tells me the tobacco he is using is from Iran, the very best. He laughs again. Has he made a deft political point? (Iran does produce tobacco, I find later. I had not known that. I should have. It grows everything else across its vast climatic spread.)

But he does regard the divide between the Shi'ites and the Sunni as dangerous. The Americans are encouraging this, he says: they have tried to introduce troublesome Sunni elements, armed gangs, in other words, into Lebanon, but Hezbollah has made every effort to keep the situation peaceful. He attributes the troubles in the Nahr el Bared camp to this American interference, at least in part. Mahmoud claims some of the fighters were financed by supporters or members of the Lebanese government, or both, and this is widely suspected, well outside opposition ranks. He says part of the unit came through Beirut airport, which would have meant Lebanese government or elements-of-government collaboration, but I do not go into all this as it is very much of the moment, if symptomatic, and no one can ever prove anything. (It is later admitted that there was some Hariri family involvement in the movement of some of the units.)

I ask him if he thinks Hezbollah is being used by Iran. 'On the contrary,' he says. 'We consider what Condoleezza Rice said to be true that last July's war on Lebanon was aimed at creating a new Middle East. It was the USA Administration that was using this war to try to get at other states, namely Syria and Iran. When we fought against Israel last year we fought in defence of Lebanon, not in defence of Syria and Iran.'

But perhaps Israel would not have attacked Hezbollah unless it had arms and was a threat?

'Is it right for the US to make Israel make war on a country because it has a resistance? We have a right to have a resistance.'

Mahmoud's history shows that not all Shi'ites come from the south or the Beka'a Valley, their main original strongholds. He is from Kilmatin, one of two Shi'ite villages,in the mainly Christian and Druze area of the Mountain. (Close to Shemlan, where the British ran the famous Middle East Centre for Arabic Studies from the late 1940s until the late 1970s, when the civil war drove it out. It became widely known, perhaps a little unfairly, as the 'spy school', a name conferred on it by Kamal Junblatt). His family were forced to flee to Beirut during the civil war, in the great transfer of populations and ethnic cleansing that took place then. Now they can return safely, he says, and do. Shi'ites still live there.

Mahmoud is a well-educated man from a lower middle-class background. His father is a tailor and Mahmoud is one of ten children. He has an MA in sociology and political science from the Lebanese University and also trained as a teacher. His CV is typical of that of many other of Hezbollah's political command. He tells me that he and his colleagues began as a religious and cultural movement in the 1970s, based on the mosques, but did not fight in the civil war, which he could easily have done as a teenager.

They did not join Amal, then the only Shi'ite political force. Those who were politically active joined other parties, presumably making their peace with the PLO groups, Nasserites, or non-sectarian groupings such as the Communists or NSSP, or even the Junblattis' PPS, which was dominated by but not confined to the Druze sect. Amal may well have been for these young men too redolent of the old, patrician and often corrupt leadership of the Shi'ites, despite Imam Musa Sadr, who disappeared just as Amal was finding its feet as a politically and militarily significant entity.

But Hezbollah was not far off. It grew, he explains, out of the Islamic Revolution in Iran in 1979: 'Our first political activity was in support of the Islamic Revolution; we had demonstrations and celebrations and formed committees to support the Revolution.'

The next development came in mid-1982, when the members of this movement fought against the Israeli invasion of Lebanon, especially in and around Beirut, which was under siege throughout that summer. These young people, from the various parties and groups, were the ingredients of the nascent Hezbollah.

He believes that Lebanon is the homeland and says Hezbollah has no intention of trying to create an Islamic Republic here: 'Look, in order to prove the opposite, we recognised the Lebanon state, we took part in elections, we have deputies and we were recently in the government.' (The departure of Hezbollah cabinet ministers helped precipitate the crisis of the mid-2000s.)

Mahmoud makes a crucial point: 'The presence of Syria in Lebanon,' he says, 'was a protection for us in the political decisions of the government and for the protection of our role as a resistance. When Syria withdrew we had to enter the government in order to protect our position as a resistance and stop the efforts to disarm us.'

But Hezbollah is not Syria's poodle: 'We have disagreed with Syria in the past.' At present, however, 'our policies converge, especially as regards Israel. We have to distinguish between two things: our own national, Lebanese interest, and what is good for Iran and Syria. At the moment we believe that the interests of Lebanon converge with the interests of Syria and Iran, and our prime purpose is to defend Lebanon.' Hezbollah must therefore be in government (or at least make sure the existing government is hamstrung) to ensure the continuation of its armed resistance and rearming.

Hezbollah, Mahmoud included, is difficult to pin down on what Iran is really doing in Lebanon. I ask him the old question: is it just paying for and arming and training Hezbollah fighters and playing a major part in its reconstruction so that this Lebanese force can be an effective opponent of Israel, a constant thorn in its side, a reminder that not every Arab has caved in – thus demonstrating Iran's crucial role in the Near East? Or is it a strategic arm of Iran, displaying Iranian revolutionary and Islamic power across the Middle East and placing Iran itself as an immediate threat on Israel's borders and challenging the world beyond?

Mahmoud says Iran does not impose on Hezbollah: the war of July 2006 was imposed by the Americans, not by Iran. 'Anyway,' he says, 'the support we get is not from Iran as a state but from the *Marjah*.' (He means Ayatollah Khamenei, the real power in Iran, as Hezbollah's guide, mentor and spiritual inspiration.) This may be seen as an example of the sinuous and devious logic of which the Persians are masters. For many Lebanese, the question is, is Hezbollah the agent for some devilish plan to suborn Lebanon's tattered but special way of life? Or work at establishing an Islamic state in Lebanon? Or is it, as Hezbollah will tell you, that Iran is helping Hezbollah enable the Shi'ites to play a larger and proper part in Lebanon's affairs? This after all adds another powerful ingredient to the balance of interests of the traditional Lebanese clans. It may be some or all of these things. There is rarely one reason for any country, or individual, to take a particular course of action.

The answers to these questions are different depending on where one sits in the Lebanese spectrum and even where one sits inside Hezbollah. But can it be wrong that the Shi'ites, who have superseded the Maronites as Lebanon's largest confessional group (around 40 per cent of the population of 3.6 million), have a better and stronger representation in the running of the country? Is this not 'democratic'? And if Hezbollah did not get it for them, who did? Or would have?

If Iran's motives and its relations with Hezbollah are a mystery and a mixture, Syria's are not. Simply, it wants to reassert itself in Lebanon. It fears US determination to weaken and subdue it – to clear the way for even greater Israeli hegemony over the region. Damascus has a way of making its points in Lebanon.

As our conversation progresses in the peace and quiet of Tent City, an incident is taking place not far from us, of which we hear nothing, which re-convinces many Lebanese, if they needed such re-convincing, that Syria is still playing a violent hand in their affairs.

It is late afternoon by now, and we say goodbye to Mahmoud. He shakes hands and tells us to meet him any time, climbs into his Mercedes with his bodyguards and rolls off through the barricades. We walk through the tents and razor wire, into the nearby office block that houses the main Western news organisations. Most of the Lebanese newspapers are downtown these days as well, *An Nahar, L'Orient le Jour, Al-Hayat* and the *Daily Star* among them. Sharzad and I enter the offices of the Associated Press, where she is a reporter, and where I can check my emails while she writes up her notes and makes a few calls.

I notice that on the TV screen monitors there is the image of a blazing car wreck. Excited people and soldiers are milling round. I take little notice. There is no sound from the screens; the other editorial people in the office seem oblivious to the scenes; I am absorbed, like they are, in my own small screen. Insofar as I register the pictures at all, I suppose I just think, 'Well that's Beirut.' In fact, it may not even be Beirut; it is not at all clear. It could well be Iraq, Afghanistan, Pakistan or even library footage.

But, it turns out, it most definitely is Beirut – Beirut at this moment. Beirut a few city blocks away. As I leave the building, dusk just faintly in the sky, Abdullah the driver tells me the news.

As we had talked to Mahmoud, some two miles to our west on the sea-front, near the Ferris wheel, an MP, his son and eight other people had been killed in a car bomb explosion. We had heard nothing. It had happened at the bottom of a narrow access-way to the Sporting Club, the beach club where the politician and his son used regularly to go to swim and play cards. The bomb was expertly placed by someone who knew the familiar route the parliamentarian was taking.

As in all these cases, no one looks like being brought to justice. Accusations will be levelled this way and that according, largely, to the political sympathies of the accuser. Many in officialdom and public life will be very careful not to make any specific charges against any specific people or regimes. But it is remarked that with his outspoken record of campaigning against the Syrians, this man, Walid Eido, was careless to say the least to have gone, as he did, the same way each day to his swimming club. At the time of writing, he was the fourth prominent Lebanese figure to have been assassinated in the two years and four months since Rafiq Hariri was blown up. All these four – three politicians and one leading newspaper columnist and writer – were outspoken critics of Syria. Similar attempts were made on others, who survived. The campaign of assassinations and attempted assassinations did not stop here. Two more prominent figures were to be killed in the coming months.

By the next morning, the day of the funeral, the streets of west Beirut are already festooned with simply but elegantly designed colour posters of Walid Eido and his son, edged by the Lebanese flag. I wonder whether some enterprising Lebanese graphics agency has stockpiled posters of all Lebanese public figures, just as newspapers hold ready obituaries of living public figures.

The funeral starts from near the house where I am staying, a few hundred yards up the road at the American University Hospital. There are no signs of grief or excitement among the knots of people standing quietly in the sun outside the hospital entrance, which so many martyrs have crossed over the years. There is almost a tired resignation: 'Another day, another martyr ... another day, another bomb. What can we do?' Most of the people here are police and security. A few young people, mainly women, wave Lebanese and Future (Hariri) movement flags. The cortège eventually moves off in a dirge of sirens towards the Sunni suburb where he lived.

By the time Abdullah and I catch up with it, it is a slowly moving parade, with the coffins of the bodyguards at the front and the hearses of the legislator and his son following some way behind, escorted by leading politicians, among them Rafiq Hariri's son Sa'ad and the Druze chieftain Walid Junblatt, flanked by mourners, bodyguards, masses of supporters and a sea of Lebanese and Future movement flags.

We look down from an overpass onto the cortège as it progresses down the Corniche Masraa, the wide boulevard that leads from the sea-front of Beirut, where Walid Eido and his son were blown up, back east into the city and into the centre of the Sunni Muslim area. I think again what a rare opportunity and excellent position this bridge I am on would be for a sniper. The roads are empty as the city is in mourning, and a professional hit man and a good driver could be away with ease. However, I put the thought away. Beirut is making me morbid. Perhaps there is an understanding that funerals are off-limits to assassins. The coffins and the politicos and their families move under us, out of sight, towards the Sunni cemetery, in Cascas, where Mr Eido will be laid to rest near the myriad martyrs of Sabra–Chatila.

For the next couple of days the city is dead and nervous. When I walk along the Corniche that weekend, practically no one is there, despite the balmy weather. On the Friday night, two days after the assassination, Sharzad and a friend and I go to a popular little restaurant in a traditional Arab house, tucked away near the old Pickwick Pub in the narrow, cosy streets at the western end of Hamra. Walima does specialised Lebanese and other regional dishes at a reasonable price in a homely, intimate atmosphere. It has popular tango night on Thursdays and people of all ages and sizes wrestle with varying degrees of poise with the dance's erotic manoeuvres. Any night, but especially Thursdays and Fridays, Walima's requires early booking. This Friday, there is one other person sitting with us. I am surprised the restaurant is open at all, given the desolation in the streets. I am sure many people think we are crazy *ajnabi*, foreigners, to be out at all.

But this is Beirut. Something, somewhere, is always open, and all of us have eaten out in worse times. Perhaps what is unnerving the Beirutis is not so much the possibility of violence itself but the uncertainty. Where is *what* coming from? And *why*?

This exodus from the streets and the life of the night does not last long, though people tend to find their entertainment and dine out in their own areas now, leaving the downtown area and some of the bar streets near it either empty or undersubscribed. Within the week the streets, cafes and restaurants are filling up again around Hamra, the spirit of the phoenix in evidence. It will take a lot to defeat these Lebanese and if it has not happened yet, after all these years of death, destruction, raised and dashed hopes, flight, return and flight again, then against all expectations one has to reckon that it is in their blood and genes that defeat is just not an option.

Mr UNIFIL   14

The sight of the UN forces rolling around the south in their white, tracked vehicles and sailing up and down the coast is perhaps a reassuring one for the baffled and war-weary inhabitants of the south. There is no doubt that in its 30 years[1] the UN 'Interim' Force in Lebanon has often defused conflicts on a local scale, catching Palestinian and other guerrillas creeping through the *wadis* towards Israel (they would be returned to their units and free to have another go) and sometimes even deterring Israel and its Lebanese allies from egregious missions out of their controlled zones.

UNIFIL also brought immediate physical and medical help to broken villages after Israel's two invasions and many bombing attacks, repairing electricity lines, patching up roads and injured or sick people, being at least one benign force in a jungle of competing armed groups and shifting alliances. Its social, medical and repair services continued in more peaceable times. They were also a much-needed link between the different battalions either side of the lines, able to talk to everyone, including the Israelis, and at least on occasion to prevent or explain misunderstandings that might have led to serious confrontations.

The villagers liked the soldiers because they were friendly and a constant source, in a benighted area, of hard currency, for food, drink, smokes, clothes, mementos and all those supplies a soldier far from home needs, although in devoutly Muslim southern Lebanon at least one of those needs, women, was in short supply.

It has also to be remembered that over the years UNIFIL has taken many casualties, some 280 killed at time of writing (2007).

I often visited Irishbatt, the Irish battalion of UNIFIL, in the late 1970s and 1980s. They were cheery, humorous, generous and philosophical about what was going on around them. The food was execrable. I remember my Lebanese driver Samih politely declining an invitation to join us at table in the officers' mess when he saw what was on offer. He wisely chose to eat in one of the local cafes in Tibnine, the town where the Irish had their HQ. But the talk was good, and in the evenings, when the whisky and the beer flowed, it was even better. Not indiscreet, but honest.

I remember early on in the Irish Army's first tour, in late 1978, one of the officers telling me over a Bushmills or six: 'Tim, as good Catholics when we first came out here we had a clear view of the problem, one we'd been brought up with at school and our press. Israel was the Good Fella, and we'd be dealing mainly with Arab and Muslim terrorists. Well, I tell you, our eyes have been opened. It just is not like that.' This was only a few months after the peacekeeping force had arrived.

The Irish, the Norwegians, the Dutch, the Nepalese, the Fijians all had similarly eye-opening experiences; the most difficult and aggressive element in the region, when it wanted to be, was Israel. But they kept cool. They were brave men, with dangerous antagonists to the front and rear, all soldiers from unwarlike countries but none the less professional for that (this was in the days when the British Army was learning, *in Ireland,* just how difficult peacekeeping is, and how different from war-making).

UNIFIL was a sort of community police and liaison force in a dysfunctional, criminalised ghetto, but with very limited powers of arrest and few of prosecution. The UN soldiers could not in the end by force of arms stand in the way of an army or a committed band of guerrillas or resistance and prevent them carrying through their objectives, whether that be full-scale invasion, cross-border guerrilla raid or rocket or shell barrage. When the big events happened they were helpless. They could and did delay events but not ultimately stop them. They were and remain the international community's only way, it seems, of applying some sort of band-aid to the deep wounds of this region, which is all it ever can be: better than nothing, but nothing like good enough – 'good enough' only attainable when peace that all can agree to arrives in the region, a prospect that recedes.

The man who knows all about UNIFIL and a lot more is Timor Goksell, a former Turkish army officer, who arrived as UNIFIL's information chief in mid-1978. He became much more than that bland title indicates. I think of him as permanent under-secretary (in the British Civil Service sense) to the long line of UNIFIL commanders he served and advised during the next two-and-a-half decades. He became the eyes and ears and often the man in the middle of the stand-off for UNIFIL, for the most part living in northern Israel, where his family were safe, and crossing the frontier between Lebanon and Israel at the only official crossing point, Ras al Nakoura, UNIFIL's HQ. This consists of a few buildings and blockhouses, once the main customs and immigration post between French-Mandate Lebanon and British-Mandate Palestine. He is a charming and articulate but tough man, who speaks English very fast and very well in a growly accent.

This enthusiastic and energetic survivor of the Lebanese troubles, these days lecturing at the AUB and living in Beirut, has become a font of wisdom to newcomers to Lebanon, students, journalists, diplomats, consultants; because, while he is in effect an insider, with nearly 30 years experience of the country at its most jagged edges, he is also an outsider, a man with no axe to grind: it is very difficult in this country to find anyone so localised and informed who does not have one such implement hidden about the person.

The first time I saw him was with friends in what used to be the Nasr Restaurant, overlooking Pigeon Rock, which was floodlit. It looked splendid, sitting out in the darkening sea, one of Beirut's more peaceable landmarks. No one was ever shot or blown up on Pigeon Rock, though it could be dangerous to swim out there in the days when the Beirut fishermen used dynamite for 'bait'.

Timor was pulling at a hookah, or *nargeela*, but put it away when the waiters brought red mullet, jumbo shrimps from Senegal and sea bass from the Gulf, accompanied by arak, beer and scotch. (One cause of civil strife in Lebanon could easily be an attempt to ban smoking.)

There was so much to try to get straight, and eat and drink at the same time, in a crowd with a lot to say. Before we got onto the UN, his speciality, I asked Timor about Hezbollah, because that surely was the main phenomenon that had arrived in his patch, not even conceived until some four years after he arrived. Since then it had grown from rough and brutal beginnings in the early 1980s into a powerful resistance, and into a social system, an entity in a way in which the PLO never was and did not aim to be. (The PLO's acquisition of power was driven by circumstances, desperation and accident. Hezbollah's route was planned and purposeful and, arguably, very Lebanese at heart and root.)

Timor said there were three strands in Hezbollah – those close to Iran, those dedicated to being purely a Lebanese resistance against

Israel, and those like the present and widely admired leader Sheikh Nasrallah who realise that Hezbollah is, like it or not, involved in the local political scene. There was a big argument in the party about getting involved in Lebanese politics, but Nasrallah's argument has been that Hezbollah must take part in the Lebanese debate and be in government so as to be seen as Lebanese and legal. If it just sat there and said, 'We are strong. What are you going to do about us?', it would be regarded as illegal and non-Lebanese, a foreign body (many see it that way anyway). Hezbollah wants the opposition to have veto power in the parliament – one of the crucial issues in Lebanon's crisis of government – because it does not want decisions made against it or to be declared illegal. But the parties who support the government are scared of the Party of God because it is so strong and organised.

He says no one, least of all the Lebanese and certainly not any UN force, can stop Hezbollah receiving arms or make the organisation surrender them. No militia, not even the army, has heavy weapons to deploy to the size and scale of Hezbollah's. The Internal Security Force, which comes under the Ministry of the Interior, is perhaps one well-armed and trained unit that could hurt Hezbollah, but probably only if Hezbollah were in serious combat with the Israelis. Therefore no one can successfully challenge Hezbollah.

I take the argument on where Timor might prefer to stay off the record. The Americans, the French, Israel, the West, want to see Hezbollah disarmed. It is a central element in their plan to undermine Iran and Syria, lock Lebanon safely into the Western camp, and maintain Israel's unchallenged role as regional 'deputy sheriff'. But there are strong reasons why such disarmament is unlikely to happen, and why it would be a dangerous idea for anyone to try to make it happen.

The problem over all, says Timor, and this is a sentiment not heard publicly or probably privately from Western diplomats, is that with Syria gone there is no one to control Lebanon. So is Hezbollah doing Iran's and Syria's bidding? He does not think so.

Timor does not think Hezbollah would turn its weapons inwards on Lebanon, unless in self-defence against some assault or serious challenge by its internal opponents. (This proves to be so, in May 2008.) There is also the increasing peril within Lebanon for Hezbollah of the extremist Sunni groups, the Salafists for example, funded by Saudi Arabia, who could try to use arms and bombs against the party and its representatives and sympathisers. But as with all organisations, much depends on the leadership, which even Hezbollah's enemies believe has been expertly and deftly conducted by Sheikh Nasrallah, with the jury still out as to how or whether he nodded off a little in July 2006 and gave the Israelis their excuse to attack. Kidnapping and hostage-taking are familiar techniques in the Middle East; it is human bargaining. Israel's massive response would have been difficult to predict. Hezbollah probably thought it was still in the cat-and-mouse game with Israel as it had operated since 1996, the two antagonists observing rules of the game. He thinks there could be a problem if Nasrallah were to be killed, die or disappear.

Getting Timor Goksell back to the subject of his former employer, UNIFIL, I ask him what practical purpose it was achieving at that time. He says it was merely a makeshift gesture by the international community. It cannot do anything; it has not the power to seize or halt weapons and weapons deliveries; it can do little more than act as observer. The Lebanese Army may have won much respect in its handling of internal riots but it is not in the game in the south, except as a reassuring presence and a support for the UN. The army has no air power and is short of fuel, so is limited in all its actions internally, though it is the only Lebanese state institution that anyone trusts. According to Timor, it is all tokenism in the south. Everyone would have to move out of the way if Hezbollah and the Israelis fought a full campaign again.

There is much scepticism. A Lebanese reporter in her 30s eating with us says the March 14 boys and girls – the core of Lebanon's nascent Orange movement, supposedly on the Ukrainian model – were dismissed after two weeks, totally disillusioned. They were told by the politicians that they had done their bit with the 'Cedar Revolution' that made all the headlines, with all those fresh-faced, fashionably styled young enthusiasts waving Lebanese flags and wearing 'I love Lebanon' tokens and tee-shirts. They could get lost.

Timor saw the glamorous ladies of Beirut abandoning their beauty parlours and going downtown with their banners. One story is that someone saw a Sri Lankan maid carrying a banner that said, 'Madame Supports March 14'. By the end of March they were all back in their luxurious boxes, and the youngsters' Cedar Revolution had been hijacked. They had had their day out. They had served their purpose.

The Americans paid for the tents, the support systems and the computers, and have been ploughing in money through all sorts of democracy-pushing but essentially unreliable NGOs. All the USA is doing is paying for the converted, she says. There is no chance, says the young woman, that US money will convert a single Hezbollah supporter. (This is a view I am to hear repeated many times in Beirut.)

The next time I saw Timor was a couple of months later, with his daughter Zeinab, at the Manara Palace, a people's restaurant used mostly by ordinary Lebanese. It was just a few days after the assassination of Walid Eido. *Al-Manara* is Arabic for 'the lighthouse', and the sprawling restaurant sits by the seashore under this new Hariri-era edifice, whose tip (and beacon) was shot off by Israeli fighter-planes during the 2006 invasion. This has now been replaced. The much prettier old *manara* is just up the hill, another peaceable landmark of the old Beirut, like the Ferris wheel along the shore and Pigeon Rock, all close together.

This is idyllic Ras Beirut. I have walked through the town, through the narrow streets and down the hill through the Manara district, a quiet and wealthy cluster of old buildings and high-rise modern blocks, past the little barracks and makeshift pokey that Walid Junblatt's forces held for a while – his picture and a few of his party symbols are still evident – and down on to the wide boulevard along the shore. The waves lap against the rocks in the hot early morning June sun; fisherman perched on struts do their best to lift such fish as might have survived the poisoned waters off Beirut. Young boys swim in these waters and emerge none the worse. Children play in a supervised nursery on rides and slides, and mothers, mostly in *hijab*, play with them or leave them for a moment of release to take coffee and chat.

There are few foreigners and no *glitterati* here. They are at the Riviera Beach, which we can see just up the bay: this is where the well-heeled acquire their bikini tans, shielded from outside view, and the waiters glide with cocktails, beer and coffee among the Lebanese businessmen and politicians and their guests; where it is unlikely even the most committed bomber could penetrate, it being accessible only through a well-guarded tunnel that runs from the hotel, under the corniche, to the pool and restaurant.

In our simpler restaurant, where liquor is not served and ordinary Arab courtesies are observed, I assume we are not targets. Timor orders scrambled eggs and tomato salad for himself and his daughter and follows it up with his customary *nargeela*. I realise after talking to him for a while that I am at the head of a queue of people waiting to consult him, other journalists, also looking for a steer through the maze, sitting patiently at nearby tables.

We try to look ahead. 'Lebanon is a feudal system,' he says. 'People do as their leaders say, and the only time there was ever a moment of national unity in recent memory was when they got rid of the Syrians with the March 14 protest, after Hariri's assassination, which was generally supposed to be the work of the Syrians. However, this feeling of national togetherness was transitory and the feudal leaders soon told the March 14 brigade to pack up and go home, the old guard of the *za'im* were taking back the reins of power.'

There is as yet little concrete sign of Timor's guidelines being proved wrong. He agrees that the Lebanese had stability under the Syrians and could get on with making money and rebuilding the country. But they turned to Syria for the tiniest decisions; the president became a satrap, his country a dependency. When the Syrians were forced to leave, the Lebanese gave themselves and the world, briefly, the impression of having restored their country to themselves; but, as soon as the Syrians left, the internecine weaknesses and rivalries quickly re-emerged. 'For instance,' says Timor, 'the Syrians kept a tight rein on the Fundamentalists and extremist Muslim groups, but once they left they emerged from the woodwork.'

So why did the Syrians fail? Timor reckons the Syrians were far too intrusive after Ta'ef, which forged an end-game and post-civil war plan for the country. The Syrians were given prime responsibility for restoring order in Lebanon, rebuilding the army and internal security, overseeing institutions, making sure there were no dalliances with Israel and keeping the lid on sectarian rivalries, disarming the militias, overseeing their neighbour's return to stability.

They did all this, but in the longer term massively overdid it. In my own view, Syria could not view Lebanon as a separate entity to be nurtured and set back on its feet, independent in the community; to Syria, Lebanon is essentially, emotionally and geopolitically part of Greater Syria. Kamal Junblatt and Antoun Sa'adeh believed this too, that the region of Greater Syria would have been better off as one single state instead of being carved into four or even five distinct parts. One sage even believed that one Mandate for all would have been better rather than having France and Britain slice it to individual tastes.

The logic of this Greater Syria approach would perhaps be more comprehensible in Lebanon and in the West were the regime in Syria less oppressive and heavy-handed. That it is so heavy-handed, however, is at least partly to do with the West's open hostility to Syria and Israel's more than 40-year occupation of extensive tracts of its most fertile southern lands, in the Golan Heights. This has not encouraged the leadership in Damascus to lighten its touch.

Back to Timor. (I am becoming nervous because I can sense his next clients getting restless as I order more Turkish coffee.) The Syrians played it tough from the start, but until 2000 were under the canny oversight and control of President Assad *pere*, than whom there was no greater exponent of the art of Levantine balance and manoeuvring. His pro-consul in Lebanon was Ghazi Kna'an, who also knew how to play all the chords on the Lebanese *oud*, and was very close, for example, to Mr Lebanon himself, the late Rafiq Hariri. After 2000 and the death of Hafez al-Assad, says Timor, the Syrians, who had always tended to be too interfering and domineering, became clumsily and terminally intrusive under the inexperienced Assad *fils*, who had been groomed for office by his father during the 1990s. (This was an emergency course after his elder brother, Basil, who had been earmarked and groomed for the succession, was killed in a car crash, in 1994.) Bashar had little real political experience.

When Bashar Assad took over, Syria became even more involved in Lebanese electioneering and assembling party lists and extending presidential terms, which latter they did so controversially in 2004. This constitutional intervention, extending President Emil Lahoud's term by three years, attracted much international as well as Lebanese anger and condemnation. (Nine years earlier, Syria had made exactly the same move, prolonging President Elias Hrawi's term by the same amount. No one said a word outside Lebanon.) However, Timor points out, 'at least half the Lebanese went along with [all this Syrian meddling]'. After Bashar, the Syrians in Lebanon had a much freer hand as he found his way though the thickets of Syrian and later Lebanese politics. Ghazi Kna'an's successor as Syrian head of Intelligence in Lebanon, Rustum Ghazaleh, was a steamroller compared with the more subtle Kna'an.

Timor says: 'The USA under Bush reckons that Lebanon is a springboard for democracy in the Middle East. Having cocked it up so badly in Iraq and Palestine, Lebanon is all that is left. But they forget that this is Lebanon, where everyone plays both ends against the middle ... it's democracy *a la Liban*, not democracy as the West knows it.'

Lebanon, he says, is an ideological battleground between East and West, despite its lack any longer of much strategic value. Here I wonder. A meltdown in Lebanon could bring Syria, Hezbollah and Israel into conflict; that is possibly to describe the beginnings of a fifth Middle East war.

One of the only solid outcomes of the uncertainty since Hariri was assassinated, the Syrians departed, the country divided and a string of selected killings began of leading figures and politicians, most of whom were publicly critical of Syria, has been the emergence into public respect of the Lebanese Army. Posters have been appearing with patriotic and inspirational slogans written on backgrounds of military camouflage (it sounds crude, but it is very effective when the Lebanese artists get to work on it).

Why is this? I ask Timor. After all, on his own admission, the army is pretty constrained in its own effectiveness, even if only by lack of resources and confused political loyalties and backing.

He points to the fighting at Nahr el Bared (where, as mentioned in Chapter 12, a desperate and disparate amalgamation of foreign and Palestinian Islamic fighters were holed up and under siege by the Lebanese Army in June 2007, which itself was taking heavy casualties). It was a disaster for the beleaguered refugees, who fled, if they could. Timor points out that the army here can show its mettle fighting Palestinians and foreigners, not Lebanese; Christian, Muslim and Druze soldiers alike have been falling alongside one another. It is unlikely, Timor says, that the army could be deployed as a force again against a Lebanese faction – half the soldiers are Shi'a, and President Emil Lahoud, when he was commander, reorganised the army so that there were no longer sectarian brigades; the army rank and file were mixed confessionally. He praises the army for its delicate touch during the troubles early in 2007 in Beirut. The army was careful and talked to people. It did not use its weapons, knowing what could happen if the soldiers came down too hard on one side or the other.

Part of the reason the army went so slowly in Nahr el Bared was because it was a Palestinian camp and it did not want to alienate the mass of Palestinians by inflicting the sort of civilian casualties that a full-scale invasion would have caused. This increased the army's casualty rate.

The army is a uniquely cross-sectarian institution, more so now than in its history. It is impossible to tell whether it could hold together in the event of another civil war; but for the moment, well-tested in the streets of Beirut during civil upheavals and against extremist Islamists in that wretched Palestinian camp in the north, in an area riddled with exponents of the most extreme interpretations of Islam, it has come out well, and won the nation's respect. (Later in 2007 the army took the camp and routed, killed or captured most of the Islamic Jihad fighters, though the organisation retains a presence in Lebanon.)

After I leave Timor to his next interlocutor and walk back through Ras Beirut, I look at the young soldiers on their armoured personnel carriers and at their sentry posts along the streets, cheery, chatting with passers-by, smart, disciplined and giving an aura of sense and stability to this nervous capital. But what could they do in practice if an even more cataclysmic version of 1975 were to erupt? How to use the army is one of the most pressing questions for Lebanon's military chiefs and politicians.

Among the Believers

15

Al Dahiya means 'the suburb' in Arabic, but in Beirut the *Dahiya* means just one thing in English or Arabic – the sprawling, mainly working-class area east of the airport road in south Beirut that has grown and grown from modest and fairly rural beginnings, over the past 40 years or so, into a self-contained city with its own identity and reputation. They do things differently here.

The 'southern suburbs', to use the English phrase – because the *Dahiya* takes up the lion's share of southern Beirut and is largely though not exclusively Shi'ite – is the urban home of Hezbollah. This conglomeration of apartment blocks, small factories, workshops, shopping streets, schools, hospitals, mosques and all the artefacts of modern urban living took the full force of the Israeli air strikes in the summer of 2006. Although Hezbollah managed an efficient evacuation of the district, hundreds of civilians were killed and many buildings devastated. The Israelis struck other parts of Beirut, including bridges near the city, the sea port and the airport, but their main purpose in the city was to hammer at the heart of Hezbollah, terrify its supporters and if possible kill the leader, Sheikh Nasrallah. This would have been a dire blow for the movement – but the sheikh went into hiding and tends to remain there.

The Israelis certainly made a massive hole in the centre of the *Dahiya*; but the strike was nowhere near fatal to the organisation and the resistance. Sheikh Nasrallah survived. It reminded me of the story during the Tet Offensive of 1968 when the US Air Force threw everything it had from B-52s at Viet Cong and North Vietnamese positions outside one beleaguered American compound, only to find that after each massive air strike there would be a moment's silence and then – one lone

Vietnamese machine-gunner would pop up and start firing again. After two or three strikes he was still there. In the end, it is said, the GIs cheered him.

Sheikh Nasrallah also kept appearing, few can know from where, on his *al-Manar* ('The Light') TV station (one of the most widely watched in Lebanon), whose technicians and artefacts had gone underground with him. The scale of the Israeli attack, and its date in July 2006, may have been a surprise, but Hezbollah knew it would come one day, and they were ready and as organised for it as any professional army and civil defence force.

There are still, only less than a year later, big gaps in the *Dahiya*, bomb sites and construction cranes everywhere; but life is largely back to pre-2006 level in this extraordinary urban landscape. Everywhere I look there are signs announcing the help that the Tehran Municipality is giving; they are not just repaving roads and repairing the infrastructure, but have built footbridges across the airport highway and florally decorated traffic islands. The phrase 'hearts and minds' comes to me, except that here the concept is more than a wistful, idle, hopeful phrase, as it became in Vietnam and as it has also become in Iraq and Afghanistan.

I suppose to someone in the West who has read only of the southern suburbs as a Shi'ite stronghold and lair of Hezbollah, the image is a grim one: bearded and black tee-shirted youths with green headscarves and combat pants toting guns at every street corner, glaring at strangers; women in black chadors scurrying from school to home trying not to catch the eye of any man; cloaked and dark-eyed mullahs eyeing the pavements for any sign of deviation; thugs measuring up possible marks, especially foreigners, for incarceration or worse.

I think it is more reminiscent of the busy, run-down but cheery high streets where I live in north-west London. The traffic is more chaotic here, and the buildings more dilapidated, even those that escaped the bombs, but I am less likely here to be mugged or have my pocket picked. There is less menace than I might well find a few hundred yards from my own London house. This is just another, virtually indistinguishable lower middle-class suburb of Beirut, apart that is from the war damage and the fact that there are no Lebanese Army or Lebanese Internal Security forces visible, the only police I see being the municipality's own employees in their blue-grey uniforms. Many of the women are not veiled, and there are quite a few young, bareheaded women in jeans, tee-shirts, high heels and wearing makeup. It is quite usual to see women dressed in Western style alongside their covered-up sisters in these city Shi'ite areas. There is a shop next to the Hezbollah press office in the *Dahiya* which sells European-style women's clothes and whose plaster mannequins are bareheaded, as is the shop assistant. Once I saw two girls crossing the road near here, in their late teens or early 20s I imagine, who could easily have walked in off Piccadilly or Camden High Street, with long hair, stiletto heels and tight jeans.

Such people are in a minority. Some of them may be Christians, as many Christians still live in this predominantly Shi'ite district, some not – not all Shi'ite or Sunni Muslim girls, especially in Beirut, wear the dull coverings that have become common since Islam has become so much stronger as a political and social force and is solace or refuge or even a political statement for many women. But Western dress does not create offence or remark. This is Lebanon, not the Islamic Republic of Iran.

The main difference between this area and other, similar areas of Beirut is that Hezbollah and the institutions they have created over the years, clinics, schools, social services for the poor, help in education, welfare and health for those in need, an inchoate welfare state in fact, have done for their people what the rest of Lebanon, and the Lebanese state in particular, have failed to do; if Hezbollah had not existed it would have been necessary to create it.

Not everyone likes it. In his garden, I sit and sip tea with a Shi'ite intellectual, listening to his stories of the 2006 blitz. He is uneasy about the party. 'It is fascist,' he says, 'it is no democracy.' He and his partner fled when the first bombs fell and came back to find Hezbollah units in their property. There had been some damage, but most of his house still stood. He asked the Hezbollah fighters to leave, and they did, but he feels watched, known as he is to be antagonistic towards the party.

It is doubtful, it is true, if there is any help for those not signed up to the cause. Hezbollah is no democratic movement (but nor is it the Nazi Party roaming the streets of Berlin in the 1930s).

These two people do not support the pro-Western Lebanese government and certainly not the USA. Like most Lebanese they are totally opposed to Israel's aggressive and acquisitive attitude towards its neighbours; but it is indicative that they are cautious about Hezbollah and its are. Are there elements in it that would like to make Lebanon an Islamic Republic? Almost certainly. But do they dominate the movement? It seems not to be so, not under the present leadership of Sheikh Nasrallah and the spiritual guidance of Sheikh Fadlallah. Is it feasible that Hezbollah could or would want to launch the sort of Holy War that would bring this complicated, brilliant and contentious people under its control? All those Sunnis, Druze, Armenians, Maronites, Orthodox, the secular, the Communists, up in their mountains, all along the littoral? It is impossible such a campaign could be won.

But if Muslims fear Hezbollah might want to change this country, then from their fears I can extrapolate the depth of trepidation that Lebanese of other persuasions have of this determined movement. Have they asked themselves, however, if it is practical for Hezbollah to contemplate much more than resistance against Israel, and against its friends and against those in Lebanon who would wish to disarm and weaken it; to seek a more profound presence in government; and to look after its people, which it seems to be doing as well as can be expected in difficult economic circumstances? If it is not democratic, what party here is? For the poor of the southern suburbs especially, most of whom have over the years fled the south, democracy is not their priority.

Hezbollah is a disciplined and efficient armed political party inside Lebanon with a will of its own, answerable to it own people, not the state, but careful of the state and its own legality. It has participated in elections and in affairs of state and government during the past 16 years. The Maronites in the 1970s and 1980s had a not dissimilar reputation for being a state within a state, with their own armed forces, discipline, taxes, security, police, ports and virtual borders. To a large extent the largely Druze PSP runs its own area, though since 1990 neither of these groups, unlike Hezbollah, has been able to wield arms (openly).

Why should Hezbollah be so special? One impressive aspect of Hezbollah's professionalism and seriousness is the academic, studious front it can present to the world, in contrast to the picture some in the West are led to perceive of fanatics running wild in the Lebanese *wadis* with bombs and rocket-launchers, foaming at the mouth, thirsty for Jewish and other Infidel blood.

I go to a modern building at the western edge of the southern suburbs, in a shopping plaza and complex of office blocks overlooking the main airport road. Dr Ali Fayyad is president of an institution called The Consultative Centre for Studies and Documentation.

He is a man of about 45, in a striped sports shirt and dark trousers; he is clean-shaven with short-cropped hair. He is obviously associated with Hezbollah and his organisation is said to be very close to Iran's Revolutionary Guards, virtually the founding fathers of the Lebanese Hezbollah movement. Dr Fayyad has an elegant, spacious office which could be anywhere in the world except for the women working in the office, most of whom are in the Islamic Revolutionary uniform of chadors; a few are merely in *hijab*.

A man studies a newspaper in an outside room, at a long table. Everywhere there are neatly filled bookshelves with books in English and Arabic. I notice that Ali Fayyad has Jimmy Carter's book on 'apartheid' in Israel and the Occupied Territories and the former BBC Correspondent Alan Hart's recent volumes on Zionism being the 'enemy of the Jews'. Somewhat rarely in a Lebanese or more particularly Middle East office, there are no icons or photos of this ayatollah or that president or *marjah*, only a modern painting that I would quite like myself. I cannot see exactly what it is, but it has an air of the 1920s about it, bright colours, lodged somewhere between the abstract and the figurative. In his room there is a big polished desk with a flat-screen computer. There is air-conditioning, but it is not the season yet.

He tells me his family is from the south, a village called Taibeh, very near the border with Palestine, but he was born and brought up in Beirut's southern suburbs, a mile or so east of where we are now. He was a young man when the civil war broke out, still at high school. His father was a government employee who had eight children; Dr Fayyad has a PhD in sociology and politics from the University of Lebanon. He went to various schools before university, including in the Christian area of Ashrafiyeh. He had to leave there when the war broke out in 1975 (if he had not left he might well have had his young throat cut by the Phalangist militia).

His story, his education, his political journey are typical of the early middle-aged Hezbollah tyros of his generation. He worked with the Hezbollah movement from its beginnings in 1983 and was in charge of its education department in Beirut, supervising students at different schools. Hezbollah was active then in the wake of the Israeli invasion, although it had not been named as such. It grew out of the failure of Amal, after Imam Musa Sadr's death, and other, leftist, Nasserite, Druze and pro-Palestinian groups to be effective in resisting Israel. They were mired in localised Lebanese rivalries and politics, often manipulated by outside Arab states without care for local issues or the successful prosecution of organised resistance.

The situation in Lebanon was hopeless, especially as far as the Shi'ites were concerned. Amal was split between an Islamist and a more secular trend. Many young Shi'ite activists were dismayed that Nabih Berri, the Amal leader, had agreed to take part in the negotiations that Philip Habib, the special US envoy, had organised among the different groups to try to end the Israeli onslaught of summer 1982.

Amal, until then the main Shi'ite political formation, had in the view of these young, Shi'ite, nascent Hezbollah activists failed to confront the Israeli invasion. The Islamic organisations that were formed in the mosques did not have the means to resist Israel even though they had mass support. Hezbollah arrived to make the difference. He does not say so, but he is referring to the Revolutionary Guards and other Iranian advisers, fresh from the Islamic Revolution of 1979, their nation caught up in a war against Iraq and its Arab and Western supporters. These young men were seeking to make their revolution real, to make converts to their cause in the wider Middle East. Ayatollah Khomeini was their leader and guru, their spiritual and political creator and mentor.

What Ali Fayyad does say is that it was the Iranian experience in 1978–9 that inspired young men and women in Lebanon to resist the occupation. He repeatedly stresses that Hezbollah is primarily a resistance movement, but this does not just mean guns. It means organising political groups and teaching, taking on social responsibilities, building institutions and building and offering what the state has failed to.

The Revolutionary Guards, says Ali Fayyad, not only came to fight and train the Lebanese militarily, but also to impart social, medical and educational ideas.[1]

Hezbollah building up its own 'state' within Lebanon is nothing new, he says. And it is true. (The Maronites did it, but their resistance was against the Palestinians and their Lebanese allies on the Left, mostly Muslims and Druze, who had reinvigorated latent Maronite separatism and isolationism. The Maronites withdrew into a defensive shell. Once the Palestinians had gone, Maronistan began to crack under the weight of its own internal contradictions and its obvious need for the Lebanese hinterland. If the Israeli threat were removed completely, Hezbollah would probably also change.)

Dr Fayyad says that if the state had fulfilled its functions, its responsibilities towards all its citizens, Hezbollah would not have had to create such an entity. As such, it took many of its models from Iran, the martyrs' foundation, the construction crusade: the expansion of services in the Shi'ite areas was because of the situation on the ground, including the long struggle to evict Israel from Lebanese soil. But he adds, the *raison d'etre* of Hezbollah is to resist Israel. All else is subsidiary.

As to the concept of 'state within a state', a phrase he does not like, he says that when there is a proper Lebanese state that serves all its citizens, 'there will be no need for our services'.

Hezbollah is strong in its resistance against Israel: partly because it has the loyalty and respect of the people to whom it alone supplies vital services – they are almost Hezbollah 'citizens'. What if there was a peace, a just peace in the Middle East, and Syria, Lebanon and the Palestinians signed on the dotted line with Israel? This is so hypothetical a question in the existing torment that consumes the Middle East, Ali Fayyad does not bother to answer the question directly. Hezbollah is not interested in dream worlds. 'Israel is not ready for peace,' he says, and I know that this means not just now, or for the next few years, but ever.

However, if a peace Hezbollah regarded as inadequate were signed, it would maintain its right to continue opposing Israel. 'We would exercise our democratic rights to refuse any compromise – resistance has many levels, social, military, it depends on the situation.' What he means is Hezbollah believes that there can be no solution in the Middle East until Israel becomes one democratic state, for Muslims, Christians and Jews. (In this situation, unlikely in the foreseeable future, unattainable in the views of many, especially Zionists, Hezbollah would no longer have anything to resist and would become a powerful but purely political and social movement.)

What does worry Ali Fayyad – this theme yet again, as from so many quarters – is the growing divide that is happening across the Middle East between Sunni and Shi'a. He describes it as a repercussion of the crisis in Iraq. 'We want good relations with the Sunnis,' he says. 'The Shi'ites in Lebanon give priority to the conflict with Israel. We give support to the Palestinians – we have great concern for the Palestinian cause, and you know that the Palestinians are mostly Sunni. The same is true of Iran, which also strongly supports the Palestinians. There is no disagreement between us and the Sunnis in Lebanon on the sectarian equilibrium, and we adhere to the Ta'ef agreement [which was not generous to the Shi'ites]. There are political differences, of course, and unfortunately these transpose into sectarian problems.'

This is not remarkable in Lebanon. It has been the recent pattern. What Ali Fayyad may mean but is not actually saying is that, in the balance of things Lebanese, the other factions are worried that the Shi'ites want more say in parliament and government, to reflect their numbers and power; and, in the old Lebanese way of things, if someone says he wants a little bit more or his fare share, that is perceived by others as someone saying he wants far too much. It is also the case that more than any single group or party in Lebanon, since its independence and including the heyday of the PLO in the 1970s, Hezbollah is by far the strongest and most singular. It is an understatement to describe it as *primus inter pares*. So its potential is disturbing, even if its intentions remain legitimate and self-preserving and to be exercised within the Lebanese rules, such as they are.

He points out also that many Sunnis, and General Michel Aoun's Christians, support the resistance and that the rest of the Arab world regard Hezbollah as heroes for having successfully fought off the Israelis and carried the battle for the first time into Israeli territory. How the Christians of Lebanon divide in the future, as between an alliance with Hezbollah and other opposition forces or supporting the pro-Western bloc, could return them a political influence they have lacked since the days of the civil war and the rearrangements of the Ta'ef agreement.

Ali Fayyad, not surprisingly, blames the USA for trying to impose its will on the region and playing up the differences that always exist among different Lebanese factions as to their respective views of Lebanon's strategic relationships – which are interwoven with geopolitics. He ends by saying, of the Sunni–Shi'a divide and the situation in Lebanon: 'It is very dangerous.' If there is one peril that all Muslims of all sects and shades of belief profess to agree on it is this; yet it does not stop international and local forces trying to play this card, all over the Middle East, the Americans and British and their Arab allies in Egypt, Saudi Arabia and Jordan making mischief in Iraq and the Gulf, and turning up the Shi'ite–Sunni volume of antagonism in Lebanon.

This antagonism is aggravated by Iran's high profile here. As we drive to another appointment there are signs by the road announcing how the Tehran Municipality is helping to rebuild the *Dahiya*. My companion, herself a Shi'ite, originally from Iran, but uncovered and not in the least religious, is not as impressed by all this as I am. As a Persian, she well remembers the indignities that were visited on liberal women like her during and after the Islamic Revolution in her homeland. 'It's a fascist state within a state,' she says of Hezbollah. 'The sort of Lebanon they want would not be worth living in.' For Iranian women particularly, clerical authority has not been benign.

Hezbollah has never disguised its *desire* to create an Islamic state in Lebanon; but this seems to remain a wish, a hoped-for outcome some day, some time, a kind of organic sea-change that would come from within the Lebanese rather than a real project or work in progress. Many Hezbollah leaders, including Sheikh Nasrallah, have gone on record repeatedly to affirm that they are aware that an Islamic Lebanese state is an impossible dream.

At Friday prayers

Sheikh Mohammed Hussein Fadlallah is the spiritual leader of Lebanon's Shi'ite community. Though he is not now a functionary within the Hezbollah movement, or a spokesman for it, his views nevertheless are held in great respect. His guidance is widely followed by Hezbollah's membership and its supporters – he is the Lebanese Shi'ites' *marjah*. Sheikh Fadlallah has never advocated an Islamic Republic in Lebanon, having always been a proponent of co-existence and dialogue among the communities. If the sheikh is not 'in' the Party of God (he was more closely associated with it officially in the 1980s), then he is very much 'of' it, and as one of the leading *marjahs* or jurists among Shi'ites everywhere his example carries great weight with Hezbollah's leadership. His words accurately reflect Hezbollah's policies and aspirations, at least, those of the current leadership.

Driver Abdullah and I go to Friday prayers on a June day in 2007. As we drive into the southern suburbs, it is still a shock to see the great breaches Israeli fighter-bombers punched through apartment and office blocks, and the collapsed wreckage of others, much of it done in that cynically arranged gap between the UN Security Council's ceasefire resolution of late July 2006 and the actual imposition of that ceasefire, thanks to Bush and Blair, who wanted Hezbollah damaged beyond repair.

The links between Hezbollah and all the citizens of this vast suburban society are so intertwined that if Israel's aim was to expunge Hezbollah in Lebanon then it would necessarily have had to destroy the civil society around the movement. This was why the Israelis liked to emphasise how, as they saw it, Hezbollah fighters and gunners were hiding themselves inside civilian areas. As guerrilla fighters defending their turf and their people, of course they were in civilian areas; the Israeli jibe was a canard, one used more than 20 years earlier against the Palestinians and just as false. One might as well argue that the British Army defences of World War II were hiding behind civilian skirts because there were ack-ack guns in Hyde Park. Here in the *Dahiyeh* there was much death and damage. Most of the people of the suburb have survived and regathered. So has Hezbollah with and around them.

But great shards of concrete still hang precariously. Abdullah points out one building that did escape the air raids, on the edge of the suburb. It is a modern petrol station, and behind it is a massive two-storey restaurant built to resemble a medieval castle, a weird construction that with its turrets and crenellations has the look of some entrepreneur's experiment in exotic restaurant design in a Californian mall. Local people, families mainly, pack the place, especially on Thursday nights and Friday evenings and for *iftar*.

This complex is owned by Sheikh Fadlallah and his foundation for orphans, *al Aytam,* and to the Mobil petrol station and fake castle-restaurant are to be added a motel and library. The proceeds of all this go to orphans, any orphans, who are cared for until they are 18 and then found employment. Opposite, on the other side of the road, is a more specific institution, *al-Rassoul al-Azzam,* the central Hezbollah mosque. Next to it is a modern hospital, which is owned and run by Hezbollah and treats free any war-wounded or members of family of its martyrs, or what we in Britain would call 'war dead'. The sick of the *Dahiya* in general, the non-war cases, have 70 per cent of their costs paid. I photograph the sheikh's food-and-fuel enterprise, but am advised not to point my camera at the mosque and hospital complex, which is party property.

We are looking at the Iranian system of *bunyads,* the Iranian clergy-run institutions that are behind the economics and the welfare provision of the Shi'ite systems in Iran and in Lebanon. The sheikh's system also owns and runs a private hospital, a religious school and a hospital.

The *bunyads* are also responsible for most of the *Dahiya*'s drinking water. They subsidise agriculture and advise and aid farmers, supply them with seeds and fertiliser, for example, and offer businessmen and farmers loans, as well as giving social security handouts.

If this is a state within a state then it is so successful that nearly half of the wealthier Shi'ites and more than half the middle-class have said in surveys that they are affiliated with Hezbollah, many of them not necessarily being actual members. It goes without saying that for the poorer and majority Shi'ite population the question hardly need be asked.

The sheikh himself has from the beginning proclaimed his radical credentials in terms of the fight against Israel, but offered a conciliatory voice and stance towards Lebanon's many other sects and parties. In October 1983, when elements of the Islamic resistance forces (what would evolve into Hezbollah) blew up the American marines and French barracks on the same day, and, in November, pulverised the Israeli occupying forces' HQ in Tyre, in the south, Sheikh Fadlallah was said to have described the missions in these terms, 'the answer of the weak to the powerful'. It is an argument some Palestinians have used to justify suicide bombs – that if these beleaguered guerrillas had jet-fighters and attack helicopters they would not have to resort to such tactics.

In March 1985, a car bomb planted near his house – said to be the work of the CIA, who saw the sheikh as a proponent of terrorism – killed 83 civilians; but not the sheikh. Some Lebanese were later arrested by Hezbollah and executed for their part in the plot.

Domestically, Sheikh Fadlallah has always tried to be friendly and co-operative towards other Lebanese factions. The month before the bomb intended for him, he wrote an open letter to a Beirut newspaper declaring that Hezbollah had no intention of trying to impose its religion or its political will by force within Lebanon.

Internally, like the Hezbollah political leadership, he emphasises a radical Islamic agenda and resistance against the Zionist enemy among his own people, but reconciliation with those of other religions and political bent beyond Hezbollah's constituency. One concrete example of Hezbollah's non-retributive restraint was after the Israeli withdrawal from southern Lebanon in the spring of 2000. There were no reprisals against the many Lebanese, Christian and Shi'ite, who had, voluntarily or under coercion, co-operated with or fought for the

Israelis. The worst that happened was that former members of the south Lebanese Army, the local force the Israelis set up to help them run their 'security zone' for 22 years, were excluded from political links or coalition deals with Hezbollah (in Lebanon, party election lists are normally made up of a kaleidoscope of representatives of different religious and political factions). SLA leaders made for sanctuary in Israel and beyond.

These cornerstones of Shi'ite loyalty – Islam, resistance, Self-Reliance and Reconciliation internally – until recently have played a tricky but largely successful game of satisfying the radical wishes of their own constituency, placating their rivals and soothing their worst fears, and establishing regionally Hezbollah's credentials as fighters for the Arab cause. 'Until recently', because with the Israeli invasion and the sustained Israeli–American–European Union campaign against Syria and Iran and their supporters it has become a more difficult exercise. But that half the people of Lebanon, including many Christians, still believe in the trustworthiness and basic honesty of Hezbollah is tribute to the leadership of Sheikh Nasrallah and the over-arching example of Sheikh Fadlallah. The evidence of what Hezbollah has done for its people resonates far beyond the boundaries of the *Dahiya*.

This Friday, Sheikh Fadlallah as usual is holding prayers at the Hosseinein (two Hosseins) Mosque. It is about five years old, a sprawling place of worship on a corner in the middle of the *Dahiya*, one single minaret over a small green dome lifting itself above the main, arched entrance. The mosque was designed by an Iranian and built with Iranian funds.

Around the mosque are bookshops filled with the writings and memoirs of the great and good of Shi'ism: on the covers are the faces of Ayatollah Khomeini, Ayatollah Khamenei, President Ahmedinejad, Imam Musa Sadr, Sheikh Nasrallah, and on posters and in windows in other shops and cafes the turbaned visage of Sheikh Fadlallah himself, smiling slightly in an avuncular way. It all seems very casual; not a gun in sight. Across the road a gutted nine-storey apartment building is being repaired. People wander about without concern or curiosity.

This weekly meeting, noon prayers, is for the Shi'ites almost the equivalent of a rally, with both political and religious messages to be imparted, not that the two are always distinguishable. A Westerner would not be advised to wander in here alone and unannounced, but Abdullah has told the right people, he says. (But have *his* right people told *their* right people?)

Maybe not. As we walk towards the mosque we are stopped by a civilian security man with his baseball cap on the wrong way round, in the West the fashion statement of the idiot, here the wearer to be taken seriously. The man looks me over. After a discussion with Abdullah, who explains that he has obtained permission for me to be there with a camera and notebook, baseball-cap refers to another, more intelligent-looking young man. They accept our story and hold on to my passport while I am inside the mosque. Like everyone else we check in our mobile phones at the entrance, and our shoes a little further on.

Inside the arena, edged by marble in subtle shades of blue into aquamarine, decorated with sinuous Arabic calligraphy, Koranic quotations and prayers, people – men on the main floor, women in the gallery, out of sight – are beginning to take their places. Soon Sheikh Fadlallah appears flanked by two security guards on a balcony-cum-pulpit under a series of filigreed arches, giving the effect of a corridor behind him, of vaulting frames in reducing perspective, a *trompe l'oeil* to place him in more impressive context. The sheikh's son, who is also a Sayyed and who wears the black turban that signifies this, sits below, looking up to his father, only moving to help the elderly Imam climb the twisting staircase.

The men at prayer around me are in sports shirts or tee-shirts and jeans or slacks. The mosque is about 200 feet square, broken by an internal octagon holding an upper level of balconies, where the women are secluded, as is the case in all main Muslim places of worship. Only occasionally does one glimpse one of them, standing up to leave with a crying baby, perhaps. Each section of the octagon is decorated in identical patterns of azure, sea-green, turquoise and gold laced with the Arabic script of the Koranic verses in white or gold. The pattern is repeated refreshingly and symmetrically around the central arena, and even more dramatically above the *minbar*, or pulpit, where the sheikh is speaking from his apparently receding arches. Beneath him – this *minbar* is in fact more like a little choir gallery than a pulpit – a sign written in white on a black cloth tells us that we are commemorating the life and death of Fatima, the Prophet's daughter.

In Islam, only the Shi'ites commemorate and revere openly and personally religious figures of the past other than the Prophet. This is a cause of concern to many Sunnis, especially the supposedly arch-devout and certainly ultra-conservative believers of the Gulf states and their militant followers spreading across the Arab and Islamic world. It is customary to see depictions, paintings of Ali and Hossein, the two great Shi'ite martyrs of Najaf and Karbala, in people's living rooms or on show in religious shop windows and in the stalls of markets in Shi'ite areas and near Shi'ite mosques. This practice of saint-recognition and personal depiction goes against the Sunni grain of shunning the human image and the indulgence instead of decoration and symmetry, though the Shi'ites have mastered and demonstrate in the most eloquent way the religious tracery of alphabet and abstract pattern. The Iranian holy places of Isfahan and Shiraz hold some of the world's finest and most inspiring religious architecture and decoration.

The sheikh wears a white robe with a black mantle draped over his shoulder and looks pale under his black turban. Around me squat the faithful, most with what appear to be pebbles in front of them that they have retrieved from a box just inside the mosque's outer corridor. These are, I am informed, pieces of sandstone – called *turba* – from the site at Karbala, in Iraq, where Imam Hossein was assassinated in the year 680. The believers touch their foreheads to these symbols of the central act of martyrdom in the Shi'ite story and Shi'ism's religious centre point as they bow to the ground in prayer.

Prayers take place after the sheikh's first message, which is largely religious, preaching the value of the spiritual as against the temporal, good deeds as against wealth, but does mention the USA, in a reference to the Prophet Musa (Moses) and his difficulties with the Pharaoh, the latter representing the USA.

No one takes any notice of the foreigner in their midst with a camera and a notebook. They know I would not be there unless Hezbollah and its system were agreeable, although it has to be stressed that this is not a Hezbollah mosque as such, and Fadlallah is the sheikh for *all* Lebanese Shi'a.

After his religious sermon comes his political address, during which he sets about America and Israel, with regard to Palestine, a struggle in which Hezbollah and its supporters have thrown all their weight behind Hamas, the Islamic resistance in Palestine. The Hamas victory at the Palestinian authority's legislative polls in January 2006, has engendered hostility on an unprecedented scale from Israel, the USA, the Europeans and even Hamas' rivals in the secular and traditionally leading Palestinian party, Fateh. What the West wants, says Sheikh Fadlallah, is a civil war between Palestinians. As he speaks it is already happening in Gaza. These tensions are reflected in Lebanon in relations between Hezbollah and some Palestinian groups, including Fateh, and between Fateh and local Hamas supporters.

For Israel, a fatal blow against Hezbollah, the mission of 2006, would have been a victory against the Palestinians as well. It did not turn out that way. Now Hezbollah is more heavily armed than ever, with rockets that can reach Haifa and even Tel Aviv. The Palestinians themselves fight on against what would seem insuperable odds.

The mosque I am in, the Hosseinein, was not hit, although many buildings nearby were. The whole area is a landscape of reconstruction. As we drive along the old airport road that skirts Bourj el Barajneh, I note the neat little Iranian-built footbridges spanning the highway. No one else would have done this. In Lebanon, you take your chance dancing amid the traffic. In one or two places gardens have been inserted where none existed before. The Iranians are devoted to gardens and flowers and the rigours of Islamic revolution have not diminished their taste for decorative horticulture. Not only are Hezbollah and Iran putting the suburb back together again, but it is going to look and to be a better place to live in than it was before the Israeli fighter-bombers visited.

As Abdullah's wife Maliki tells me over lunch at their little flat near the airport: 'We love Hezbollah. We support them. They do much for us.' 'We need them more than they need us,' says Abdullah. Years ago I would have been tempted to disregard such remarks as propaganda or leader-worship. In this case I feel these views are genuine. Abdullah is a smart young man. If he had been able to afford university he would have gone much further than a taxi company, and may yet do so. He does not mouth slogans, but thinks for himself. In his position I too would support Hezbollah.

Abdullah's modest, sparsely furnished flat is in a run-down block just east of the airport. The electricity is off, as it often is for up to eight hours a day, as the authorities divert power to Beirut to keep up the spirits of the Lebanese – families, businessmen, politicians – in the wealthier districts. These are also where the diplomats and other foreigners reside.

In the vast regions where such as Abdullah live, many people pay extra money for generators. Millions, even billions, of dollars must have been made out of glass, generators and cable in this country during the past 30 years; perhaps almost as much as out of guns and ammunition. There is no drinking water available in the *Dahiya* except from Hezbollah water trucks or, for those with enough money, the purchase of bottled water.

Abdullah and his wife and children, Ali, nine, and Zeinab, 11, the latter already in *hijab*, all speak some English. Although taken by surprise, Maliki produces an instant meal of bread, tomato and *kibbeh*. She apologises for the paucity of the meal and does not believe me when I tell her with a throat-cutting gesture that any British husband who produced a foreign visitor for a meal without warning at some 20 minutes' notice during the school holidays would be facing domestic strife.

Abdullah produces pictures of himself with Sheikh Nasrallah, the hero in this house. There is a framed portrait-poster of the Shi'ite martyr Hossein in his main living room. There are tens of thousands of identical homes in the *Dahiya*, all with much the same thought processes: Thank God for Hezbollah. Whatever you may think of the Party of God, and its *marjah* in Iran, Ayatollah Khamenei, it is not going to be possible to shift it from the Lebanese scene, though the Americans will doubtless keep trying, unless their new president is really as grand a change in American global thinking as some would have the world believe.

The fact that the USA has just created the first Arab Shi'ite-run state, in Iraq, has also been of enormous assistance to Hezbollah; it also has to be remembered that Hezbollah's and Iran's closest ally in the Middle East, Syria, does not number indigenous Shi'ites in its population – more than 80 per cent Sunni, with about 10 per cent Allawi and the rest Druze or Christian or other much smaller minorities.

As I drive back to my lodgings in the largely Sunni Muslim quarter of Ras Beirut, at about 4.30 in the afternoon, for reasons I cannot decipher, the Maronite Church of the Rosary just up the road is ringing its bells enthusiastically. Half past four? On a Friday? Yet it is somehow reassuring that all this religious – this *overt* religious – variety exists for so much of the time in peace and tolerance.

New Lines in the Sand

Tolerance is easily stretched, then snapped. Sami, a 30-ish student doing a PhD at Princeton and lecturing at AUB, is someone rare among Lebanese of his political awareness and education – refusing to be clearly identified with any faction, of the secular, liberal tendency. He says of Sheikh Nasrallah that after defeating Israel and setting up his protest downtown the Hezbollah leader cannot move away without gaining something. A year after this conversation (which took place in April 2007) the opposition's Tent City is very much in place. As I write, the 18th attempt in six months (since November 2007) to put a new president in place has failed. Neither side has made progress, and the opposition's, Hezbollah's and others' attempts to change the shape of the government and the electoral system have failed, so far.

American, French, Western and 'moderate' Arab efforts have kept the existing pro-Western government in office if not in action. But Sami says, and many would agree with him, that this is a government with no agenda except the trial of those who are alleged to have killed Rafiq Hariri (since, apparently, virtually abandoned). He goes on to say of the Hariri case that justice would be fine, but many in Lebanon do not trust the international justice system – they view it has having been hijacked and suborned by the Americans and their Western acolytes.

Few would trust a local trial. Many would echo Sami's observation: 'Why all the fuss about Hariri when so many assassinations here and abroad have gone unsolved?' As Sami observes, a state cannot ground a policy in the conduct of a court case. The opposition says the result of any trial is predetermined. The four main defendants have been locked up without much concern for *habeas corpus* or a rigorous committal hearing, and will have presumably stayed locked up in Lebanon

229

until the International Tribunal sits and considers and reaches a verdict (quite a few years from now), after which, if it goes against them, they will remain locked up for a good deal longer.[1]

It is undeniable, given the pro-Syrian record of the suspects, that this would be the outcome most devoutly wished by the Americans in particular, the West in general and the existing Lebanese government and the March 14 movement. Equally unhappy would be the Lebanese opposition and its many sympathisers and supporters, and the Syrian government and its agents, all of whose capacity for changing the course of events in Lebanon is well proven. 'Justice' for Hariri's alleged assassins would not bring with it forgiveness and forgetting, commodities in short supply around here.[2]

Lebanon's present government is not a government of the people, says Sami. And when people talk of the rule of law, whose rule of law is it? He thinks the prime minister, Fuad Siniora, made a terrible mistake in December 2006, when he asked those who stand by Lebanon to put a flag in their window or on their wall. This immediately identified who was with and who was against the government and therefore was divisive. Whereas a flag is intended to unite people, in Lebanon it can often divide them. It depends on the circumstances. In this case, flying the flag identified the flyer as pro-government.

Sami mentions Samir Makdisi's book, *The Culture of Sectarianism*, in which the argument is that sectarianism does not have to be regressive or backward. Everyone is 'against' sectarianism here, just as everyone is 'against' racism in the USA; but there racism has spawned affirmative action, which militates against racism. Here you cannot say 'stop sectarianism' or try to stop it, because it would not allay people's fears. Even if a president or prime minister were elected by popular vote instead of sectarian-based MPs, he would, whatever he was, continue to seek support and put trust in people from his own community. Sectarianism is endemic. It is also a convenient scapegoat. People can blame sectarianism for the civil war and thus dodge responsibility or attempts at reconciliation. In Lebanon, identity is based on sectarianism.

Sami's uncle was a fighter with Dany Chamoun, younger son of the former President, Camille, and who led the Christian militia 'The Tigers' during the civil war, then was murdered at its close in 1990. That uncle is now an Aounista, seeing General Aoun as a leader who signed a genuine electoral and political pact with Hezbollah – at the St. Mikhail Church in south Beirut, on the edge of the *Dahiya*.

Sami also thinks it simplistic to say, as many Christians are saying, that Sunnis are only now becoming 'Lebanon-firsters'. They might always have been Lebanon-firsters but just had a different view from the others as to what Lebanon should be: 'connectedness' with the rest of the Arab world as opposed to 'isolation' from it. His point is that just because the Sunnis argued for greater contact with the Arab world beyond Lebanon's borders it does not mean that they wish to be subservient to that world; there is also much of that world to play on and with. The Sunnis now are torn beyond two separately developing Arab worlds – the one that more or less falls in with or behind Iran, the radicals, the 'street' and the Palestinians; and the bigger states like Egypt and Saudi Arabia who go along with the USA. There are also elements in the Sunni parts of the alliance that are sympathetic to the Wahhabism of Saudi Arabia, that puritanical desert code of Islam that has been taken up by Al-Qaeda and its sympathisers and imitators, but is also strong in the Saudi ruling elite.

There is plenty of evidence that extremist Sunni groups are lurking in disturbing numbers in the Lebanese undergrowth, a fertile habitat for irredentists and fanatics. This has been borne out to some extent by the fighting between the Army and Islamic Jihad at Nahr el Bared, and continuing reports since the jihadists were routed of their *confreres* setting up cells in Lebanon.

A few months later, I meet Sami again at a cafe called Bardot's, next to the Armenian Hagazian College in the Rue Mexique, in Ras Beirut, just up the road from the Central Bank.

It is, I realise, a redevelopment of the site of the old Wiener House, which was run by an Austrian *émigré* called Hans before and for much of the civil war. It was one of the few places we could eat decent food during the war, which in late 1975 very much eddied around and about this area. The location, in quiet, residentially inclined Rue Mexique, is up the hill from the coast, to the south of the hotel district. Though this neighbourhood, Kantari, is a classy one full of tall old villas and 1920s apartment houses, it was severely damaged by the Phalangists and Palestinians and others as they fought on the western side of the Green Line. The area was dominated by the Murr Tower to the south-east, held then by units sympathetic to the Palestinians, and the Holiday Inn to the north-east. You had to be careful to stay out of the line of fire, to keep concrete between you and these sniper nests. If, as we did so often, we walked from the Mayflower or Commodore

Hotels eastwards to Hans' restaurant, as it were from Palestinian lines, there would be no trouble from marksmen in the Murr Tower. It was fairly safe to walk up Hamra, past the Central Bank, *an-Nahar* newspaper offices, which housed UPI and Newsweek in those days, and the Ministry of Information. But it was even safer to sneak up to Hans' wiener schnitzel, rosti and Chateau Musar via the side streets, past Walid Junblatt's Beirut house and the Trad Hospital, and the many fine old houses with their arches, traceries, rococo pillars and high windows behind deep balconies.

Bardot's is a pleasant successor to the dark Viennese trappings of Hans' old eatery. It is a bar and bistro patronised mainly by the young and the studious, including Hagazian College undergraduates from next door.

Sami and I, in June 2007 are to retrace some of the steps he took in January 2006, when rioting broke out in the Muslim parts of Beirut. There was a momentary frisson as the lines appeared to divide seriously for the first time between Sunni and Shi'ite in the middle, lower-middle and working-class Muslim districts in the centre of Beirut.

The tensions did not descend into extreme violence or civil strife. The Lebanese Army acquitted itself well in defusing the worst of the clashes. But it was an unpleasant augury of what could, and might still (and was, briefly, to), come if the political tensions exploded beyond speeches, meetings, sit-ins, verbal exchanges, newspaper and TV debates and a stranglehold on the nation's life and progress.

We begin at Ras el Naba, near Sodeco, the most northerly crossing-point between east and west Beirut during the civil war between the Palestinian–Muslim–leftist alliance and the Christian Maronite militias. Ras el Naba is near the old Green Line and there displayed are the flags of the *Morabitoun*, one of the old so-called Nasserite Sunni militias who fought with the Palestinians in 1975 and 1976. They subsequently became a menace in west Beirut as many were criminals. Now they seem to be reappearing, possibly as the Sunnis cast around for muscular support, in which they are deficient compared with other groups.

One of the perennial problems for the Sunnis is that while the Shi'a, the Druze, the Christians, the Communists and the NSSP have all in their time mobilised fighting groups, the Sunnis (apart from the PLO guerrillas when they were here) have been short of organised armed strength. It would appear that the Sunnis, the establishment and the middle and working classes have tended to put their faith in the arms of the state, when those were active and working, which for much of the period between 1975 and 1990 was not the case.

We also see here pictures of Rafiq Hariri, Gamal Abdel Nasser and the very recently late Walid Eido and his son Khalid – so Ras el Nabaa is with March 14 and strongly Sunni in identity.

Just a few metres away on Bishar el-Khoury Boulevard, a wide avenue driving north to south from the downtown area towards the airport, and near the old Sodeco crossing point, the Shi'a and opposition demonstrators were burning a car that day in January when Sami was there. There were mounds of sand as barricades – the opposition were making mayhem in a very Sunni enclave. But there was no serious fighting. Burning cars and tyres is hardly raising your eyebrows in terms of Beiruti rioting technique.

We walk about half a mile down to the Corniche Masraa and head west towards the coast. The Corniche is the main artery that cuts through west and south Beirut. These days it separates at its eastern end, near the racecourse, the essentially Sunni working-class suburb of Tarek el-Jedidi (where Walid Eido has just been buried in the Sunni graveyards of Cascal) from the districts of Mousseitbeh and Mar Elias, which are mixed Shi'a and Sunni. Here, in January 2006, a new, incipient 'green line' began to form, at right angles to the old one, as Sunnis on one side and Shi'a on the other threw stones at one another over the heads of the army.

This rivalry is made manifest by the banners, flags, images and slogans. Over the road, on the Tarek el-Jedidi side of the street, is a poster depicting the studious image of Fuad Siniora, the Sunni prime minister, which repeats three times 'We're Staying', a reference to the influx of Shi'a into Sunni areas. There are the usual pictures of Sa'ad Hariri, son of the assassinated ex-prime minister and, by the big Nasser Mosque, a landmark on the corniche and a home to Salafists, there is a trio of massive portraits of the late Sunni Mufti of Lebanon, of Gamal Abdel Nasser and one Ibrahim Kleilat, the head of the aforementioned *Morabitoun* (which means 'marauders' or 'ambushers'). This is the holy Sunni Trinity as seen in a particular part of working-class Sunni Beirut.

'ARAB NATIONALISM IS THE SOLUTION', says another poster, echoing the dreams of Nasser (most Arabs are Sunni, and Arab nationalism was in a way both popular with and coterminous with the

Sunni *umma*, or religious 'collective'). Another banner, more complex, recommends the Security Council's decision to enforce a UN tribunal on Lebanon to try to do justice in the Hariri affair and the subsequent string of assassinations. It also exhorts everyone to criticise Qatar for abstaining on the vote in the UN body. All this is very Sunni, very pro-government.

On the north side of the street, at the entrances to Masraa, there are pictures of the Shi'ite Amal leader and speaker of parliament (and opposition supporter) Nabih Berri, the founder of Amal, Imam Musa Sadr, and, reflecting perhaps the mixed nature of this quarter, a picture of Rafiq Hariri. Just to confuse matters there are posters calling for support for and solidarity with the army. They are mostly in the new fashion in Beirut these days for camouflage-pattern posters and advertisements: outlines of the shape of Lebanon placed in serried ranks of green, brown, yellow and khaki, emblazoned with such slogans as 'The Decision is Yours'. Further west, going up Mar Elias, another main road, running north to south through the Muslim areas, we see no posters at all and no Lebanese flags. This may mean it is so mixed an area that no one dares put out any flag. As we walk up nearer the old sector, Basta, we finally see a very large poster of Sheikh Nasrallah, the Hezbollah leader, giving thanks to Ayatollah Khomeini's spirit and to Iran for all its help.

So, at the moment, the 'green lines' might be changing. But how permanently or definitively it is impossible to predict. It, or they, look a deal more devious and interwoven than the old Green Line, reflecting the traditional spread of Muslim population whichever type of Muslim one was.

The Shi'ite–Sunni relationship has had its ups and downs in Lebanon over the centuries, but there has never been as clear-cut a separation familially between these two sects of Muslims as there has been between Christians and Muslims. The panic emanating from Iraq, and the power of Hezbollah have alarmed the Sunnis; and comments from Arab leaders warning of a 'Shi'a Crescent' in the Middle East, holding sway from Persia to Lebanon, via Iraq and Syria, have injected poisonous thoughts into many souls.

In Search of Sunnis

17

Looking back over this book it strikes me we are missing something, some vital people. Most of the *dramatis personae* have been Shi'ite, Christian, Druze, Palestinian, from big movements and small parties or militias; leaders and activists and talkers of various sizes, strengths and calibres: artists, social workers, academics, drivers, reporters, intelligent observers; but hardly any of these have come from that section of society which is the glue of Lebanon – the Sunnis. With the exception of the Hariri family, assassinated father Rafiq and his prime ministerial son, Sa'ad, and the emergent but secretive and militant Islamic extremist groups, the Lebanese Sunnis seem to be grey, low-profile, *there* but not saying or doing much; disorganised, and certainly bereft of the military power that, in varying degrees, most other factions or confessions can and do summon up when necessary.

To explore this, I visit one of my very favourite old houses in Beirut. It is a villa we used to call the Pink Palace, a property that emanates 'Sunnidom' in the same way Buckingham Palace does royalty. It is the epitome of tasteful Ottoman and Arab style, rich yet discreet: it is full of class and history. It is not that class does not exist elsewhere in Lebanon, but here, and in a few other remaining houses not far from the shore in Ras Beirut, it is subtle and dignified.

This is the way the Sunni elite do things: they are quiet; perhaps too quiet? (The Hariris are exceptional, with their ostentation and brashness, much disapproved in some Sunni circles.)

The Pink Palace, not far from the vast fortress of the Saudi Embassy, in Marie Curie Street, is a three-storey villa in just that colour. It is set with a (just-remaining) view of the sea in broad and beautiful gardens on all sides and behind a guardian wall. A short, curved driveway

235

divides in crescent form round an islet of front lawn and trees in a short route to the grand entrance – steps up to a balcony in front of French windows. In the gardens that surround the villa on all sides are pines, palms, firs and a hundred gardenia trees; below them bougainvillea, geraniums, mimosa and jasmine glowing against the rich green grass. I am here in late spring and the display is at its best. The house, the flowers and the lawns are lit by what sharp sunlight darts through the trees.

Behind the villa is a pool, the oval of bright blue water reflecting its protective penumbra of bushes and trees; to its side there is a vegetable garden in the villa's eastern shade. Through the trees is another, more classical villa, taller and off-white in colour, even more hidden from public view, though what looks like a derelict lighthouse standing at the edge of the grounds indicates that privacy was not always guaranteed. This was a French observation tower. From here, the Mandatory authorities could survey and spy on their troublesome subjects between 1923 and 1944. This rear villa is part of the same family property, that of the Daouks, a wealthy, upper-class merchant Sunni family that came to Lebanon from the Maghreb about 600 years ago.[1]

The Daouks are profoundly Lebanese and Sunni, but it is in the house itself and its own story that is to be found the thread back to recent Lebanese history, to the struggle against the Turks and then the French and then against the various forces that have swirled up and down and around the streets by the Pink Palace.

Raya, the striking widow (a Druze) of the late Omar Daouk, with her little Italian greyhound Romeo, invites me in. Though I have visited her and her husband many times over the past 15 years or so I never fail to be consumed again by this striking home, Levantine in history and warmth.

The villa is essentially in a cross-shape. Two long, tall rooms, a dining-room to the left, a sitting-room to the right, as you enter, form the lateral stroke of the cross, while the other is formed by two more rooms, a reception room and, beyond, a parlour that opens on to the rear garden. If the front French windows remain open, and those to the garden also, the sea breeze from the Mediterranean fans gently through, under the high ceilings and past the heavy drapes and brick-red blinds that let in the sun only in narrow stripes and dappling spots. (If they ever shoot *The Big Sleep* again, this would be the ideal location for the mansion where Marlowe first meets Carmen.)

236

Persian rugs lie ahead of the visitor like soft-fabric stepping stones across the marble floor; ottomans and chairs in dark maroons and greens line the walls under the Persian miniatures. The further room, the parlour, is mainly hung with David Roberts' prints of Cairo Street life, the Palestinian, Lebanese and Egyptian countryside of the nineteenth century, including the famous *Interview with the Viceroy*, with the view of the Royal Navy off Alexandria in the mid-nineteenth century – 'Imperial Echoes', both Ottoman and British. There are inlaid Damascene sideboards; the bust under glass of a pharaonic Egyptian. Below the high lintels are deep strips of decorated linen giving a top line of coloured balance to the room and its detail below. Everything is rich but subdued, deep greens and browns and crimsons, as if to defy the bright light outside.

What catches my eye, though, are two portraits, each about two-foot square, facing each other across the point where the reception area stops before the rear parlour. These are two solid-looking, dignified, moustachioed men in suits and scarlet tarbouches, the Daouk ancestors. One is the man who in the early 1900s bought the villa, which had been built on a property considered in those days to be laughably far out of town (now it is almost as central in Beirut as the Serail itself); across from him is his father, who lived in the Souk Tawili and owned shops and a factory in Bliss Street that made railings and balconies. He was the foundation of the family's success and prosperity. This patriarch built the pretty little Green Mosque in Bliss Street, opposite the old Saudi Embassy and near the AUB, so that his workers would not have far to travel for noon prayers each day. This strikes me as a classic piece of Sunni practicality: the conflation of altruism and religious respect with the guarantee that workers' lunch breaks would not over-run.

The first picture is of the purchaser of the house, much smaller as it then was, Omar-bey, Raya's grandfather-in-law and a considerable player in Lebanon's story. There is also in the parlour a massive black and white photograph of him in full diplomatic fig, medals and other decorations, taken in the early 1920s. This was probably when he was Governor of Beirut. Well before that, Omar-bey was in the forefront of the struggle for Lebanese freedom from the Ottoman Empire, then in the harsh hands of the Young Turks during World War I. He became Lebanon's first president under the French after the Turks were defeated in 1918. Through this house passed many great figures, including that of the Hashemite King Feisal, bold but traduced ally of Britain. It may well have been here that the king was told that his reign over Syria, under the French, was being transferred to rule over Iraq, under the British, a scene of treachery as the victorious allies tricked the Arabs, reneging on promises of freedom and independence for an inglorious – and long-planned – colonial division of the spoils.

The villa was a grand and dignified establishment – a meeting place for the diplomats and the great and the good under Governor Omar-bey and beyond. Omar-bey was no more impressed by French rule than he had been by Turkish. Raya tells me that when, at a French reception on Bastille Day, the French High Commissioner raised his glass and pronounced 'Vive La France', Omar-bey raised his and echoed: 'Vive La France, *en France*'.

In the picture is visible among his many decorations one from the Vatican, awarded to him for his efforts during the famine in Lebanon during the middle of World War I, a famine exacerbated by the Turks' blockade of Lebanon. Omar-bey ensured that shipments of wheat that were eventually allowed through the Turkish-, Muslim-controlled port under allied pressure were distributed equally among Muslims and Christians. He was a close friend of Riad el-Solh, Lebanon's first prime minister, and of the eminent Karami family of Tripoli. All these were Sunni advocates of ridding their country of the empire of their co-religionists in the Ottoman system and, later, persuading the Christians to join the campaign to rebel against French rule. (Riad el-Solh was assassinated, in 1948, as was one of the most notable Karamis, Rashid, eight times prime minister, in 1987.)

More recently, there was more diplomacy at the villa, in 2005, when Raya hosted a reconciliation between her friends Michael Aoun and Selim al-Hoss, who had been rival leaders of Lebanon in the chaotic last years of the civil war. The former was a Christian general, claiming his authority at the point of guns from the presidential Palace; the latter, the legitimate (Sunni) prime minister, whose power was, if very limited, constitutional. It is a very Sunni story. The French rescued Aoun from the Palace, finally; the rule of law and the Syrians, not quite the same thing, saved Selim al-Hoss. Fifteen years on, the two old rivals met here for the first time since those days of national meltdown. Raya is too discreet to volunteer what they said, and I am too discreet to ask, but the fact is that Aoun is an opposition leader now, while Selim al-Hoss has moved well into the background of politics and may be the nearest to a neutral public personality that Lebanon possesses.

If the Pink Palace has been an occasional repository of diplomatic finesse it has also been the still centre of military storm down the years. Most recently, not a few days before I make my latest visit to Raya, the battles between pro-Hezbollah forces and the few units loyal to the March 14 movement have been swirling around her perimeter. The villa is neighbour to the Hariri complex at Koreitem and the Future TV station, all of which became the focus of the Hezbollah onslaught. During the civil war, various militias at various times fought for territorial gain in the byways of Marie Curie Street. Outside the windows of one of Raya's downstairs rooms has been erected a breeze-block wall, to defend against stray bullets and shrapnel. It is to this shelter Raya and her family and staff repair when the bullets fly.

In the summer of 2006 the Daouks had to replace much of the villa roof after it was shredded by the explosive detritus of Israeli bombs. Interestingly, for all its subtle splendour and obvious wealth, no group has tried to seize the Pink Palace. There are lengths in this Arab society to which a street-fighter just does not go.

The Daouk family – led by Raya's late husband – led the long and finally failed resistance to the Hariri takeover of Beirut, especially his coup in acquiring by commercial storm the ruins of the downtown area, in which the Daouks and many like them, and many others not so well off, had property. It was a campaign in which Rafiq Hariri used his massive, Gulf-style wealth almost forcibly to purchase or bribe the landowners out of their properties in favour of his Big Plan. Hariri-land sits there before us today, grandiose and fun maybe, but bearing as much relationship to the spirit and style of the old merchantman port–city as Bluewater does to Regent Street.

The Sunni discrepancies

The Sunnis may have become a little subdued now, but were the cutting edge of the struggle against the disintegrating Ottoman Empire despite the fact that as Muslims they were the top layer of society during most of the Empire, a long and formative 400 years. They were the establishment. However, the Turks gave privileges to all and sundry. In the end it was an idea of that 'Lebaneseness', the Mountain fused with the coast, that attracted the Sunnis. Here was an entity in which they could rule and prosper, arm in arm with their Sunni brethren throughout the Middle East, but not subject to them. By 'Arabising' the Christians in Lebanon they could co-opt them into the Lebanon enterprise, but use them as an essential and productive part of the mosaic. It worked at first. The Turks went very suddenly, under foreign force; the French eventually went, but very reluctantly, a handover that took three years. Lebanon had its tensions, but until the 1970s they were manageable, and the Sunnis were at the centre of life, politics and business.

Arab nationalism had its ideological attractions to the Sunnis in its various forms, Nasserism and Ba'athism, mainly because of its attraction as a prideful defence against the Zionists and the shame that Israel's creation had brought all Arabs. The Baghdad Pact, of Iraq, Iran, Turkey and Pakistan, a Western plan to unite Muslims against the Soviet Union, also had its attractions. The leading Sunnis of Lebanon steered a middle course between these polar alternatives, concentrating on building their state, keeping it as 'Arab' as possible and trying not to inflame their neighbours, yet keeping it separate.

The Sunnis continued to see their power and their personality as reflected in the state itself. In a sense, they were the state: everything else was an add-on, a complement. The constitution had given the Sunnis almost as much power as the Maronites, the prime minister-ship. These two groups divided the nation up. 'Christians' meant Maronite; 'Muslim' meant Sunni. It was a neat pact. Even when it all went wrong in the 1970s, the Sunnis had the military power of the (mainly Sunni) Palestinians to protect them, although many in the Establishment were nervous. When the war ended, the Sunnis gained again: the Ta'ef agreement adjusted the political balance in their favour. As the Syrians more or less ruled Lebanon for the next 15 years, all the Lebanese Sunnis had to do was keep in line, much as many of them resented it, while the even more resentful Christians – shattered by the long war – could do little more than nurse their wounds.

A good Sunni friend of mine from a well-known political family explains it like this: the Sunnis have relied on what might be called Arab depth for their assured position inside Lebanon. The Arab world was theirs, and they were part of it. Yet within it, they were the Lebanese state and the state was the machine they could use for their betterment and survival. The Christians might be tougher and make more noise, but the Sunnis were the foundation.

There may also be an Islamic dimension to the Sunnis' apparent lack of individualistic profile, their dearth of prime personalities – of larger-than-life characters like the Junblatts, the Aouns, the Nasrallahs and the Sadrs, the Gemayels and the Chamouns, in their day. Until recently, a trend only recently beginning to be bucked by the Palestinians, in their long and endless crisis, the Sunni have tended to bury their egos in the wider anonymity of the *umma*, the communal whole of Sunni, majoritarian Islam, the main religion of the Arab world. The cult of the Sunni personality existed mainly in the *rais*, the chief, the leader – the Sultan, the Caliph, Gamal Abdel Nasser, Yasser Arafat, King Hussein, Saddam Hussein, Hafez al Assad (an Alawite, a heterodox branch of the Shi'a), King Faisal, Crown Prince Abdullah, the more memorable Lebanese prime ministers, the al-Solhs, the Sa'eb Salams, the Karamis. The Palestinians in their special category of revolutionaries, national liberationists and exiles defied this generality. They recently have broken away from Sunni tradition by writing their stories, their individualistic experiences, their autobiographies, their poems. They have been encouraged not only by their seemingly hopeless situation, but probably by their wide experience of and immersion – in exile, in the diaspora – in other, often Western cultures. There the cult of 'me' has paid off, as it has paid off for the Israelis and the Jews, who never cease telling their stories and relating their agonies and their triumphs in prose, poetry, diary, film, on stage and in music.

But I think it still goes against the general Sunni grain – this fierce drive to appear as a 'celebrity' to tell the tale to the world. Perhaps this will change, is changing, in the era of the Internet, of al-Jazeera, and the shrinking of the world and the agglomeration of our ideas and ways. But such a shift takes its time. In Lebanon even the most assiduous political commentator would be hard-pressed to name any likely, talented Sunni leaders waiting to lead their people and their country forward in a moment of inspirational glory.

The seeds of the Sunnis' present difficulties were in part laid in 1990 when the Syrians took over the country after the Ta'ef agreement. All the militias were disarmed, the Palestinians having been effectively eviscerated militarily in 1982, except Hezbollah, which was – was it not? – a resistance against an Israel still much in occupation of a great swathe of Lebanon, a regional menace to Arabs in general and Lebanese, Syrians and Palestinians in particular. Who could complain when Hezbollah was given permission by Syria to stay strong and fully armed? It certainly would have been difficult if not hazardous and counter-intuitive for the Sunnis, of all people, to argue then for the disarmament and enfeebling of a nascent army aimed against the occupying Zionists.

The Syrians, further, have been in a close alliance with Iran since the Islamic Revolution of 1979. They were not going to disarm Iran's favourite son in the Levant and would not have been able to even had they wished. For most of the Sunnis, if they had thought about it all, they would have written off Hezbollah in those early days as a resistance group facing Israel and doing the Lebanese government's dirty work for it, defending Lebanon but not having that much to do with the centrality of Lebanese domestic politics.

Meanwhile, Rafiq Hariri was rebuilding Lebanon and was close to Syria. He was a Sunni, even if some of the old guard thought he was flamboyant and more redolent of the Gulf than his modest home town of Sidon. Many Sunnis, and others, were making money out of the connections and Hariri's individualistic ways. He brought in his own people to create a kind of parallel civil service in Lebanon, appealing to that Lebanese fixation with the dramatic and the new, and to that can-do spirit the Lebanese cherish and deploy.

All this played into Sunni confidence. Why have your own political organisation, like the Druze or the Maronites or the Shi'a? Why have your own militia, when there is the Internal Security Force and the Army? *'L'etat c'est nous'* might have been the Sunni motto. When Hariri was killed and the Syrians suddenly left, the Sunnis were high and dry. They had a paralysed state; they had no defences; they had no militia. When Hezbollah attacked in May of 2008, the Internal Security Force, sometimes jokingly known as the Sunni militia, faded away; and the Army, that arm of the state, played only intermediary. Hezbollah itself was by now very concerned with domestic politics; and the Sunnis had a Christian hinterland and population that was splintered, half of it apparently going in with Hezbollah, at least in tactical voting terms.

The Sunni glue that held Lebanon together had melted. Even the March 14 movement, in which most of the Sunnis had invested themselves, was then, and until mid-2009, effectively led by a Druze, Walid Junblatt.

The Sunnis are virtually leaderless. There are no characters at the helm, the types needed in the tribal politics of Lebanon who were side-lined during the Syrian era, unless they operated as obedient servants. The Hariris are the strongest element, but not that popular since Rafiq

was murdered. My Sunni friend says of him: 'Rafiq Hariri had no prin-
ciples. He tried to use in Lebanon his experience in Saudi Arabia, his vast
fortune, Big Money on a Vast Scale [I hear the capital letters], and he created a system which bypassed government. His consultants were being
paid far more than our most senior civil servants. He did not believe in
procedure. He also used money to play religious groups off one another.'

Some of this is hypocritical: no one in Lebanon has ever been averse
to using money or acquiring it or playing one religious group off
against the other: it is a question of scale and style. Hariri played Rome
to Lebanon's Greeks, and many of them did not like it. He became
essentially one of theirs when he was blown up by those most people
assumed to be the Syrians or their people.

But the point about Hariri, whether he was a Mr Toad, pro- or anti-
Syrian, or a bedfellow of Jacques Chirac and his manoeuvres to build
bridges with the Americans,[1] is that he *did* something. He acted. For
better or for worse, he re-envisioned and re-made downtown and
rebuilt Lebanon and its infrastructure. It was at vast cost and brought
vast debt, but what he did restored Lebanon and its people's confidence. The Sunnis who complain about him may have a point about
his lack of class and his coercive tactics, but he was a doer. A Druze
friend of mine who is close to the Sunnis, says to me: 'Tim, the Sunnis
are flat. They don't do anything. They are traders, merchants, they
made money from Hariri and his bonds, but they don't make anything
or create anything.' This is an oversimplification and an unkind gener-
alisation. Many Sunni entrepreneurs, politicians of bygone days and
ordinary brave people I have worked with in the most demanding and
dangerous of circumstances do not deserve such a dismissiveness sen-
tence: but there is a kernel of truth in it these days. If Lebanon is to
reassert itself, it needs the Sunnis to pull themselves together, yet they
seem disunited, scared and demoralised. (As for the one leader they do
have, the Prime Minister Sa'ad Hariri he is generally regarded as
young and inexperienced, only in power because of his father's sudden
and early demise, and his and his family's enormouse wealth.)

Ras Beirut

From the Pink Palace I stroll downhill, back towards the familiar landscape of Ras Beirut and Hamra: past the City Cafe, where the older

politicians and a handful of émigrés, Iraqis, Syrians, sip their coffees or watery scotches and watch the world walk by outside as they argue quietly over their *an-Nahars* and *al-Hyatts* and *Herald Tribunes* how to put their troublesome region to rights; down to Lenas, one of a new chain of bright, continental-style sandwich bars, or perhaps to a street stall for *manouche* and a coke, or to the excellent fast-food Kebabji. New bars have sprung up, though my feet usually walk me back to the Duke of Wellington, unchanged since I first drank there in 1975 before making a mad dash with the British Consul, Terry Gardner, to rescue a British girl from the hotel district. She said she would rather stay with her boyfriend.

The elderly newsagent across the way, as he has done for 30 years, is still selling the foreign newspapers, and I buy a *Sunday Times* ('and can I interest you in the *Guardian Weekly*, sir? *Le Monde literaire*?'). The flower shops are bursts of colour down Jeanne d'Arc, and round the corner the strains of modern jazz from the Blue Note reach the Greek Orthodox Church, just up from the side entrance to the AUB. Churches, mosques, pubs, cafes, the fast-food emporiums of Bliss Street: one of the latter – Thank God It's Friday perhaps, it is hard to remember the old landscape – has replaced the legendary Abu Feisal's, where generations of students sat with their Gitanes and Turkish coffees and plotted the creation of new worlds: Out with Capitalism, Down with Zionism, Long Live Nasser, Hurrah for Fateh, Hail Dr George, Junblatt for Ever, Chamoun Go Drink the Sea; or maybe just dodged the classes across the road; or all of the above. Old men with dusty degrees who shouted at the Vichy French remember Abu Feisal's, and in the 1950s and 1960s it must have fomented more dissent than any other coffee shop in the Middle East.

The Starbucks and Costas in Hamra do not appear to have replaced Abu Feisal's in any other sense than that they serve coffee – espresso, cappuccino and mocha, not Turkish.

Otherwise, Hamra does not change that much. It is not as seedy as it became 20 years ago, when the city was falling apart and there were more beggars than customers, more guns than credit cards. Now there are smart hotels disgorging brisk young men and women with well-cut suits and laptops into the loud traffic and cruising taxis. The windows of Red Shoe, the steps down to the old bookshop, the neat little menswear kiosks with their jaded attendants lurking in the door, the luxuriant bedding on offer at Sleep Comfort, the nonchalance of the easygoing shoppers and soldiers, strollers and policemen – it remains much the same, through war and peace and the more common berth that exists somewhere between, and in which the Lebanese most consistently dwell. No one gives a foreigner a second look, unlike everywhere else in the Middle East; everyone will answer a 'Good Morning' or a 'Salaam Aleichem'.

Anyone can be at home here and almost everyone is, from the mendicant slumped against a shop-front to the merchant in his glass palace to the student to the traveller. There is nowhere like Ras Beirut in the Arab world. If it has survived more or less as is in the past 35 years that I have known it, and from what I am told for a lot longer than that, then it is going to survive the next 35 and far beyond. It is the spirit of the place. It is irrepressible. It is never parochial. Ras Beirut does not 'do' parochial.

It is June 2008. I have an urge to stop a pretty young girl sauntering by and ask her: 'Was there really once a battle here?' I do not. Not because I am shy or she will not answer, but because I know her reply will be: 'Why, yes, *habibi*. Just a couple of weeks ago. *Ahlan Wa Sahlan!*'

The Lebanese are a highly intelligent, resourceful, enterprising, entertaining and hospitable people whose charms and dramatic tendencies reflect their magnificent landscape. More than anywhere else in the Arab world, here you can still discover some of the warmth, grace and culture that has informed the Arab world through all its fortunes; Lebanon retains elements of the traditional Levant in a kind of living museum that keeps old and new intact, more or less, side by side.

In too many other Arab countries, where the artefacts and manners of the past remain, the people have had their hopes, energies, excitements and freedoms ironed out of them by repressive and monolithic regimes or by foreign occupiers. There is also a disturbing tendency among Arabs to associate the past, the authentic and the historic with lack of progress, regression; to prefer brutalistic modernity to antiquity, memory, tradition and continuity. Lebanon is not immune from these trends. But somehow a past of the mind as well as the physical remains here, endangered yet not quite extinct.

In different circumstances Syria, Iraq and Palestine could have remained more like Lebanon. Dictatorships and comprehensive invasions prevailed. Only in Lebanon today can be experienced that creative fusion of West and East, the Janus-facing people mixing, when they can, the best of Western freedoms and technological advance with the traditional grace, centrality of family and religious observation of the Arab world, so much of the latter, indeed most of it, not extreme or distorted, or not yet. Listen to the church bells of Muslim west Beirut.

The Lebanese are often criticised by their Arab neighbours and some foreigners for flashiness, shallowness, unreliability, chicanery, obsession with façade, fashion and the latest gadgets. There are elements of these traits. But for the most part this criticism usually comes with a flavour of sour grapes or tinge of envy. The Lebanese have made ghastly inroads into their landscape, wrecking much of the coastline, burying many of the glories of the Mountain and its towns under concrete high-rises. It has to be said that in some ways the wars and the economic stagnation may have saved some of the countryside and old-fashioned houses and districts from destruction. But the Lebanese are no worse than the Spanish, the Italians, the Turks or the Cypriots when it comes to despoliation by development, and more than with any of those comes that magical, almost erotic sense of being on the edge of two worlds, an entry and an exit point.

Perhaps Constantinople, Alexandria and Jaffa once contained this essence, but Ataturk, Nasser and Zionism beat these cities into different and duller shapes. There are echoes there of the Old East Mediterranean, but they do not breathe as freely as they do in Lebanon.

Lebanon has not been well served by its two powerful neighbours and is treated callously by the powers further away, even the superpower two oceans away that is supposed to be such a progenitor of the freedoms the Lebanese cherish. But in this power's book these must be the correct freedoms, exercised in its approved way.

The tensions that most closely affect these people can be reflected in recent indirect peace talks between Syria and Israel. What a boon peace could be to the Lebanese. What changes a successful outcome of this barely nascent peace process would bring to Lebanon. Yet it is also announced that Bashar Assad has been seeking new arms imports from Russia. Why should he not? But here is just one small if vital example of how a Lebanese poring over his *an-Nahar* or *as-Safir* with his morning *wasad* can have his hopes raised and then dashed within the hour. It happens as surely and regularly as the five daily calls to prayer.

The Lebanese not only live with this constant tension, but seem to thrive on it. They have a powerful sense of irony and ridicule. During the Syrian time, the joke went, a Lebanese entered a lift with two Syrian soldiers inside. Nothing happened. 'Why aren't we moving?' asked the Lebanese. One of the Syrians pointed at the weight restriction sign: 'We are waiting for fourth person.' Bleak humour too. A Syrian stops a Lebanese in Hamra and asks him, 'What do you think of our leader President Assad?' The Lebanese looks nervously about him and beckons the Syrian to follow him down a tiny, empty alleyway. At the bottom he looks nervously round again, then leans forward to whisper in the Syrian's ear: 'Frankly, *habibi*, I don't think he's such a bad guy.' Lebanese resilience is leavened with arts and entertainment. The girl I heard in the Gemmayzeh cafe was right: no dictator could ever change this.

Good food and drink is the vital underlay to all this, a *sine qua non*. In 1988, when the Christians were at each other's throats, I was on the highway north out of east Beirut, towards the port town of Jounieh, then the main Christian outlet to the world, except that the coastline was under Syrian siege. It was winter: cold and wet and grey. I stopped at a popular restaurant I had known in peaceful times.

When I walked in I could not believe what I saw. Though the establishment was empty but for myself, my driver and a journalist companion, the waiters were immaculate in their tartan jackets, white shirts and bow-ties as black as their patent-leather shoes, the food emporium at the entrance to the shop a miniature Harrods Food Hall: Italian and Hungarian hams; French and Dutch cheeses; Argentinean beef; freshly baked bread in a score of different styles: European, Persian, Arab; tray upon tray of sweets: *baklava, mamoul, knaffe*; spices, herbs, sauces; imported as well as fine Lebanese wines and beer; and any Scotch, vodka, gin or arak you cared to name. Inside, the lunch we had was exquisite: *mezze*, steak, frites, Bellini, superb Turkish coffee or espresso or cappuccino if we preferred.

It was not cheap, but then nor should it have been. We deserved it. The weather was foul and we were in a war zone. I felt a pang of guilt – after I had eaten. The owner soon shimmered over to us, a famous restaurateur, well-groomed like his waiters and smiling at our enjoyment. It could have been Saturday evening on the Rue Fauborg St.

Honore. I said, 'Isn't all this a bit much? All this beautiful, rich food, all this choice, while outside, all around, the Lebanese are under siege, dying, eking out meagre rations, shivering without enough *mazout* to heat their houses?'

'Monsieur,' he said, 'if I allowed standards to drop in my restaurant these Lebanese would really think we had come upon hard times. They expect this. Without it they would be in despair.'

Endnotes

Chapter 1

1   My friend and former Associated Press Middle East Correspondent, Ed
     Blanche, tells a wonderful story of Amal's ban on Christmas
     celebrations. The PPS, street rivals of Amal then, but not actually
     fighting them, were undeterred. As (mainly Greek Orthodox) Christians
     they were going to have their Christmas, at any cost. When Ed asked a
     street-side Santa Claus in full scarlet rig and white beard if he was
     worried about Amal trying to enforce its views on this public celebration
     of the Nativity, Father Christmas assured him he had no worries at all,
     opening his red robes to reveal a sub-machine gun.

Chapter 4

1   Geagea is not alone in his preference for bunkers: Aoun has one nearer
     Beirut, in Rabieh; Walid Junblatt, the Druze chieftain, spends a good
     deal of the time in his splendid palace-cum-fortress in Moukhtarra, in
     the Shouf; the remaining Hariris live in a walled-off zone of Ras Beirut
     called Qoreitem, shielded by many layers of uniformed and un-
     uniformed protectors; the Prime Minister of the time (mid-2007) was
     spending a lot of time in the Serail, the government House, also behind
     layers of protection. All Lebanese leaders do much the same, whatever
     their persuasion, and so do most notables in the country, including most
     of the important Ambassadors and their immediate staffs. Given
     Lebanon's recent experiences it is more wisdom than paranoia.

Chapter 5

1   In April 2009, the four generals were freed on the orders of the UN Tribunal after prosecutors said there was insufficient evidence to justify their continued detention. A key witness was said to have withdrawn his evidence. Sceptical Middle East observers however, reckoned that in the general atmosphere of attempted Western reconciliation with Syria after President Barack Obama's election in November 2008, and the calmer climate in Lebanon after its presidential election earlier the same year, the international political will to put Syria in the dock had evaporated.

2   The East side of Beirut had its advantages. The food was better and the women more enticingly dressed, even if the atmosphere was more hostile. We visitors were definitely from 'over there', and suspected Palestinian-lovers and Muslim-sympathisers. Very few foreigners any longer lived or worked among the Christians – those who remained for the war years had largely found themselves on the Muslim-Palestinian side of Lebanon, or had been forced to locate there because that was where the head offices, banks, embassies, missions, the AUB and its feeder private schools were, including those bankers, insurance brokers, chandlers, traders and hoteliers whom the battles and ethnic cleansing had forced from the downtown area.

3   It is said that when Yusuf returned from that trip, in 1976, he met Abu Hassan Salameh, a senior figure in the PLO's Intelligence unit, Force 17, who was the PLO's point man in contacts with the Christians and had good relations with them. Abu Hassan clicked as to what was happening between the Christians and the Israelis when Yusuf carelessly remarked to him, 'You have a wonderful country there. It is worth fighting for.' It is a good example of how naive and careless, how isolated, the Lebanese Christians were sometimes in their thought processes.

Chapter 6

1   This was the plan hatched by the British MP Sir Mark Sykes and the French diplomat and political activist Francoise George Picot, in 1916, to divide the Near East into spheres of British and French influence or, more precisely, control. The arrangement that subsequently came into effect under League of Nations Mandates after World War I and the various post-war treaties and deals was different in territorial detail from that which the two schemers devised on behalf of their respective governments, but not in overall effect. The best and most entertaining

description of this colonialist conspiracy is to be found in A Peace to end all Peace: Creating the Modern Middle East 1914–22, by David Fromkin, published in 1989 by Andre Deutsch.

Chapter 7

1   The only exceptions to this were some foreign doctors and medical teams working at the Gaza Hospital, who were trapped by the Israeli siege and the subsequent Christian militia onslaught. Later, they emerged physically intact.
2   The refugees are from the 1948 Palestine that has now become Israel. For such a solution of Return or Compensation, the Israeli government would have to admit the responsibility for this Palestinian catastrophe it shares with Britain and the UN, which it certainly neither wishes nor is likely to do.

Chapter 8

1   The Druze religion is a mystery to those outside it, and conversion to it is not possible these days. It appears to draw on many disciplines, from the Greek philosophers such as Plato, Aristotle and Socrates, as well as Islam and the teachings of Hindu mystics and gurus, the latter much patronised by Kamal Junblatt himself. The Druze have their own religious books and appear to be free to draw on a wide variety of texts. They do not have mosques or obvious and elaborate temples of worship such as the main monotheistic religions require, but do have places of gathering perhaps more akin to the informal structures of the Quakers and some other Nonconformist Christian branches. It is a meditative religion based on self-knowledge rather than laws, commandments, deistic instructions or faith in one god. It contains aspects of reincarnation and unitarianism. It is significant that unlike other heterodox Middle Eastern religions, such as Baha'ism and the smaller sects of Islam, even, in these harsh and extremist days the Shi'ites, the Druze have not in recent years been apostatised and persecuted with any consistent vigour. This may well have to do with their military prowess, their mountain refuge and their fearsome reputation among those who have crossed their path.
2   It was generally reckoned that the Syrian leadership's anger at Kamal Junblatt was further inflamed by his public references to the

membership of the Asad family and its political, military and Intelligence entourage in the minority Allawite sect, another schismatic branch of Islam. Everyone knew this for a fact, but it was not done or wise to mention it publicly. It was especially sensitive at a time, in the 1970s, when Sunni Muslim extremists were carrying on a violent campaign against Syrian leaders and their supporters in general, and the Allawites in particular.

Chapter 9

1   After the first hours of the invasion, a French officer of the UN Interim Force in Lebanon, which had come in 1978 to try to keep the sides apart and oversee Israeli withdrawal, said he counted more tanks crossing from Israel into Lebanon than there were in the entire French Army.

Chapter 10

1   This is not unusual in the Middle East. Long after Israel and Egypt had signed their peace treaty in 1979, they were arguing about who owned the tiny resort of Taba, on the Red Sea Coast, another matter of vague delineations going back into the mists of the Ottoman Empire. The Gulf is replete with disputes over such vagaries of boundary, clashes over lines in the sand that flare up, or are flared up, from time to time between states: the most recent and consequential example being Iraq's decision in 1990 to root out ancient quarrels about whether or not Kuwait was actually Iraq's 'nineteenth province', who owned what oil where, where exactly did the border sit, and so on. We know how that ended, if indeed its consequences have.

Chapter 11

1   I am not sure I believe this. Timor Goksell, a former UN peacekeeper and expert on Lebanon, of whom more later, says there are three lines in Hezbollah these days: the pragmatic line of Nasrallah, which is now heavily involved in local politics; the hard religious line, which would follow Khamenei and press for Hezbollah to be more a representative of Iran's interests and wider Islamic Revolution; and the line which wants

to continue as purely a resistance against Israel, staying out of Lebanese politics qua Lebanese politics. Timor says that the following for Hezbollah in Lebanon is really a following for Nasrallah. If he were to be killed or to die or disappear, Hezbollah might fracture.

Chapter 14

1   UNIFIL achieved its 30 years of service in Lebanon in the spring of 2008.

Chapter 15

1   It is a model used by previous resistance organisations, including the North Vietnamese, the PLO and, ironically, the Zionists, as they resisted and exploited and manipulated the British Mandate authority at the same time as building their institutions, not just the secret army and the terrorist attack groups, but the trade union movement, the immigration service, universities, the Jewish Agency, a government in waiting. Hezbollah would not wish to take this last comparison too far, not just because of the Israeli connection but because, they insist, they are not preparing to take over Lebanon and remake the nation in their own image.

Chapter 16

1   See endnote 1 of Chapter 5 on p.250 concerning the freeing of the generals.
2   This last piece of information, incidentally, reminds me how everyone comes from somewhere else, how peoples from Arabia, from the eastern redoubts of Persia and Mesopotamia, from the Caucasus and far beyond swept across these lands, and how so many stayed and how flexible is the notion of nationality here – perhaps anywhere. It illustrates the nerve of some proponents of Zionism who have accused the Palestinians of being opportunistic interlopers from other Arab lands, especially as most of the Israeli establishment are European Jews with no blood ties to the region at all. Even the Israelis may one day belong to this area as part of the same process – if they ever learn how to fit in with rather than try to rule over their neighbours and steal more and more of their land.

Chapter 17

1 France and the USA commenced a mutual diplomatic and political froideur in late 2002, when the French government made clear it would not support the Anglo-American adventure in Iraq or its attempts to give the enterprise UN Security Council cover.

Bibliography

Barrakat, Halim, *Lebanon Student Preludes to the Civil War*, Austin, Texas, and London, 1977.

Blanford, Nicholas, *Killing Mr.Lebanon, the Assassination of Rafik Hariri and its Impact on the Middle East*, London, 2006.

Bulloch, John, *Death of a Country, the Civil War in Lebanon*, London, 1977.

Bulloch, John, *Final Conflict, the War in Lebanon*, London, 1983.

Chehabi, H.E., *Distant Relations, Iran and Lebanon in the Last 500 Years*, Oxford, London, 2006.

Glass, Charles, *Tribes With Flags, a Journey Curtailed*, London, 1990.

Glass, Charles, *The Tribes Triumphant, Return Journey to the Middle East*, London, 2006.

Hanf, Theodore, *Co-existence in Wartime Lebanon, Decline of a State and Rise of a Nation*, London, 1993.

Iskandar, Marwan, *Rafiq Hariri and the Fate of Lebanon*, London, 2006.

Jaber, Hala, *Hezbollah, Born with a Vengeance*, London, 1997.

Johnson, Michael, *All Honorable Men, the Social Origins of the War in Lebanon*, London, 2001.

Joumblatt, Kamal, *I Speak for Lebanon*, Paris, London, 1982.

Harik, Judith Palmer, *Hezbollah, the Changing Face of Terrorism*, London, 2004, 2005.

Housepian, Nubar (Editor), *The War on Lebanon, a Reader*, Northampton, Mass., 2008.

Mujais, Salim, *Antoun Saadeh, a Biography, Volume 1. The Youth Years*, Beirut, 2004.

Nasr, Vali, *The Shia Revival, How Conflicts Within Islam Will Shape the Future*, New York, London, 2006, 2007.

Noe, Nicholas (Editor), *Voice of Hezbollah, the Statements of Sayyed Hassan Nasrallah*, London, New York, 2007.

Randal, Jonathan, *The Tragedy of Lebanon, Christian Warlords, Israeli Adventurers and American Bunglers*, New York, London, 1983, 1990.
Salibi, Kamal S., *Crossroads to Civil War, Lebanon 1958–1976*, New York, 2007.
Salibi, Kamal, *A House of Many Mansions, the History of Lebanon Reconsidered*, London, 1998, 1989.
Traboulsi, Fawwaz, *A History of Modern Lebanon*, London, 2007.

Index

Iran 13, 50, 167, 185
  and Hezbollah 148, 160, 195,
    196, 197–8, 206, 218–21,
    222–3, 242
  holy places 226
  Revolutionary Guards 218
  Shi'ites in 143
  struggle with Syria 51
Iranian Committee for
    Reconstruction in Lebanon
    139
Iraq 50
  Karbala 226
  as Shi'ite state 228
  War 13
Irish Army (UNIFIL) 203–4
Isfahan holy places 226
Israel
  border with Lebanon *see* Southern
    Lebanon, border with Israel
  creation 84, 86
  Dahiya district attacks 213–14,
    215, 221–2, 227–8
  and Hezbollah 13, 14, 30, 50, 69,
    70–1, 82–3, 163, 218–19,
    223–4, 227
  interest in despotism/fragmentation
    44, 81–3
  1967 War 23, 88, 90, 105–6
  occupation/invasions 25, 27, 41,
    60, 67, 92, 123, 128
  occupied territories 13, 100–1,
    104, 126, 140, 141, 145, 147
  political influence 11–12
  relations with Phalange 35, 41, 42,
    45, 51, 55, 58–60, 68–9, 93–4
  Sabra-Chatila massacre 89, 91–9
  and Southern Lebanon 23, 88,
    90, 105–6, 136, 138–9,
    140–3, 146–8, 159, 167
  sympathy for 55
Italian soldiers 177, 187

Jamal Pasha 62, 77
Jamil Ismail Hamad 99–102
Al-Jazeera 241
Jeanne d'Arc 15
Jebl Amal 48, 152
Jebl Lubnan see Mount Lebanon
Jebl Sheikh 169
Jerusalem 68, 109, 147
Jesus Christ 189
Jewish Brigade 158
Jiyeh 135
Jordan 29–30, 86
  River 153
Jounieh 35, 47, 247–8
Junblatt family 112–14, 116, 124,
    125, 241
Junblatt, Kamal 53, 84, 112,
    117–19, 122, 181, 196, 209
Junblatt, Walid 17, 112, 115, 120–1,
    122–6, 128, 131, 132–3, 162,
    200, 208, 232
Junblatti area 16, 19

Kadisha, Holy Valley of 32, 48
Kantari district 16, 231–2
Kaouk, Sheikh Nabil 179
Karam, Yusuf 116
Karami family 238, 241
Karbala, Iraq 226
Kateab House 64–5
  see also Phalangist Party
Kebabji restaurant 15
Kennedy, President 13
Khalet Wardeh 140–1
Khalidi Hospital 15
Khalil Gibran 48
Khalil Museum 43
al-Khalil, Yusuf 178
Khalil, Yusuf Abu 65, 66–72
Khamenei, Ayatollah 145, 152, 167,
    185, 228
al-Khatib, Dr Mohammed 103–4